The Hellenistic Worl

Coinage is one of our key so
of the Hellenistic world (32
the period with an up-to-d   r
and bronze coins in their cultural and ____   o
offers new perspectives on four major themes in conte..₊ _ .ry
Hellenistic history: globalization, identity, political economy and
ideology. With more than 250 illustrations, and written in a lucid
and accessible style, this book sheds new light on the diverse and
multicultural societies of the Hellenistic world, from Alexander to
Augustus. The author assumes no prior knowledge of Hellenistic
history, and all Greek and Latin texts are translated throughout.

Peter Thonemann is Fellow and Tutor in Ancient History at
Wadham College, University of Oxford. His first sole-authored
monograph, *The Maeander Valley* (Cambridge, 2011), was awarded
the prestigious Runciman Prize in 2012. More recently, he has published a large corpus of inscriptions from Roman Asia Minor
(*Monumenta Asiae Minoris Antiqua XI: Monuments from Phrygia
and Lykaonia*, 2013) and has edited two collections of essays on the
history of Asia Minor in antiquity (*Attalid Asia Minor*, 2013 and
Roman Phrygia, Cambridge, 2013).

Guides to the Coinage of the Ancient World

General Editor
Andrew Meadows, *University of Oxford*

Coinage is a major source of evidence for the study of the ancient world but is often hard for those studying and teaching ancient history to grasp. Each volume in the series provides a concise introduction to the most recent scholarship and ideas for a commonly studied period or area, and suggests ways in which numismatic evidence may contribute to its social, political and economic history. The volumes are richly illustrated, with full explanatory captions, and so can also function as a numismatic sourcebook for the period or area in question.

Titles in the series

The Hellenistic World: Using Coins as Sources
by Peter Thonemann

The Hellenistic World

Using Coins as Sources

PETER THONEMANN

CAMBRIDGE
UNIVERSITY PRESS

University Printing House, Cambridge CB2 8BS, United Kingdom

Cambridge University Press is part of the University of Cambridge.

It furthers the University's mission by disseminating knowledge in the pursuit of education, learning and research at the highest international levels of excellence.

www.cambridge.org
Information on this title: www.cambridge.org/9781107451759

© Cambridge University Press 2015

First published 2015

Printing in the United Kingdom by TJ International Ltd. Padstow Cornwall

A catalogue record for this publication is available from the British Library

Library of Congress Cataloguing in Publication data
Thonemann, Peter, author.
The Hellenistic world : using coins as sources / Peter Thonemann.
    pages   cm. – (Guides to the coinage of the ancient world)
ISBN 978-1-107-08696-8 (hardback) – ISBN 978-1-107-45175-9 (paperback)
1. Hellenism – History.   2. Greece – Civilization.   3. Coins, Greek – Sources.
4. Coinage – Greece – History.   5. Alexander, the Great, 356 B.C.-323 B.C.
6. Greece – History – Macedonian Expansion, 359-323 B.C.   7. Mediterranean
Region – Civilization – Greek influences.   8. Globalization – Economic aspects –
Mediterranean Region.   9. Group identity – Mediterranean Region – History.
I. Title.
DF235.A2T46   2015
737.4938–dc23

                                                                        2015013718

ISBN 978-1-107-08696-8 Hardback
ISBN 978-1-107-45175-9 Paperback

Contents

Maps

Figures

Preface

This book is an introduction to the coinages of the Hellenistic world, from the campaigns of Alexander the Great in the late fourth century BC to the Roman conquest of the eastern Mediterranean. Rich and fascinating as it is, this period poses particular challenges for historians. For much of the Hellenistic era, narrative sources are entirely lacking. The Hellenistic historian therefore has to master a wide range of different kinds of source material: inscriptions, papyri, archaeology, Alexandrian poetry, and of course coinage. The aim of this book is to show how coins can help us to understand the varied societies and cultures of the Greek-speaking world during the last three centuries BC.

The book is structured around four main themes, all of them concepts of central importance in recent work on the period. The first theme (covering Chapters 1 and 2) is *globalization*. The Macedonian conquest of the Near East created a new monetary 'world-system', stretching from northern Gaul to the central Asian steppe. The coinages of Alexander the Great and his early successors served as a kind of common language for monetary cultures throughout this 'big' Hellenistic world. Chapters 3 to 5 explore the second major theme of *identity*. Greek cities, regional leagues, and Hellenized peoples on the fringes of the Graeco-Macedonian world all used coinage as a means of representing their distinctive cultural and political identities. The third theme, discussed in Chapters 6 and 7, is *political economy*. The use of coined money underwent radical changes during the Hellenistic period, both at the macro-level of state and civic economies, and at the micro-level of coin use by individuals. The fourth and final theme is *ideology*. In Chapters 8 and 9, we shall look at the representation of power on Hellenistic coins, first by the rulers of the major Graeco-Macedonian kingdoms, and finally by the Romans who succeeded them across much of the Greek-speaking world during the second and first centuries BC. The book also has an unobtrusive forwards motion, travelling from the decades after Alexander's death (Chapter 1) to the organization of Rome's eastern provinces in the last decades of the Roman Republic (Chapter 9).

Like all specialist disciplines, 'numismatics' (the study of coins, *nomismata* in Greek, *nummi* in Latin) has its own technical jargon: obverse and reverse, dies, weight-standards, denominations and so forth. The reader is urged to make use of the Appendices on pp. 193–200 (Glossary of numismatic terms; Denominational systems; The manufacture and material of ancient coinage). All ancient sites and mints mentioned in the text will be found on the maps on pp. xxvii–xxxi.

I am grateful to Volker Heuchert, Chris Howgego, Lisa Kallet, Jack Kroll, Sarah Thonemann and Liv Yarrow for their critical comments on earlier drafts of this book. Volker Heuchert (Ashmolean Museum), Victor England (Classical Numismatic Group), Paul Hill (Baldwin's), Shanna Schmidt (Harlan J. Berk), Alain Baron (Numismatica Genevensis), Philip Kinns, Rick Witschonke and Richard Ashton kindly assisted with coin images. Financial support was generously provided by the Leverhulme Trust and the American Numismatic Society. I am once again indebted to Michael Sharp, my editor at Cambridge University Press. My warmest thanks are reserved for Andrew Meadows (American Numismatic Society), *il miglior fabbro*. The book is dedicated to Sarah, with love.

Abbreviations

Abbreviations of Greek and Latin authors and works follow *The Oxford Classical Dictionary, Third Edition Revised*, eds. S. Hornblower and A. Spawforth (Oxford, 2003). The following special abbreviations are also used:

BCD Akarnanien	Münzen und Medaillen GmbH, Auktion 23 (18. Oktober 2007), Sammlung BCD: Akarnanien und Aetolien.
BCD Peloponnesos	LHS Auction 96, 8–9 May 2006, Coins of Peloponnesos: the BCD Collection (A. S. Walker).
BCD Thessaly	Triton XV, 3 January, 2012, The BCD Collection of the Coinage of Thessaly.
CH	*Coin Hoards*. London, 1975–2002 (vols. I–IX); New York, 2010 (vol. X).
FGrHist	F. Jacoby, *Die Fragmente der griechischen Historiker*. Berlin and Leiden: 1923–.
I.Délos	*Inscriptions de Délos*.
I.Ilion	P. Frisch, *Die Inschriften von Ilion*. IGSK 3. Bonn, 1975.
IG	*Inscriptiones Graecae*
IGCH	M. Thompson, O. Mørkholm and C. M. Kraay, *An Inventory of Greek Coin Hoards*. New York, 1973.
NAC	*Numismatica Ars Classica*
OGIS	W. Dittenberger, *Orientis Graecae Inscriptiones Selectae* (2 vols). Leipzig, 1903–5.
RPC I	A. Burnett, M. Amandry and P. P. Ripollès, *Roman Provincial Coinage Volume I: From the Death of Caesar to the Death of Vitellius (44 BC–AD 69)*. London and Paris, 1992.
RRC	M. H. Crawford, *Roman Republican Coinage*. Cambridge, 1974.
SEG	*Supplementum Epigraphicum Graecum*
SNG	*Sylloge Nummorum Graecorum*

Maps

Map 1 The Peloponnese and southern Greece

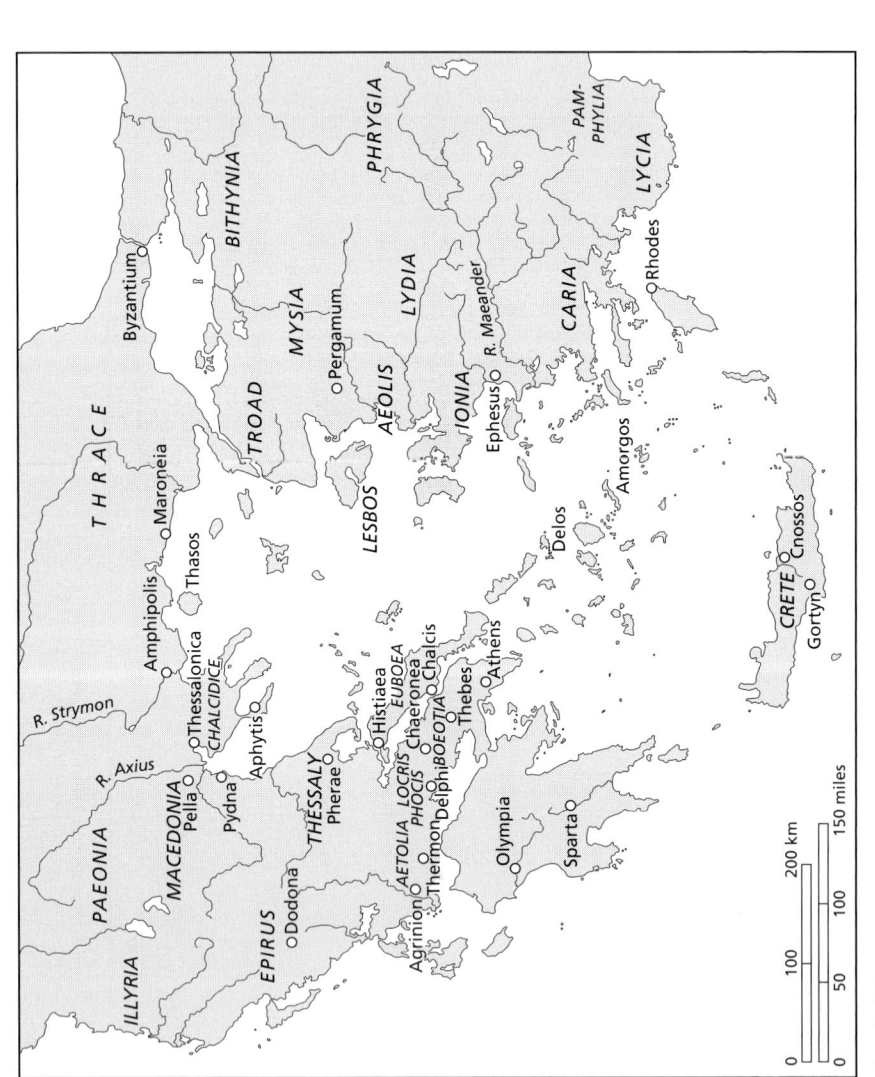

Map 2 The Aegean

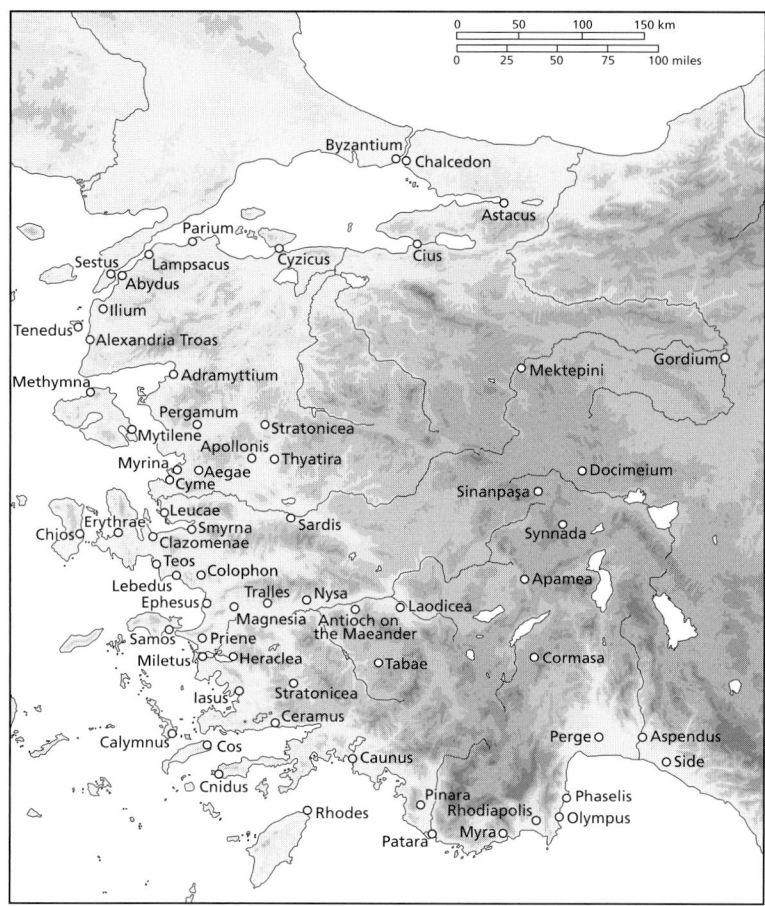

Map 3 Western Asia Minor

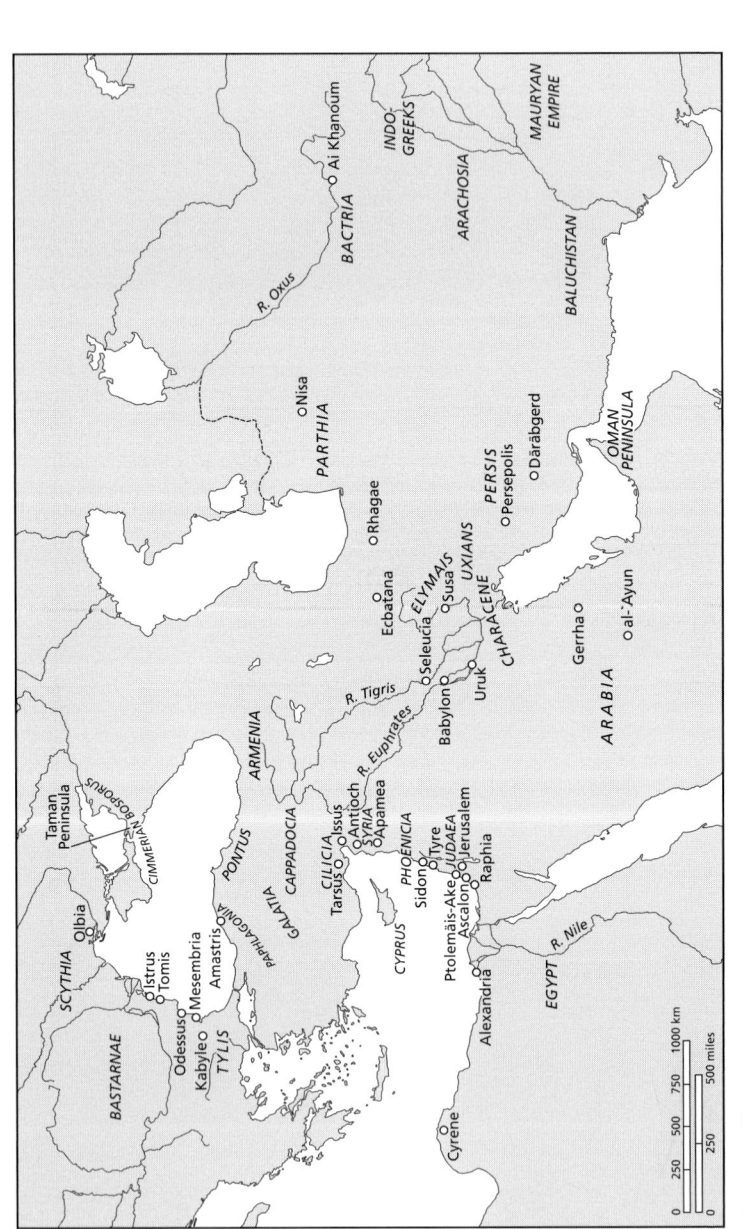

Map 4 Hellenistic Asia

Map 5 Western Europe

Part I

Globalization

1

Alexander and the transformation of Greek coinage

I The Sinanpaşa hoard

In the early years of the twentieth century, a poor Turkish farmer made his fortune overnight. Somewhere near the modern town of Sinanpaşa, deep in the highlands of central Turkey, the soil gave up an enormous hoard of ancient silver coins, buried there more than 2,200 years earlier (Fig. 1.1). We will never know how many coins the farmer originally dug up from his fields, since the coins were quickly dispersed on the international antiquities market. Still today, this remains the fate of most large coin hoards discovered outside of official excavations. As I write this paragraph, on 15 August 2013, a US coin-dealer called 'zoderi' is offering on eBay thirty-two tetradrachms of Alexander the Great, all evidently from a single hoard, for between $320 and $780.

Between 1919 and 1927, the American scholar and collector Edward T. Newell (1886–1941; Fig. 1.2) tracked down hundreds of coins from the Sinanpaşa hoard from coin-dealers in Athens, London and the United States. Thanks to Newell's efforts, we can today identify 670 coins which are known for certain to come from the Sinanpaşa hoard, almost all of them (640 out of 670) now in the collection of the American Numismatic Society in New York (*IGCH* 1395; Thompson 1983: 86–9).

From the surviving coins, we can be pretty sure that the hoard was buried in 317 or 316 BC. All of the Sinanpaşa coins are drachms on the so-called 'Attic' weight-standard (named after the abundant coinage of Classical Athens), weighing around 4.30 g. These drachms all carry the same images on their two faces. The front, or 'obverse' face, depicts a bust of Heracles, the legendary ancestor of the Macedonian royal house, wearing a lion-skin headdress. The back, or 'reverse', shows a male deity seated on a throne, holding an eagle on his right hand, with the name (in Greek) of a Macedonian king running vertically to the right of the throne. Most of the coins carry the name of the young conqueror who, between 334 and 323 BC, changed the course of world history: Alexander III ('the Great') of Macedon (Fig. 1.3).

Figure 1.1. Drachms from the Sinanpaşa hoard, buried in 317 or 316 BC, probably by a Macedonian veteran of Alexander's army. ANS.

The Sinanpaşa hoard bears silent witness to the dramatic events which had played out across the whole of the Near East, from the Mediterranean to India, in the twenty years or so before its burial. In 336 BC, Sinanpaşa lay deep within the Persian empire, a vast patchwork of different societies and cultures stretching from Egypt to the Himalayas, ruled over by the Achaemenid dynasty of western Iran. This empire had enjoyed a remarkable stability for more than two centuries, in large part thanks to the Persian kings' hands-off style of government (Wiesehöfer 2009). Persian rule often meant little more than a token payment of tribute to the far-off Iranian royal court, leaving the empire's subject peoples to enjoy very substantial religious and cultural freedoms.

Despite its long and prosperous history, the Persian empire was in effect little more than a loose confederation of heterogeneous, quasi-autonomous culture-zones, bound together solely by the person of the Great King and his tribute-collectors. This helps to explain why the Macedonian invasion of Asia enjoyed such brutally swift success (Briant 2010). In less than four years, between his crossing to Asia Minor in 334 BC and his capture of the

Figure 1.2. Edward T. Newell (1886–1941). Newell's personal collection of more than 87,000 coins is now held by the American Numismatic Society in New York. ANS.

Figure 1.3. Silver drachm of Alexander the Great, from the Sinanpaşa hoard (Lampsacus mint, *c.* 323–317 BC). The reverse legend reads ALEXANDROU, 'of Alexander'. 4.26 g ('Attic' weight-standard). ANS 1944.100.29876.

Persian heartlands in 331 and 330 BC, Alexander of Macedon swept this vast empire into the dustbin of history. By the time of Alexander's death at Babylon in the summer of 323 BC, the inhabitants of Egypt, Syria, Iran and

Bactria were learning to live with a new ruling elite of Greeks and Macedonians.

No one has evoked the impact of the Macedonian conquest better than John Keegan, in his wonderful book *The Mask of Command*:

> Imagine a highland Napoleon. Imagine a Bonny Prince Charlie with European ambitions who, having won back Scotland from King George II, sets off at the head of his clans not just to conquer England – a mere preliminary – but to cross the Channel, to meet and beat the French army on the River Somme, then journey south into Spain to besiege and subdue its principal fortresses, return north to challenge the Holy Roman Emperor, twice confront and defeat him at the head of his own forces, seize his crown, burn his capital, bury his corpse and finally depart eastward to cross swords with the Tsar of Russia or the Sultan of Turkey. Imagine all this compressed into, say, the years 1745–56, between the princeling's twenty-second and thirty-third birthdays. Imagine on his death, at the age of thirty-two, the crowns of Europe shared between his followers – Lord George Murray ruling in Madrid, the Duke of Perth in Paris, Lord Elcho in Vienna, John Roy Stewart in Berlin, Cameron of Lochiel in Warsaw, a gaggle of tartaned chieftains braying for whisky in the small courts of south Germany and London garrisoned by a crew of bare-kneed highlanders. (Keegan 1987: 13)

The Sinanpaşa hoard almost certainly belonged to one of this 'crew of bare-kneed highlanders', a grizzled veteran of Alexander's expeditionary army, many of whom settled permanently in the East in new city-foundations like Docimeium, a Macedonian colony 45 km east of Sinanpaşa (Thonemann 2013b: 15–24). Quite probably, as we shall see in a moment, the 670 silver drachms of the Sinanpaşa hoard represent the remains of this veteran's back pay for his long and bloody service on Alexander's Asiatic campaign.

But even at the moment that the Sinanpaşa hoard was buried, a mere seven years after Alexander's death, the new Macedonian empire was beginning to fracture. Alexander's sudden death at Babylon in 323 had left his kingdom without an obvious heir. In the end, the kingship was shared between his as yet unborn son by the Bactrian Roxane, the future Alexander IV, and his mentally disabled half-brother Philip III Arrhidaeus (Bosworth 2002: 29–63). The short reign of Philip III Arrhidaeus has left its traces on the Sinanpaşa hoard: eighty-eight of the drachms in the hoard carry Philip's name in place of Alexander's (Fig. 1.4). But Philip III and

Figure 1.4. Drachm in the name of Philip III Arrhidaeus, from the Sinanpaşa hoard (Abydus mint, *c.* 323–317 BC). Large numbers of Alexander-style coins with Philip's name on the reverse (PHILIPPOU, 'of Philip') were struck between 323 and 317 BC. 4.29 g. ANS 1944.100.84469.

Alexander IV were kings in name only. Real power was held by the generals who commanded the remains of the great Macedonian royal army (Perdiccas, Eumenes, Antigonus the One-Eyed) and, above all, by the Macedonian nobles who governed the various provinces or 'satrapies' of the Macedonian empire (Ptolemy in Egypt, Lysimachus in Thrace, Seleucus in Babylon).

By the time the Sinanpaşa hoard was buried, Philip III was probably already dead, murdered at the hands of Alexander's mother, Olympias, in the autumn of 317. The young Alexander IV was killed on the verge of adulthood, probably in 309 BC. Between 306 and 304, the strongest of the Macedonian 'successors' – Antigonus in Asia Minor, Ptolemy in Egypt, Lysimachus in Thrace, Cassander in Macedon and Seleucus in Babylon – all claimed the title 'king' in their own right (Gruen 1985). By 277 BC, the former Macedonian empire was left divided among three new great powers: the Antigonids, by now installed in Macedon and mainland Greece, the Ptolemies in Egypt and much of the eastern Mediterranean, and the Seleucids in Asia.

The cultural impact of the Macedonian conquest of the Near East can be seen wherever you look. In some regions, such as Asia Minor (western Turkey), the encounter between Graeco-Macedonian and non-Greek cultures was a creative and mutually beneficial one, with Lycians, Carians, Phrygians and others enthusiastically adopting the cultural trappings of Greek life (Vlassopoulos 2013: 290–302). Elsewhere, such as in Egypt, more sharply stratified colonial societies developed, with a small Greek ruling class enjoying very different lifestyles from the native Egyptian masses (Bingen 2007: 215–55; Manning 2010: 73–116). In a few places, such as Judaea, the meeting of cultures ended in violent and destructive conflict (Millar 1978; Gruen 1993). The old Greek world of the Aegean, too, was transformed by the great Macedonian adventure in the East. The globalization of Greek culture lent a renewed importance to the cultural centres of the old Greek world (Athens, Delphi, Delos), and the old Greek *poleis* pursued federal institutions more vigorously than ever before in the face of Macedonian power (Chapter 4 below).

In 1913, William Tarn began his magnificent biography of Antigonus Gonatas with a memorable evocation of the mindset of the early Hellenistic man:

> All the horizons have widened and opened out; civilization pulsates with new life, and an eager desire to try new things. . . For there is so much to be done; nothing less than the conquest, material, social, intellectual, of a whole new world. In his desire to master that world, he shrinks from no effort, and he achieves. The dark places of the earth contract before him; one language now takes him from the Rhone to the Indus, from the Caspian to the Cataracts. (Tarn 1913: 1)

Coinage is a wonderful category of evidence for the cultural and linguistic globalization which Tarn rightly saw as a hallmark of the centuries after Alexander's death. As we shall see in Chapter 2, the late fourth and the third century BC saw the emergence of a numismatic common culture – what the Greeks would call a '*koinē*' – stretching from northern Europe to central Asia, and from Carthage to Arabia. This was also an era in which cultural identities underwent dramatic transformation, not least in the traditional Greek world of the Aegean (Chapters 3 and 4). Cultural change is perhaps particularly stark along the outer fringes of the Macedonian empire; Chapter 5 will show some of the ways in which coin iconography can help illuminate these new hybrid 'Hellenizing' identities. The existence of the great Macedonian imperial states had profound effects on the shape and scale of local and regional economies, which we can only understand through close analysis of coin-finds and minting patterns (Chapters 6 and 7). Finally, royal coinages tell us a great deal about how Macedonian kings wished to be seen by their subjects (Chapter 8) – just as, in a slightly later period, coinages minted by Roman generals and provincial officials show us how the Roman conquest of the Greek world was 'spun' for a Greek audience in the late second and first century BC (Chapter 9).

The Sinanpaşa hoard, the abandoned wealth of some anonymous Macedonian infantryman, living out his last years deep in the quiet grey hills of central Turkey, is a poignant emblem of the transformation of the Near East wrought by Alexander and his Macedonian successors. But to understand the full significance of this cache of silver drachms, we need to take a more detailed look at the remarkable coinage of Alexander the Great, where the whole story of Hellenistic coinage begins.

II   The royal coinages of Philip II and Alexander III of Macedon

On his accession to the Macedonian throne in 336 BC, after the murder of his father, Philip II (ruled 359–336 BC), Alexander inherited a long tradition of royal coinage stretching back to his ancestor Alexander I 'Philhellene' (ruled *c.* 498–452 BC) (Westermark 1989; Dahmen 2010; Kremydi 2011). Philip's own gold and silver coinages were struck in very large quantities, particularly towards the end of his life, and offer vivid evidence for how Macedonian kings wished to be seen, both at home and abroad, in the mid-fourth century BC (Le Rider 1977; 1996).

The royal gold coinage of Philip II was struck on the 'Attic' weight-standard, based on a 'stater' ('standard coin') of *c.* 8.60 g. These coins carried a bust of the god Apollo on the obverse, with a two-horse chariot and charioteer and the legend Philippou ('of Philip') on the reverse (Fig. 1.5). As Plutarch tells us, this last image was chosen to commemorate Philip's chariot victory at the Olympic games in 348 BC (Plut. *Alex.* 4.9). Philip, like his predecessors, was intensely conscious of the Macedonians' ambiguous ethnic status as a people on the fringes of the Greek world (Engels 2010; Hatzopoulos 2011). The Greek historian Herodotus recounts an illuminating episode around 500 BC, when the 'Greekness' of Alexander I of Macedon was very publicly called into question at the Olympic games:

> When Alexander decided to compete at the Olympic games, and came down to Olympia to do so, the other Greek competitors tried to stop him on the grounds that the contest was not for barbarians but only for Greeks. But when Alexander proved that he was actually an Argive, he was judged to be a Greek, and competed in the foot race, where he came equal first. (Hdt. 5.22)

Figure 1.5. Gold stater of Philip II, struck at Amphipolis (*c.* 340–328 BC). The types commemorate Philip's Olympic chariot victory of 348 BC. 8.58 g. ANS 1944.100.12024.

Evidently Alexander's ethnicity was, to say the least, a matter of perspective. His claim to be a Greek rested on the Macedonian kings' alleged descent from the legendary Argive hero Heracles; but in the eyes of the other Greeks competing at Olympia, Alexander was very definitely not part of the 'club' (Hall 2002: 154–68). This story beautifully explains why Philip chose to commemorate his Olympic victory so prominently on his gold coins. To have competed successfully at Olympia was the best possible proof of the 'Greekness' of the Macedonian royal house.

Philip's abundant silver coinage, based on a local Macedonian drachm of *c.* 3.60 g, embodies a similar set of messages. His silver didrachms ('two-drachm pieces', weighing *c.* 7.20 g) carry a bust of a youthful Heracles wearing a lion-skin headdress on the obverse – a reminder of the legendary ancestry of the Macedonian kings – with a horse and jockey on the reverse, perhaps celebrating Philip's victory in the Olympic horse-race of 356 BC (Plut. *Alex.* 3.8) (Fig. 1.6). His tetradrachms ('four-drachm pieces', weighing *c.* 14.45 g) also carry a horse and rider on the reverse – some, like the example illustrated in Fig. 1.7, possibly showing the king himself on horseback – but this time with a bust of Zeus as the obverse type.

In the early years of his reign, Alexander III seems to have struck no coinage in his own name, but to have continued minting with his father's coin-types. This phenomenon of 'posthumous' minting would go on to

Figure 1.6. Silver didrachm of Philip II, struck at Pella (*c.* 342–336 BC). The obverse type recalls the legendary descent of the Macedonian kings from the hero Heracles. 6.73 g. ANS 1944.107.1.

Figure 1.7. Silver tetradrachm of Philip II, struck at Pella (*c.* 356–348 BC). These coins were struck in vast quantities in Macedon, both before and after Philip's death in 336 BC. 14.36 g. ANS 1967.152.197.

Figure 1.8. Tetradrachm in the name of Philetaerus of Pergamum (ruled 282–263 BC), struck by Eumenes II (*c.* 165–150 BC). This coin-type remained effectively unchanged from *c.* 270 to the mid-second century BC. 16.92 g. ANS 1971.260.2.

become very common in the Hellenistic world. To take an extreme example, the silver coin-types of Philetaerus of Pergamum (ruled *c.* 282–263 BC), the founder of the Attalid dynasty, continued to be used virtually unchanged by all of his successors right down to *c.* 150 BC (Fig. 1.8; Westermark 1961; Meadows 2013: 154–81). 'Posthumous' coinages of this kind served various purposes. For a new king, they were a way of indicating dynastic continuity with a popular predecessor. More practically, when a coin-type had become familiar through widespread use (as was certainly true of Philip's huge gold and silver coinages), carrying on with the same types would help ensure that one's own coins would be widely accepted.

At an uncertain date, but probably before the beginning of his Asiatic campaign in 334, Alexander introduced a new gold coinage in his own name alongside the 'posthumous' gold staters of Philip (which in fact continued to be struck in Macedon right down to *c.* 315 BC: Le Rider 1993). Alexander's gold staters and distaters carried on the obverse a portrait of Athena wearing a Corinthian helmet, closely imitating her portrait on contemporary coins of Corinth (Figs. 1.9–1.10). This 'Corinthian' Athena surely refers to Alexander's status as leader (*hēgemōn*) of the League of Corinth, an alliance of Greek states founded by Philip II after his victory at Chaeronea (Poddighe 2009). The reverse type carries the legend ALEXANDROU ('of Alexander') alongside a winged figure of Nike, a personification of victory, grasping a *stylis* (a kind of flagpole which stood on the stern of a warship: Sergueenkova 2006).

Figure 1.9. Gold distater of Alexander the Great, struck in Macedon in the first years of his reign (*c.* 336–332). This was Alexander's earliest coinage in his own name. 17.20 g. ANS 1944.100.319.

Figure 1.10. Fourth-century silver stater of Corinth. The portrait of Athena was imitated by Alexander for his gold coinage. 8.48 g. ANS 1955.54.303.

Although this image clearly refers to a naval victory, it is far from clear which victory is meant. Since these coins were probably first struck shortly before the beginning of Alexander's expedition against the Persian empire, the Nike-type may have been meant to recall the great Athenian naval victory over Persia at Salamis in 480 BC (Price 1991: 29–30). If so (and other interpretations are possible), Alexander will have been trying to link his new campaign with the famous Greek victories over Persia in the early fifth century BC.

Alexander apparently did not begin to strike silver coins with his own types until late 333 or early 332 BC, around the time of his first major victory over the Persian king Darius III at Issus (November 333 BC). These coins were initially struck at mints near Issus in Cilicia and Phoenicia, before being taken up by royal mints back home in Macedon, and eventually right across Alexander's new empire (Le Rider 2007). Unlike Philip's earlier royal silver coinage, Alexander's new silver coins were struck on the Attic weight-standard: the main denominations were a drachm of *c.* 4.30 g and a tetradrachm of *c.* 17.17 g (Fig. 1.11). The obverse is a traditional Macedonian royal type, a portrait of Heracles in a lion-skin headdress, already found on Philip's silver didrachms and on the coinage of several earlier Macedonian kings (above, p. 10). The new reverse type shows a bearded deity seated on a throne, holding a sceptre in his left hand, with an eagle perched on his right hand.

Figure 1.11. Silver tetradrachm of Alexander the Great, struck at Tarsus in Cilicia (*c.* 333/2 BC). Alexander's army rested at Tarsus for several weeks in late summer 333 BC; these were the first silver coins struck by Alexander with his own types. 17.17 g. ANS 1965.77.80.

Figure 1.12. Silver stater of the Persian satrap Mazaeus, struck at Tarsus (*c.* 361–333 BC). The image of the seated god Ba'al on the obverse was adapted for the reverse of Alexander's tetradrachms. 10.91 g. ANS 1967.152.502.

The identity of this seated deity is a fascinating problem. A Greek or Macedonian viewer would naturally see it as an image of Zeus, the chief deity of the Graeco-Macedonian pantheon, whom, notoriously, Alexander would soon claim as his own father (Badian 1981). But in fact, the image is closely modelled on a contemporary Persian coin-type: the image of the Semitic god Ba'al of Tarsus which appears on coins minted by the Persian satrap Mazaeus in Cilicia (Fig. 1.12; Troxell 1997: 87–9; Casabonne 2004: 207–36). Alexander seems to have carefully chosen an image which would carry different connotations for two different audiences: continuity with Persian rule for his new subjects in Cilicia and Phoenicia, and traditional Hellenic piety for his own Macedonian army. Here, as elsewhere, we see Alexander brilliantly juggling his two *personae* as Graeco-Macedonian conqueror and as legitimate successor to the Achaemenid kingship of Asia (Briant 2002: 817–71; 2010; Lane Fox 2007).

III   The triumph of the 'Alexander'

As we have seen, the iconography of Alexander's gold and silver coinages was tailored to the political issues of the day: propaganda for his Panhellenic campaign against Persia (gold, *c.* 335/4 BC) and the need to appeal to newly conquered peoples of the Near East (silver, 333/2 BC) (Stewart 1993: 158–61). However, both coinages would live on long after the immediate political needs that originally inspired them. In the winter of 325/4 BC, Alexander and his army returned from India. The last eighteen months of his life saw a massive retirement programme, encompassing both his own ageing Macedonian troops and the large Greek and Thracian mercenary forces scattered across the satrapies of his new empire (Diod. Sic. 17.106.3). In 324, 10,000 Macedonian soldiers were discharged at Opis in Babylonia and sent on their way back home to Macedon – among them, I assume, the original owner of the Sinanpaşa hoard with which our story began. The historian Arrian tells us that each of these 10,000 soldiers received a personal gift of a talent (6,000 silver drachms), along with their back pay for the campaign (Arr. *Anab.* 7.12.1). That same year, Alexander also paid off the accumulated debts of his army, to the sum of 20,000 talents (Arr. *Anab.* 7.5.3).

These are almost unimaginably vast amounts of money. If all of these expenses were paid in silver tetradrachms, we would be talking about something like 54 million tetradrachms (36,000 talents) being paid out to Alexander's army in the summer of 324 BC *alone* (Price 1991: 25–7; Le Rider 2007: 64–6). Payments on this heroic scale were, of course, only possible thanks to the accumulated wealth of the Persian royal treasuries captured by Alexander in 331–330 BC, supposedly equivalent to 180,000 talents of silver (Strabo 15.3.9); by the time of Alexander's death in the summer of 323, we are told, only 50,000 talents remained (Justin 13.1.9).

It is no surprise to find that the years 325 to 323 BC saw an explosion of coin production by Alexander's royal mints, above all in Macedon, western Asia Minor and Babylonia. We can give only very rough estimates for the actual number of coins struck by any given mint. To take a single example, in the course of 324 and 323 BC, the main Macedonian royal mint at Amphipolis (in the far east of Macedonia) used something like 330 different obverse dies for striking silver 'Alexander' tetradrachms (Fig. 1.13; Troxell 1997: 86–98). If we assume that 20,000 coins were struck off each obverse die (Callataÿ 2005), that would mean that the Amphipolitan mint produced something like 6.6 million tetradrachms (4,400 talents) over these two years alone. During the same period, the Amphipolis mint also struck around 300,000 gold staters and 150,000 double staters, representing about 2,000 talents (the equivalent of another 3 million tetradrachms) (Le Rider 2007: 65–6).

This tremendous burst of production by the Amphipolis mint was surely intended to meet the costs of paying off decommissioned soldiers returning

Figure 1.13. Tetradrachm of Alexander the Great, struck at Amphipolis (324–323 BC). Vast numbers of these coins were struck as back pay for Alexander's veteran soldiers. 16.88 g. ANS 1947.98.38.

to Macedon from the East (Thompson 1984). Similarly, in western Asia Minor, half a dozen new royal mints started operating around 325 BC, all specializing in the production of 'Alexander' drachms (Touratsoglou 2004: 184–7; Le Rider 2007: 85–110). More than 96 per cent of the 670 surviving drachms from the Sinanpaşa hoard were struck at one of these western Asia Minor mints. We ought to picture our battle-scarred Macedonian infantryman finally arriving back on the Asiatic shore of the Aegean some time in the late 320s or early 310s BC, collecting his overdue back pay (plus bonus talent) of 9,000 or 10,000 silver drachms, before tramping back up country for the last time to hang up his *sarissa* in a comfortable Macedonian veteran colony somewhere near Sinanpaşa in central Turkey. The Sinanpaşa hoard represents what was left after his final blow-out on whores, booze and a nice big country villa.

The last years of Alexander's reign – and the last quarter of the fourth century BC more generally – form a massive watershed in Greek monetary history. Between 325 and 300 BC, the accumulated wealth of the Persian empire flooded out into the Greek and Near Eastern economy in the form of gold staters and silver drachms and tetradrachms on the Attic weight-standard – initially in order to pay off Alexander's veteran troops, and later to fund the huge armies of his successors. Quantifying the total amount of coinage produced by Alexander's royal mints across this entire period is far from easy. Recent estimates suggest that between 333 and 290 BC Alexander's royal mints may have struck some 60 million tetradrachms, 66 million drachms and 12 million gold staters (Callataÿ 2005: 87; 2011b: 23). Since gold and silver were valued at a 10:1 ratio in this period, this represents the equivalent of *c.* 91,000 talents of coined silver in total (51,000 talents in silver, 40,000 in gold). To give some idea of scale,

91,000 talents would buy 182 Parthenons (one Parthenon = 500 talents) – or, from another perspective, is probably a little more than the aggregate revenue of the fifth-century Athenian empire throughout its entire seventy-three-year existence (477–404 BC, *c.* 1,000 talents per year).

This vast new mass of coinage exercised an irresistible gravitational pull on all the other currency systems of the Greek world. Before 325 BC, Greek silver and gold coinages had been struck on a bewildering variety of different weight-standards, with a rich and diverse repertoire of local types. In the late fourth century, these local coinages went into a sharp decline. From around 300 BC, many cities, particularly in Asia Minor, abandoned their distinctive civic types and moved over to minting local imitations of Alexander's coinage (and, in a few cases, Philip's), with discreet civic symbols and mint-marks on the reverse (Fig. 1.14; Ashton 2012b: 192–3). These so-called 'civic Alexanders' (discussed in more detail in Chapters 2 and 3 below) were still being struck in the Black Sea region as late as the first century BC. Likewise, the influence of Alexander's coinage meant that the Attic standard became effectively the sole weight-standard used for international transactions, although many cities continued to run their own miniature epichoric ('local') currency systems alongside (see Chapters 6 and 7 below).

The sheer volume of gold and silver 'Alexanders' struck between *c.* 333 and 290 BC meant that the period *c.* 290–225 BC saw relatively little coinage being minted anywhere in Greece and the Near East: there were quite enough coins in the system already. Royal 'Alexanders' of the late fourth century make up a huge proportion of the coin hoards buried in Asia Minor and the Near East throughout the third century BC (Le Rider and Callataÿ 2006: 71–99). For instance, a hoard from Gordium in central Turkey, apparently buried at the very end of the third century BC, consists of fifty silver drachms

Figure 1.14. 'Alexander-style' tetradrachm, struck by the city of Miletus in western Asia Minor (*c.* 275–240 BC). The reverse type carries a lion (the civic blazon of Miletus) and the letters MI in a monogram. 17.02 g. ANS 1944.100.32002.

in a pot (*IGCH* 1401). No fewer than forty-six of them are fourth-century 'Alexander' drachms struck in western Asia Minor, still happily circulating in inland Turkey more than a hundred years later (Le Rider 2007: 97).

IV   The successors and a new numismatic 'koinē'

Take a look at Figures 1.15 and 1.16 – a lifetime tetradrachm of Alexander and a tetradrachm of the early Seleucid king Antiochus I (ruled 281–261 BC). No one would mistake one coin for the other. The two portraits (of Heracles and Antiochus I, respectively) are very different in style, and the reverse type of Antiochus' coin depicts a different deity altogether (the god Apollo, seated on an *omphalos*, checking his arrows). But at the same time, Antiochus' coinage is obviously modelled in some very basic ways on the earlier 'Alexanders'. Both coins depict a right-facing beardless male profile on the obverse, with a full-length portrait of a seated deity on the reverse, facing left with his right arm extended. Even certain minor details of the coinages are the same, such as the legend running vertically from top to bottom on the reverse, or the border of dots on each face.

Now compare Figure 1.17, a tetradrachm of the Armenian king Tigranes II (ruled *c.* 95–56 BC). We are now in a very different visual world from that of Alexander's coinage. In his portrait on the obverse, the king sports a stupendous pearled tiara, and the figure on the reverse (the Tyche or 'fortune' of

Figure 1.15. Tetradrachm of Alexander, struck at Babylon late in Alexander's reign (*c.* 325–323 BC). 17.20 g. ANS 1944.100.80183.

Figure 1.16. Tetradrachm of the Seleucid king Antiochus I, struck at Seleucia on the Tigris (*c.* 281–261 BC). 17.14 g. ANS 1946.89.93.

Figure 1.17. Tetradrachm of Tigranes II of Armenia, struck at Antioch (*c.* 75–69 BC). 14.92 g. ANS 1944.100.76964.

Antioch in Syria) is resting her feet rather awkwardly on a personification of the river Orontes. The border of dots has mutated on one face into a bead and reel pattern, and on the other into a laurel wreath. Nonetheless, a full 250 years after Alexander's death, much of the basic iconographic format and 'vocabulary' remains essentially unchanged (right-facing male profile, full-length seated deity and vertical legend).

These two examples were chosen pretty much at random; dozens of other coin designs would have made the same point. Virtually every king who ruled anywhere in the Hellenistic period took Alexander's coinage as his model. The desire to link oneself visually with the great conqueror is of course part of the story. But remember the huge numbers of 'Alexanders' sloshing around the Greek and Near Eastern economy in the third century BC. The greater part of any third-century soldier's pay-packet would have been made up of Alexander-style coinage. No doubt the average infantryman expected the rest of his pay to look like 'proper coins' too: good metal, nice portrait on the front, god on the back and so on. Some of this was probably subliminal – I doubt many people looked at a border of dots and said 'Oooh, isn't that just like Alexander's coins!' What we are seeing here is the growth of a new numismatic common language, a growing sense of what a 'proper coin' is supposed to look like (Bracey 2011: 46–9).

In the generation or so after Alexander's death, most of the generals and satraps who succeeded to his vast empire (Perdiccas, Antipater, Antigonus and others) continued minting coins with his royal types. As we have seen, between 323 and 317, many of these Alexander-style issues carried the name of the short-lived Philip III Arrhidaeus on their reverse (Fig. 1.18). The first of the successors to break away from this conservative pattern was Ptolemy, appointed as satrap of Egypt in 323 BC. This ought to come as no surprise: Ptolemy, firmly entrenched in his wealthy Egyptian satrapy, was

Figure 1.18. Alexander-style tetradrachm in the name of Philip III Arrhidaeus, struck at Sardis (*c.* 323–319 BC). 17.10 g. ANS 1944.100.31284.

by far the earliest of the successors to show strong separatist tendencies (Diod. Sic. 18.39.5; Hölbl 2001: 9–34).

Around 319 BC, Ptolemy introduced a new silver coinage on the Attic weight-standard (Lorber 2005; Lorber 2012a: 211–14; von Reden 2007: 33–43). These coins carried the traditional 'Alexander' type on the reverse, with Zeus/Ba'al seated on a throne and the single word ALEXANDROU, 'of Alexander' (Fig. 1.19). The obverse type, however, is entirely new: it shows Alexander wearing an elephant-skin headdress, with a ram's horn sprouting from his right temple, indicating his descent from Zeus Ammon. A few years later, perhaps around 311, Ptolemy changed the reverse type of his coinage as well. The seated Zeus/Ba'al was now replaced with an image of Athena Alkidemos ('protector of the people') striding to the right and brandishing a spear (Fig. 1.20).

The period between *c.* 305 and 294 saw Ptolemy gradually moving away from the Attic weight-standard: the weight of his tetradrachms drops in stages from *c.* 17.25 g to *c.* 14.20 g, for reasons which will be discussed in detail in Chapter 6. Around 298/7 BC, Ptolemy introduced a new series of gold staters, which for the first time carried his own diademed portrait on the obverse; the reverse type is also new, and depicts Alexander riding a chariot drawn by four elephants, accompanied by the legend BASILEŌS PTOLEMAIOU, 'of King Ptolemy' (Fig. 1.21). Finally, around 294 BC, Ptolemy scrapped his Alexander/ Athena tetradrachm series and created a new silver coinage, with his own portrait on the obverse and an eagle perched on a thunderbolt on the reverse (Fig. 1.22; Lorber 2012b).

The reason why the early development of Ptolemy's coinage is so complicated is that every step was an innovation: the introduction of a coin portrait of Alexander (*c.* 319 BC); the decision to move away from Alexander's types altogether (*c.* 311 BC); the decision to move off the

Figure 1.19. Tetradrachm struck by Ptolemy son of Lagus, satrap of Egypt (*c.* 319–311 BC). The reverse is modelled on Alexander's tetradrachms, but the obverse portrait of the deified Alexander is Ptolemy's own innovation. 17.17 g. ANS 1957.172.1269.

Figure 1.20. Tetradrachm of Ptolemy, first as satrap (*c.* 311–305 BC), then as king (*c.* 305–294 BC). These coins still carry Alexander's name on the reverse (ALEXANDROU). 15.71 g. ANS 1957.172.2020.

Figure 1.21. Gold stater of King Ptolemy I (from *c.* 298/7 BC). These were the first coins struck by Ptolemy in his own name and with his own portrait. 7.10 g. ANS 1967.152.621.

Figure 1.22. Tetradrachm of King Ptolemy I (from *c.* 294 BC). Note the light weight of these coins: this weight-standard was distinctive to Ptolemaic Egypt and the overseas Ptolemaic empire. 14.75 g. ANS 1944.100.75453.

Attic weight-standard (*c.* 305 BC); and the introduction of Ptolemy's own portrait (*c.* 298–294 BC). The coinages of the other major successors are, for the most part, much more straightforward.

In Thrace, the former satrap Lysimachus (reigned *c.* 305–281 BC) started striking his own royal coinage around 297/6 BC, clearly in

Figure 1.23. Tetradrachm of Lysimachus, minted at Lampsacus (*c.* 297–281 BC). The spectacular portrait of Alexander recalls Lysimachus' earlier career as one of Alexander's bodyguards. 17.11 g. ANS 1944.100.45301.

Figure 1.24. Tetradrachm of Demetrius Poliorcetes (*c.* 292–287 BC). The idealized image of Demetrius may be modelled on the portrait of Alexander on Lysimachus' coins. 16.97 g. ANS 1967.152.208.

response to Ptolemy's new gold portrait coins (Fig. 1.23; Thompson 1968b; Lund 1992). Lysimachus' silver tetradrachms carry a bare-headed portrait of Alexander on the obverse, with a diadem bound around his head and a ram's horn growing from his right temple. The reverse type depicts a seated Athena holding in her right hand a little figure of Nike, who is reaching out to place a wreath on the name Lysimachus. As we will see in Chapter 2, this coin-type went on to have a long Hellenistic afterlife in the Black Sea region.

Very similar in style was the royal coinage of Demetrius Poliorcetes (ruled 306–286 BC), probably also first struck in the mid-290s BC (Fig. 1.24; Newell 1927). The obverses of the gold and silver coins carry a youthful portrait of Demetrius, with his features and hairstyle closely resembling the portrait of Alexander on Lysimachus' coins, although the ram's horn of Zeus Ammon is replaced by a small bull's horn poking out from his hair (Thonemann 2005). The reverse type of Demetrius' silver depicts the god Poseidon, an allusion to the awesome power of Demetrius' fleet.

Finally, the Seleucid dynasty of Mesopotamia. Amid the luxuriant variety of the early Seleucid royal coinage (Houghton and Lorber 2002; Erickson 2013), two types stand out. At some point after 301 BC, Seleucus I (ruled *c.* 311–281 BC) struck an issue of Attic-weight tetradrachms at Susa, with a male bust wearing a horned helmet on the obverse and a Nike crowning a

Figure 1.25. Tetradrachm of Seleucus I from Susa (perhaps *c.* 301–295 BC). The male figure on the obverse, wearing a panther-skin helmet with horns, is probably Seleucus himself, although Alexander the Great and the god Dionysus have also been suggested. 16.89 g. ANS 1944.100.74108.

Figure 1.26. Tetradrachm of Antiochus I from Sardis, with a portrait of the deified Seleucus I (*c.* 281–261 BC). The reverse type, with Apollo seated on an *omphalos* ('navel-stone') and holding a bow, was used by several third- and second-century BC Seleucid kings. 17.03 g. ANS 1967.152.671.

military trophy on the reverse (Fig. 1.25). The identity of the helmeted figure has been much debated, but the consensus now seems to be that it is our earliest extant portrait of Seleucus himself (Hoover 2002). His son and successor, Antiochus I (ruled 281–261 BC), struck coins with a portrait of his father in a very similar style to that which we have already seen on the coinages of Lysimachus and Demetrius: Seleucus is now depicted with the same shaggy mane of hair as Alexander and Demetrius, and a bull's horn protruding from underneath his diadem (Fig. 1.26; Hoover 2011).

As will be clear from the past few paragraphs, and as we shall see in more detail in Chapter 8, Hellenistic royal coinages are a fascinating source for the changing ideologies of kingship in the Hellenistic period. The point that I wish to make here is a much simpler one. A quick flick back through the images of coins on the past few pages will, I hope, show very clearly how all these coinages share essentially the same iconographic and stylistic vocabulary (Kroll 2007). For all their myriad modulations of detail (horns, diadems, headdresses; male and female gods, standing and seated), every single one is basically a variation on the theme of Alexander's original royal coinage.

This fundamental point will recur again and again throughout this book. Today, two currencies, the dollar and the euro, effectively play the role of 'global money', dominating international exchange and serving as the main reserve currencies worldwide. In the Hellenistic world, the coinage of Alexander the Great played a similar global role, with countless royal and civic mints adapting their types and weight-standards to fit this new universal norm. Chapter 2 will map out the size and shape of this vast Hellenistic monetary civilization, which, as we shall see, eventually stretched all the way from the Atlantic to India, and from northern Europe deep into the deserts of Arabia.

2
A 'big' Hellenistic world

I Defining the Hellenistic

We all know *when* Hellenistic history happened: from the death of Alexander in 323 BC down to the death of Cleopatra in 30 BC. Most periodizations in history are pretty arbitrary, and the 'Hellenistic' is no exception (Shipley 2000: 1–5). At the lower end, the 'Hellenistic period' goes distinctly ragged around the edges: parts of the eastern Mediterranean tend to drop quietly out of Hellenistic history and into Roman Republican history at the point when they become part of the Roman empire (Macedonia in 146 BC, Asia Minor in 129 BC, Syria in 64 BC). Still, we cannot always be talking about 'the period roughly from the break-up of the Persian empire *c.* 334–301 BC to the fall of the major Graeco-Macedonian kingdoms *c.* 146–30 BC', and – so long as we remember that it is a kind of shorthand – the notion of a Hellenistic period is no worse than most.

But *where* was the Hellenistic world? This question makes much more of a difference. In practice, historians usually treat the Hellenistic world as roughly co-extensive with the short-lived empire of Alexander: Greece and the southern Balkans, the eastern Mediterranean including Egypt, and western Asia from Turkey and the Levant to Afghanistan and Pakistan. That is to say, the Hellenistic world is usually studied as though it were confined to the various Graeco-Macedonian successor kingdoms and the Greek *poleis* of Europe and Asia (Walbank 1981; Errington 2008). Regions outside this supposed core zone – the entire western Mediterranean, central and northern Europe, the kingdoms of east and south Arabia – are studied separately, as though they were part of a different world altogether. For most historians, phrases like 'Hellenistic Gaul' or 'Hellenistic Carthage' feel intuitively just as odd as 'Renaissance Ethiopia' or 'medieval Australia'.

Since the whole idea of a 'Hellenistic world' is a modern invention, our intuitions are frankly neither here nor there. A recent book, combatively titled *The Hellenistic West* (Prag and Quinn 2013), urges us to think through the consequences of regarding the western Mediterranean (including Rome and Carthage) as part of a single, 'big' Hellenistic world. Nicholas

Purcell has made a case for taking the whole, densely populated zone from Cadiz to Susa, the Mediterranean in the west and the Fertile Crescent in the east, as a single unit of study (Purcell 2013). Needless to say, this is only one of several possible right answers. We can pick any unit of study that we like: Eurasia, the Mediterranean, land below 1,000 m altitude. The point is that the questions we ask about Hellenistic societies should not be constrained by arbitrary preconceptions about what the Hellenistic world 'really is'.

In this chapter, I will suggest that coinage offers one possible way of mapping and defining a 'big' Hellenistic world. The third and second centuries BC saw the emergence of a kind of monetary 'common language zone', stretching from the Atlantic to the Indian subcontinent. Regions far beyond the Graeco-Macedonian kingdoms, to both the east (Pakistan, the Arabian peninsula) and the west (Spain, north-west Europe), became monetized for the first time in this period. More importantly, monetization took very similar forms right across these widely dispersed regions. The huge coin issues of Alexander the Great and Philip of Macedon served as the model for coins struck everywhere from East Anglia to eastern Arabia.

As it happens, this notion of a 'big' Hellenistic world – Britain to Sri Lanka – reflects the outer limits of Greek geographical exploration in the period rather well (Cunliffe 2001; Geus 2003). This is no coincidence. The Hellenistic monetary 'language zone' was created by the aggregate physical movement of peoples across western Eurasia, both itinerant mercenary soldiers (particularly Thracians and Celts) and long-distance traders (particularly in Arabia and the Far East). The aim of this chapter is to map out the particular human networks reflected in our surviving coin evidence. We will focus on two distinct phenomena: the physical migration of coins far away from their original place of minting, and the imitation of Graeco-Macedonian coin-types outside the major successor kingdoms. Many of these themes will be taken up again in Chapter 5, which deals with new 'Hellenizing' identities on the outer fringes of the Graeco-Macedonian world: the Parthians, Graeco-Bactrian and Indo-Greek kingdoms will be discussed in more detail in this later chapter.

II   The north

As we have already seen, the royal coinages of Alexander the Great and Philip II were very widely imitated by Greek cities in the third and second centuries BC (Chapter 1 above, p. 16). It is important to be clear that these were not in any sense official royal issues: any city could choose to mint

Figure 2.1. Alexander-style tetradrachm of Rhodes (*c.* 205–190 BC). Note the Rhodian rose symbol on the reverse, and the letters *rho* and *omicron* (the first two letters of 'Rhodes' in Greek) under Zeus' throne. The coin also carries the name of a Rhodian civic mint-magistrate, Diophanēs. 17.19 g. ANS 1947.98.216.

Macedonian-style coinage whenever it wished. So when the island-city of Rhodes struck a small issue of Alexander-style tetradrachms in *c.* 205–190 BC (with a discreet Rhodian rose symbol on the reverse), this need not indicate any loyalty to Macedon, or any special Rhodian connection with Alexander (Fig. 2.1; Ashton 2001: 88). All it means is that Rhodes suddenly found itself in need of a widely acceptable international Attic-weight silver currency, and the well-known Alexander-type fitted the bill.

Most modern studies of Hellenistic coinage draw a sharp distinction between these 'civic' Alexander- and Philip-style coinages (largely in Greece and Asia Minor) and 'barbarous' Alexander and Philip imitations minted outside the Greek world. But the distinction is a fuzzy one at best. In both cases we are dealing with what Peter van Alfen has called 'marked imitations': imitative coins which stick very closely to their prototype in metal, weight and iconography, but which clearly indicate (through the use of legends, symbols or monograms) that they are the product of a distinct issuing authority (van Alfen 2005: 333–4). In formal terms, there are few grounds for distinguishing between a 'civic' Alexander-type from the island of Samos, carrying a Samian trireme prow and the abbreviated ethnic SA on the reverse, and a 'barbarous' Alexander-type from (say) north-west Arabia, with the name of the Hagarite king Abyatha in South Arabian script on the reverse (Figs. 2.2–2.3).

Perhaps the best sense of the global impact of the late fourth-century Macedonian royal coinage can be gained by looking at northern Europe, and the various Iron Age peoples collectively known to modern scholarship

Figure 2.2. Alexander-style tetradrachm of Samos (*c.* 250–225 BC), with a Samian trireme prow and abbreviated ethnic (Sᴀ) on the reverse. 16.92 g. ANS 1974.26.537.

Figure 2.3. Alexander-style tetradrachm of Abyatha (*c.* 220–204 BC), with the name Abyatha ('byt') in South Arabian script on the reverse. 16.58 g. ANS 1986.44.1.

as 'Celts' (James 1999; Collis 2003). The earliest 'Celtic' coinages date to the early third century, and are all based on Macedonian royal types (Nash 1987; von Reden 2010: 55–63). The imitation of Philip's and Alexander's coinages in temperate Europe was not the result of long-distance trade, but rather of the large-scale use of Celtic mercenaries by Macedonian kings. Hellenistic royal armies were a rag-tag mix of mercenary soldiers, many of them Celts from north of the Danube (Archibald 2011: 46–51). The Roman historian Livy describes how the Macedonian king Perseus (reigned 179–167 BC) tried to enlist a 20,000-strong Celtic mercenary force (the Bastarnae of the middle Danube) in the lead-up to the battle of Pydna in 168 BC (Livy 44.26–7). The Celts demanded a one-off payment of ten gold pieces for each cavalryman and five for each infantryman, with a further thousand gold coins for their commander. If this is at all typical, it is easy to see how Macedonian gold and silver could have travelled northwards in vast quantities.

The new coinages of Iron Age Europe divide fairly neatly into a 'silver zone' to the south-east (the middle and lower Danube) and a 'gold zone' to the north-west (stretching from south-east Britain to Bohemia) (Allen and Nash 1980). Different coin-types served as the model in different regions: so the Celts of the middle and lower Danube copied the silver tetradrachms of Philip II and Alexander III respectively, while in north-west Europe,

Philip's gold staters were imitated in the lands west of the Rhine, with copies of Alexander's gold staters predominating further to the east in Bohemia. Genuine Macedonian coins are surprisingly few and far between in coin hoards from northern Europe (Wigg-Wolf 2008). Apparently local Iron Age societies preferred to melt down their imported gold and silver coins and remint them with their own types.

The first Celtic imitations stuck fairly closely to their Macedonian models, but increasingly distinctive local styles emerge over the third and second centuries. By way of example, let us take a look at the imitations of Philip's gold staters in north-west Europe (Allen and Nash 1980: 68–82). Philip's original gold staters carried on the obverse a beardless head of Apollo wearing a laurel wreath, with a two-horse chariot and rider and the legend Philippou on the reverse. The first Celtic imitations come from north-west Switzerland (early third century BC) and stay very close to their original model, both in types and weight (Fig. 2.4; Keller 1996). By the second century BC, gold imitations of Philip's staters were being struck across much of northern Gaul. But by now the types had been radically adapted to suit the styles and images favoured in the Celtic world (Harding 2007: 212–15). The types became less and less 'realistic', with an increasing emphasis on patterns and abstract curvilinear shapes. The horses and charioteer on the reverse undergo a particularly striking series of transformations: we find a female rider (perhaps the Celtic goddess Epona), horses with human faces, and defeated enemies or wild boar being trampled under the horses' hooves (Fig. 2.5). The coins of the Parisii, in the Seine valley, or the so-called 'Gallo-Belgic A' coins, struck in Belgic Gaul and found in various parts of south-east England, illustrate quite how far the Celtic types eventually travelled from their original Macedonian model (Figs. 2.6–2.7).

Figure 2.4. Celtic imitation of gold stater of Philip II, struck in north-west Switzerland (*c*. 300–250 BC). Note the slightly stylized horses' heads. 8.54 g. ANS 1944.100.71838.

Figure 2.5. Celtic imitation of gold stater of Philip II, struck by the Treveri, near modern Trier (second century BC). The horse on the reverse now has a human face. 7.56 g. ANS 1944.100.74208.

Figure 2.6. Celtic imitation of gold stater of Philip II, struck by the Parisii, in the Seine valley (*c.* 125–50 BC). The rider on the reverse has disappeared, and the weight-standard has dropped significantly. 6.74 g. ANS 1944.100.74136.

Figure 2.7. Celtic imitation of gold stater of Philip II, struck in northern France or Belgium ('Gallo-Belgic A', *c.* 150–100 BC). Coins of this type were imported into south-east England in large quantities; they were the first coins of any kind to circulate in Britain. 7.26 g. ANS 1944.100.74142.

Clearly the people of Iron Age Europe were not just slavishly copying Macedonian coinage: the 'globalized' Philip and Alexander types were creatively adapted to Celtic tastes and interests. The same could well be true of day-to-day coin use in Iron Age Europe. Just because Celtic coins look like other Hellenistic coinages does not mean that they were actually used in the same way (Bloch and Parry 1989; Howgego 2013). The evidence for the use of coins for trade and exchange in Iron Age Europe is very limited. Instead, gold and silver coins are very often found in ceremonial ritual deposits alongside other prestige objects such as torcs and brooches. Coins seem not to have had their own distinctively economic niche in Hellenistic Celtic society: they were just one of a whole range of socially valuable material goods, including decorative weapons and jewellery.

A second major group of Celtic imitation coinage dates to the late second and the first century BC. One of the largest silver coinages of the Greek world in this period was the tetradrachm coinage of the Greek island of Thasos (*c.* 160–80 BC). These coins bear a bust of Dionysus on the obverse and a standing Heracles on the reverse, with the name of 'Heracles Saviour' and the ethnic of Thasos (THASIŌN) in Greek (Fig. 2.8; Callataÿ 2008; Psoma 2013: 289–92). Thasian-type tetradrachms were struck in very large quantities during the early first century BC, almost certainly by officials in the Roman province of Macedonia, in order to pay Roman auxiliary troops

Figure 2.8. Tetradrachm of Thasos (*c.* 160 BC). 16.95 g. ANS 1966.75.86.

Figure 2.9. Thasos-style tetradrachm of the early first century BC, probably minted by a Roman official (Prokopov 2006: Group XIV). The types are identical to the genuine Thasian tetradrachms of the mid-second century. 16.78 g. ANS 1948.19.586.

recruited from Thrace and the lower Danube basin (Fig. 2.9; Callataÿ 2009a: 59–70). As we will see in Chapter 9, this was very characteristic of the early Roman empire in the east: Roman governors and generals often struck imitations of pre-existing Greek coin-types, rather than trying to impose the use of the Roman denarius or a new 'provincial' coinage.

Between about 120 BC and 70 BC, very large numbers of these Thasian-type coins travelled north into modern Bulgaria and Romania in the hands of retired mercenaries. As a result, many of the Celtic peoples of the lower Danube began striking their own imitations of Thasian-type tetra-drachms, which circulated as far north as modern Hungary (Prokopov 2011). As with earlier Celtic coinage, the first of these imitations followed their Thasian models quite closely (Fig. 2.10), but by the mid-first century BC they have taken their own distinctive stylistic path. On the late Celtic Thasian-type tetradrachms, the Greek legend on the reverse has been transformed into a horseshoe-shaped pattern of dots, and the bust of

Figure 2.10. Celtic imitation Thasos-style tetradrachm of the early first century BC. The Greek legend on the reverse has become mangled, and the style is distinctively 'Celtic', but on the whole this coin stays fairly close to its original model. 16.32 g. ANS 1948.19.2354.

Figure 2.11. Celtic imitation Thasos-style tetradrachm of the later first century BC. The Greek legend on the reverse has been replaced with an abstract pattern of dots. 16.07 g. ANS 1944.100.75440.

Dionysus on the obverse has fractured into a kaleidoscope of geometric shapes (Fig. 2.11).

III   The Balkans and the Black Sea

In the Balkans, as in Celtic Europe to the north, several non-Greek kings and chieftains struck coins with types imitating the silver coinage of Alexander. By the last years of the fourth century BC, King Audoleon of Paeonia (the mountainous region north of Macedon) was striking Alexander-style coins bearing his own name and title on the reverse, BASILEŌS AUDŌLEONTOS, 'of King Audoleon' (Fig. 2.12; Waggoner 1983). His example was followed in the third century BC by King Monounios in Illyria and by two Thracian rulers, Orsoaltios and Kersibaulos, all of whom

Figure 2.12. Alexander-style tetradrachm of Audoleon of Paeonia (late fourth century BC). 16.79 g. ANS 1981.67.1.

Figure 2.13. Alexander-style tetradrachm of Kavaros (*c.* 225–215 BC). 16.73 g. ANS 1968.19.3.

minted imitation Alexander tetradrachms in their own name (Peter 1997: 249–50). Most striking of all is a series of Alexander-style coins struck by the Celtic chieftain Kavaros at the fortress of Kabyle in inland Thrace (*c.* 225–215 BC). Unlike the Celtic 'Philips' and 'Alexanders' of northern Europe, Kavaros' coins stuck very closely to their Macedonian models, with only the legend Basileōs Kauarou ('of King Kavaros') to indicate their Celtic origin (Fig. 2.13; Price 1991: I, 173–4; Manov and Damyanov 2013).

The third and second centuries BC saw large quantities of gold and silver coinage flowing northwards from the Greek cities of Aegean Thrace and the Black Sea into the non-Greek kingdoms of inland Thrace and south Russia. Much of this coinage was directly extorted by powerful non-Greek states, demanding tribute from their Greek neighbours, rather like the Danegeld later levied by the Vikings on the Anglo-Saxon kingdom of England. The Greek historian Polybius describes how, in the mid-third century BC, the city of Byzantium was forced to pay protection money of 80 talents per year (in gold staters) to the neighbouring Celtic kingdom of Tylis (Polybius 4.45–6; Gabrielsen 2007). At Istrus, near the mouth of the Danube in modern Romania, a large Thracian army on the verge of ravaging the city's territory was bought off by a one-time payment of 600 gold staters (Austin 2006: no. 116). Finally, at Olbia, in modern Ukraine, the Scythian king Saitaphernes repeatedly demanded 'gifts' of several hundred gold coins at a time, to be paid whenever he passed near the city.

'Gifts' for Saitaphernes

A long honorific decree for a certain Protogenes of Olbia (c. 200 BC) gives a vivid picture of the tense relationship between Greek cities and their non-Greek neighbours on the northern shore of the Black Sea. Saitaphernes, king of the Scythian tribe of the Saii, turned up from time to time on the borders of the city's territory, demanding 'gifts' from the Olbians. When the city's magistrates were unable to find the necessary cash, they called on one of their wealthiest citizens, Protogenes, to help out:

> When King Saitaphernes arrived at Kankytos and demanded the gifts due for his passage, and the public treasury was exhausted, Protogenes was called upon by the *dēmos* and gave 400 gold pieces... [Some time later], when the Saii came by to receive their gifts, the *dēmos* was unable to provide them, and called on Protogenes to help out in this crisis; he came forward and promised 400 gold pieces. When he was elected as one of the city's Nine magistrates, he lent 1,500 gold pieces to be repaid from the city's future revenues, out of which several chieftains were placated in good time, and several gifts were gainfully provided to the king.

The city's relationship with Saitaphernes was clearly a delicate one. Some years later, the king took great offence at some perceived insult in the exchange of 'gifts', and seems to have threatened to sack Olbia:

> When King Saitaphernes arrived on the far side of the river to receive his gifts, the magistrates called an assembly, reported on the king's arrival, and said that the city's revenues were exhausted; Protogenes came forward and gave 900 gold pieces. But when the ambassadors, Protogenes and Aristocrates, took the money and met with the king, the king rejected the gifts, flew into a rage, and broke up his camp...

This episode beautifully illustrates the clash of two very different economic systems. From Saitaphernes' perspective, his regular protection money from Olbia took the form of 'gifts': the point was not to draw 'tribute' from Olbia, but to receive a token of honour and goodwill. Similarly, back in the fourth century BC, whenever the Persian Great King crossed over the mountainous territory of the Uxians between Persepolis and Susa, he would exchange compulsory 'gifts' with the

Uxians as a means of showing mutual respect. When Alexander the Great crossed through these mountains in 331 BC, he was outraged to find that the Uxians expected to receive presents from him, and launched a vicious campaign against them (Arr. *Anab.* 3.17.1). The Uxians, like Saitaphernes, did not perceive their actions as extortion, but simply as part of a system of regular gift exchange (Briant 1982: 57–112). Greeks seem often to have disastrously misinterpreted this cycle of gift and counter-gift (Mauss 1990 [1925]) as simple brigandage. (Austin 2006: no. 115; Müller 2011.)

The main model for local coinages in Thrace and the northern Black Sea was the royal gold and silver coinage of Lysimachus. Lysimachus had been appointed as satrap of Thrace after Alexander's death in 323. After 301, he took possession of much of western Asia Minor, and between 288 and his death in 281 he controlled Macedonia itself (Lund 1992; Shipley 2000: 47–51). His gold and silver coins, minted in large quantities from *c.* 297/6 BC, carried a diademed portrait of Alexander on the obverse, with a prominent ram's horn (indicating his descent from Zeus Ammon) sprouting from his forehead; the reverse depicted the goddess Athena, carrying a little Nike figure in her right hand, who reaches out to lay a wreath on the name Lysimachus (Fig. 2.14; Thompson 1968b).

Despite the collapse of Lysimachus' kingdom in 281, his coinage and its later imitations continued to act as the common international currency in Thrace and the Black Sea throughout the third and second centuries BC. Coins with Lysimachus' types may have been favoured precisely because of Lysimachus' disappearance from the political scene: minting 'Lysimachi' could well have been a way of signalling neutrality *vis-à-vis* the Seleucid, Ptolemaic and Antigonid dynasties (the three main rival powers in the region in the later third century).

Perhaps even before Lysimachus' death in 281, a dynast in inland Thrace by the name of Skostokos struck his own silver tetradrachms with Lysimachus' royal types (Fischer-Bossert 2005). These coins are in most respects identical to royal and 'civic' Lysimachi, apart from the single word Skostokou, 'of Skostokos', added at the bottom of the reverse type (Fig. 2.15). It is unclear whether Skostokos was a local Thracian vassal of Lysimachus, or whether he was an independent Thracian chieftain imitating the coinage of his more powerful neighbour.

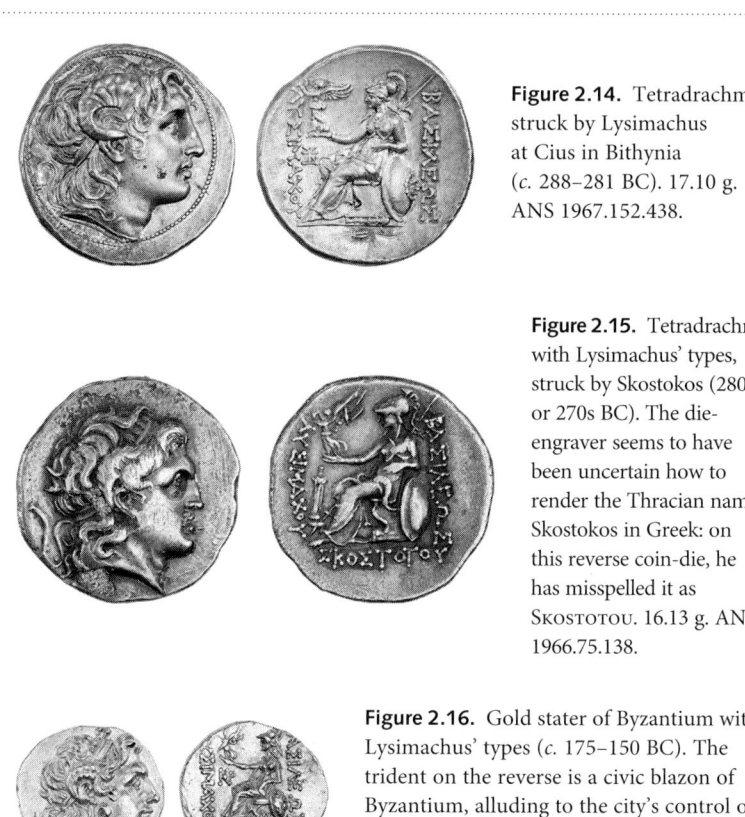

Figure 2.14. Tetradrachm struck by Lysimachus at Cius in Bithynia (*c.* 288–281 BC). 17.10 g. ANS 1967.152.438.

Figure 2.15. Tetradrachm with Lysimachus' types, struck by Skostokos (280s or 270s BC). The die-engraver seems to have been uncertain how to render the Thracian name Skostokos in Greek: on this reverse coin-die, he has misspelled it as Sᴋᴏsᴛᴏᴛᴏᴜ. 16.13 g. ANS 1966.75.138.

Figure 2.16. Gold stater of Byzantium with Lysimachus' types (*c.* 175–150 BC). The trident on the reverse is a civic blazon of Byzantium, alluding to the city's control of the Black Sea straits. 8.51 g. ANS 1967.46.111.

From the 260s BC, the cities on the two shores of the Bosporus, Byzantium and Chalcedon, began striking large numbers of gold staters and silver tetradrachms with Lysimachus' types (Fig. 2.16; Marinescu 1996). Their huge third-century issues of gold staters were probably struck primarily as 'protection money' for the Thracian Celts. Various Greek cities in the western Black Sea (Istrus, Tomis, Kallatis, Odessus, Mesembria) also minted Lysimachus-style gold staters from the mid-third century onwards, no doubt for similar reasons (Petac and Vîlcu 2012). These coins were particularly favoured by the Celtic, Dacian and Scythian peoples of the Black Sea hinterland: gold staters with Lysimachus' types appear in large numbers in hoards from Romania and south Russia, and an enormous find of some 40,000 gold staters from southern Transylvania, buried in the first century BC, consisted almost entirely of gold Lysimachi (*IGCH* 670).

In the far north of the Black Sea, local gold coins based on Lysimachus' types were struck by the Spartocid dynasty of the Cimmerian Bosporus (today's eastern Crimea). Between about 180 and 120 BC, a succession of Bosporan rulers struck gold staters modelled on the Lysimachus coinage of Byzantium. The obverse of these Bosporan staters carried a ruler portrait based on the image of Alexander on Lysimachus' coins, but lacking the prominent ram's horn: this modified portrait was presumably intended to depict the Spartocid king. The reverse types are identical to those of the Byzantine Lysimachi, except for the legend, which reads (in most cases) Basileōs Pairisadou, 'of King Pairisades' (Stolyarik 2000). The example illustrated here (Fig. 2.17) probably dates to the 170s BC.

Around 140 BC, a Bosporan king named Spartocus struck an unusual issue of silver didrachms, carrying the same modified portrait of Alexander on the obverse, but with a distinctive local reverse type, a bow-case flanked by the title Basileōs Spartokou, 'of King Spartocus' (Fig. 2.18; Stolyarik 2004/5). Strikingly, this reverse type still carries the characteristic mint-mark of Byzantium below the bow-case (trident with two dolphins). Apparently the kings of the Bosporus mechanically imitated this symbol on their own royal coinage, without understanding its 'original' meaning as a Byzantine mint-mark.

Just as with the north European Celts, the gold coinage of Lysimachus and its local imitations may have played a role more symbolic than

Figure 2.17. Gold stater with types imitating the 'Lysimachus' coinage of Byzantium, struck by King Pairisades III of the Cimmerian Bosporus (*c.* 180–170 BC). Note the 'Byzantine' trident on the reverse. 8.40 g. ANS 1944.100.40974.

Figure 2.18. Silver didrachm of King Spartocus of the Cimmerian Bosporus (*c.* 140 BC). Didrachms are a relatively unusual denomination; the choice of denomination may be influenced by the prevalence of gold staters (also of didrachm weight) in this region. 8.32 g. ANS 1954.67.1.

economic in the aristocratic society of the Cimmerian Bosporus. In a large funerary barrow of the mid-second century BC (the Artjukhov *kurgan*, from the Taman peninsula), a husband and wife were buried side by side with a lavish assemblage of gold and silver jewellery and vessels. Among the grave goods were a gold stater of Pairisades on the man's chest, and a Byzantine gold stater of Lysimachus by the woman's body (Minns 1913: 430–3). Out here on the Scythian and Celtic fringes of the Black Sea, gold coins clearly served as prestige goods in their own right, not merely as instruments of monetary exchange.

IV   The south and east

Local imitations of Macedonian royal coinage were also struck along the eastern and southern peripheries of the Graeco-Macedonian world. Coin hoards are much less well recorded here than in Europe and the Mediterranean, and so it is often hard to say where particular imitations may have been struck. A major hoard from modern Baluchistan (western Pakistan) allows us to identify an imitative mint in ancient Arachosia, in the far south-east of the Hellenistic world. Arachosia had briefly formed part of Alexander's empire, before being handed over by Seleucus I to the Indian king Chandragupta Maurya *c.* 305 BC. Despite now being part of the Mauryan empire, the Arachosians continued to strike rough local imitations of the silver coinages of Alexander and Lysimachus right down through the third century BC (Miller 2010). The kingdoms of the Greek 'Far East' – Bactria and India – also struck their own distinctive local coinages, which will be discussed in Chapter 5 below.

Much the broadest and liveliest repertoire of Hellenistic Alexander-type coinage comes from the Arabian peninsula (Callot 2010). Arabia was never part of any of the major Hellenistic kingdoms, although the Ptolemies and Seleucids had extensive trading links with south and east Arabia respectively (Kitchen 2001), and parts of the Persian gulf were directly administered by the Seleucids (Kosmin 2013). It is no surprise to find that Alexander-style coinage had already made its way far into the Arabian peninsula by the early third century BC. An extraordinary hoard of thirteen Alexander tetradrachms, mostly from Macedonian mints, was buried shortly after 300 BC at al-'Ayun, deep in the central Arabian desert south of Riyadh (Potts 2010: 68). Later South Arabian hoards show the continuing influx of Alexander-style coinage from the Greek world far to the north.

Figure 2.19. Alexander-style tetradrachm struck at Gerrha (*c.* 230–220 BC). The figure of Zeus/Baʿal on the reverse has been reworked to represent the sun god Shamash. 16.41 g. Vienna (photograph courtesy of P. van Alfen).

Figure 2.20. Alexander-style tetradrachm struck in Oman, in the name of Abiʿel daughter of Nšyl (third century BC). 15.71 g. ANS 1989.121.1.

Around 225 BC, the great caravan city of Gerrha (probably modern Thaj, in the east Arabian desert) began striking its own Alexander-style tetradrachms and obols (Fig. 2.19). The types are very similar to genuine Alexander coins, but the seated Baʿal/Zeus on the reverse of Alexander's coins has been re-interpreted as a figure from the local Gerrhan pantheon. The deity is now beardless and wears a diadem; immediately to his left, the coins bear the name of the Semitic sun god Shamash in South Arabian script. Presumably these coins were struck in the context of the lucrative Gerrhan spice trade with the Seleucid and Ptolemaic kings.

Further to the south, a large series of Alexander-style tetradrachms, drachms and obols was struck in the Oman peninsula between the third century BC and the first century AD (van Alfen 2010). In place of the Greek legend ALEXANDROU, these coins carried an Aramaic legend with the names of a series of south-eastern Arabian queens (Fig. 2.20). All of these queens were known as Abiʿel, distinguished from one another by the name of their father (Abiʿel daughter of Nšyl, Abiʿel daughter of Mʿšmš, etc.). Over time, the Abiʿel coins drift further and further away from their original Macedonian model: the weight of the tetradrachm drops from *c.* 16.80 g to *c.* 14.70 g, the metal degenerates from pure silver to base metal alloys, and the types become increasingly stylized.

Figure 2.21. Sabaean imitation of the Old Style coinage of Athens (third century BC). The reverse type carries a rough copy of the Greek legend ATHE to the right of the owl, with letters in South Arabian script to the left and below, and also on Athena's cheek on the obverse. 5.45 g. ANS 1944.100.69454.

The kingdoms of southern Arabia – Saba' (the biblical Sheba), Qataban, Hadramawt, Ma'in, and later Himyar – also struck abundant silver coin issues throughout the Hellenistic period, this time modelled on the 'Old Style' fifth- and fourth-century coinage of Athens (Fig. 2.21; Huth 2010). The earliest South Arabian imitations of Athenian coinage date back to the mid-fourth century BC, when Athenian coins were widely imitated in the Near East. Hence the persistence of this tradition in south Arabia during the Hellenistic period (when Athens' coinage was of relatively little international significance) should probably be seen as a matter of inertia, rather than a positive wish to distinguish themselves culturally from the kingdoms of eastern Arabia. Still, it is remarkable that when the Athenians eventually shifted over to their 'New Style' coinage in the 160s BC, the Sabaean kingdom promptly followed suit and started imitating the Athenian New Style coinage instead – clearly the South Arabian kingdoms were able to respond to changes in the coin traditions of the remote world of the Mediterranean.

V   The 'Hellenistic west'?

Finally, the western Mediterranean. The real surprise here is quite how little Macedonian coinage made it west of the Adriatic at all. A few silver and gold coins of Alexander and later Macedonian kings travelled to Sicily during the late fourth and third century BC (Cutroni Tusa 1990), but the absolute numbers of Macedonian coin finds in Sicily and Italy are remarkably small, in comparison with the vast scale of Alexander's coinage (Williams and Burnett 1998: 380–3). Still more meagre quantities of Macedonian royal coinages made their way as far west as Spain and Morocco, with a concentration of imported coinage around the time of the Second Punic War (Ripollès 2008; *CH* X 469). In southern Gaul, coins of any kind from the eastern Mediterranean are extremely few and far between during the Hellenistic period (Feugère and Py 2011: 409–19). Very few Macedonian royal coins seem to have passed through the great commercial harbour of Massalia; in south-east Gaul, they are even outnumbered by stray finds of silver coins from Histiaea in Euboea (Robert 1951: 179–216).

Seen as a whole, the western Mediterranean seems to have been remarkably little affected by the huge Macedonian monetary zone to the north and east. The reasons for this are far from obvious, especially given how intimately connected the eastern and western parts of the Mediterranean basin had been in the Archaic and early Classical periods. The main Hellenistic coinages of Iberia and southern Gaul show no iconographic or metrological influence from the East whatsoever. Coin circulation in Spain during the third and second centuries BC was dominated by local silver drachms of Emporion and Rhoda and their imitations, struck on a distinctive weight-standard of *c.* 4.70 g (Fig. 2.22; Ripollès 2012: 357–61). Iberian silver coinage seems to have been widely used by various Celtic peoples on the French side of the Pyrenees, who struck several series of crude imitations of the coins of Rhoda, the so-called 'monnaies-à-la-croix' (Fig 2.23; Boudet and Depeyrot 1997). Further to the east, in the Rhône valley and the Alps, the dominant currency was the silver and bronze coinage of Massalia, modern Marseilles, which was struck in huge quantities throughout the Hellenistic period (Fig. 2.24; Depeyrot 1999).

Examples of Macedonian coin iconography are very rare in Sicily, Italy and Punic North Africa (Williams and Burnett 1998: 383–7). Around

Figure 2.22. Hellenistic silver drachm of Rhoda in Iberia, with stylized rose figure on the reverse. 4.50 g. ANS 1944.100.79724.

Figure 2.23. Silver imitation of drachm of Rhoda, struck near modern Toulouse in south-west Gaul, dating to the late third or second century BC. The rose on the reverse has been transformed into an abstract cruciform pattern. 3.38 g. ANS 1944.100.73273.

Figure 2.24. Hellenistic silver drachm of Massalia, with Artemis on the obverse and a prowling lion on the reverse. 2.61 g. ANS 1957.172.747.

300–290 BC, a Carthaginian mint in Sicily struck silver coins with an obverse type closely based on Alexander's tetradrachm coinage, perhaps indicating Carthage's aspirations to build its own Macedonian-style empire in the West (Chapter 5 below, p. 104). But most Carthaginian coin iconography in the Hellenistic period owes nothing whatsoever to the Greek East. Only two places in the western Mediterranean seem to have responded to Hellenistic royal coin iconography in a serious and consistent way. The first was Syracuse, where two tyrants, Agathocles (ruled 317–289 BC) and Hieron II (ruled *c.* 269–215 BC), presented themselves as successor-style kings: their remarkable royal coinages are discussed further in Chapter 8 below (pp. 161–3).

The other city was Rome. Roman coinage of the third century BC bears a wide range of types, a few of which can plausibly be seen as creative adaptations of royal coin iconography from the Hellenistic East (Burnett 1986). Figs. 2.25 and 2.26 illustrate two silver didrachms struck at Rome in the mid-third century BC. The first of these carries a portrait of the hero Heracles on the obverse, with a she-wolf suckling Romulus and Remus on the reverse (*RRC* 20/1). However, the portrait of Heracles – unbearded, with idealized features, a diadem, curly Alexander-style hair and side-whiskers – is fairly clearly modelled on contemporary coin portraits of Greek Hellenistic rulers. Likewise, the coin portrait of the god Mars in Fig. 2.26 has straggles of unruly hair and side-whiskers poking out from underneath his helmet (*RRC* 25/1); once again, the idealized features seem to derive from Hellenistic royal portrait coins. This receptivity to the contemporary coin-styles of the Greek East is part of a wider 'Hellenization' of Roman culture in the third century BC (Morel 1989; Wallace-Hadrill 2008: 17–28).

Figure 2.25. Roman Republican silver didrachm, with 'Alexander-style' portrait of Heracles on the obverse (*c.* 260 BC). 6.86 g. ANS 1944.100.15.

Figure 2.26. Roman Republican silver didrachm, depicting the god Mars wearing a Corinthian helmet (*c.* 230 BC). 6.67 g. ANS 1944.100.22.

However, we ought not to overstate the significance of these visual echoes: the Greek coinages of south Italy were a far more significant influence on early Roman coins than the coinages of the Macedonian kings (Crawford 1985: 25–51).

From the perspective of coinage tradition, the 'Hellenistic West' has turned out to be something of a world apart. The western Mediterranean basin, from Italy, Sicily and Carthage in the east to Spain and southern Gaul in the west, formed a distinct and separate cluster of monetary zones (Massaliot, Punic, Iberian and eventually Roman). As we will see in Chapter 5, many of the non-Greek peoples of the western Mediterranean (including the Carthaginians, Sikels and the non-Greek inhabitants of southern Italy) developed strongly 'Hellenizing' coinage traditions in the course of the Hellenistic period. But none of these coinages (with the partial exception of Rome) were ever strongly influenced by the Macedonian numismatic tradition, which held sway everywhere else from north-west Gaul to Baluchistan. Looked at through the lens of coinage, the traditional exclusion of the western Mediterranean from the Hellenistic world proper does have something to be said for it.

Part II

Identity

3
Civic identities

I   Introduction

For one grouchy Athenian orator, Philip II of Macedon's victory over Athens and Thebes at Chaeronea in 338 BC was the moment that 'the affairs of Greece fell into slavery' (Lycurgus, *Against Leocrates* 50). Then again, he would say that. For aggressive imperialists like the fourth-century Athenians, the rise of the great Macedonian kingdoms was nothing but bad news (Habicht 1997). Other Greeks saw things differently. The average Greek city had spent two centuries being pushed around by the Athenians, Spartans and Thebans: in small towns like Sicyon, Chalcis and Mytilene, I imagine that the humbling of the Athenians at Chaeronea was met with street parties.

Most Hellenistic Greek *poleis* enjoyed far more freedom of action than they had ever had in the fifth or fourth century BC (Ma 2000). Hellenistic kings had little reason to meddle with the internal affairs of Greek cities in their zone of influence, and inter-city diplomacy and *polis* warfare were pursued with a new enthusiasm. Despite the doubts of some modern scholars (Gruen 1984: I, 133–42), when Hellenistic cities celebrated their 'freedom and autonomy', they really did mean what they said.

The civic coins struck by Greek cities in this period are vivid evidence of the continuing vitality of civic life and civic identity in the third and second centuries BC. Yet they bring surprises too. In the Aegean and western Asia Minor, city coinages go through periods of sharp decline (such as the early third century BC), alternating with sudden revivals (most obviously in the mid-second century BC). These unexpected rhythms of minting cry out for explanation. Can changes in the volume and character of civic coinages be explained by the cities' changing relationships with Hellenistic kings? Or did civic mints respond in a pragmatic way to the amount of royal coinage in circulation, striking their own coins only when there was an immediate financial need? Or – the most interesting possibility of all – might we be dealing with a series of positive choices by the cities about how to represent their own civic identity?

The civic coinages of the Hellenistic world are bewildering in their quantity and variety. In this chapter, I shall focus on the city coins of a single region, western Asia Minor and the offshore islands. The coinages of Asia Minor are abundant and fascinating in their own right, and have been at the heart of several major modern debates: the relationship between coinage and *polis* autonomy; civic identities in the Hellenistic period; and the economic functions of local coin issues. They have also been the object of some particularly impressive recent scholarship. This chapter will be entirely concerned with the large-denomination silver coinages of the cities; their bronze coinages are discussed separately in Chapter 7 below.

II   Civic coinage in decline: western Asia Minor, 325–275 BC

The fourth century BC was something of a golden age for civic coinages in western Asia Minor. Between 400 and 325 BC, several dozen civic and dynastic mints were active in western Asia Minor and the offshore islands. Most of these cities and dynasts (around thirty-five mints in total) struck silver coins on a single regional weight-standard, based on a tetradrachm of *c.* 15.3 g (Meadows 2011). The most abundant of these coinages was the huge fourth-century silver coinage of Ephesus (Fig. 3.1; Kinns, *CH* IX 172–206), followed by the coinages of the Hecatomnid satraps of Caria (Konuk 2013) and the islands of Rhodes, Chios and Samos (Kinns 1989a; Ashton 2001: 98).

The use of a single weight-standard across this entire region suggests that the civic economies of western Asia Minor formed a well-integrated economic zone in the last years of Persian rule. It also shows how little the Persian royal state intervened in the production of coinage by its Greek subjects in Asia Minor (Le Rider 2001a: 165–205). In inland Asia Minor, away from the Greek cities of the coast, the dominant silver coinage was

Figure 3.1. Fourth-century tetradrachm of Ephesus, with a bee and the ethnic Eph on the obverse, and a stag and a civic magistrate's name (here, Zōilos) on the reverse. 15.20 g. ANS 1944.100.46012.

Figure 3.2. Silver Achaemenid Persian *siglos* ('shekel'), perhaps struck at Sardis. Note the ancient test-cuts on the reverse, confirming that the coin is silver all the way through. 5.43 g. ANS 1944.100.73500.

the Persian *siglos* of *c.* 5.60 g, carrying an image of the Persian archer-king (Fig. 3.2). The Greek cities of western Asia Minor seem to have been free to ignore the existence of this official Persian royal coinage, even to the extent of minting coins on a different weight-standard with their own local civic types.

This picture changes dramatically in the last quarter of the fourth century, in the wake of the Macedonian conquest of Asia Minor (Delrieux 2007). Between *c.* 324 and 290 BC, as we have seen, vast numbers of gold staters and silver tetradrachms and drachms in the name of Alexander the Great were struck at various mints in western Asia Minor (above, pp. 13–17). These coins were probably struck in order to pay veteran soldiers from Alexander's army on their way back home to the Balkans, although later issues may have been intended to fund the great armies of his successors.

This flood of royal silver and gold coins on the Attic weight-standard had a profound effect on the existing civic coinages of the region. By *c.* 300 BC, the minting of silver city coinages with local types had all but come to an end in western Asia Minor. Many cities did go on striking their own silver coins in the early third century BC, but these now largely took the form of imitation tetradrachms in the name of Alexander (the so-called 'civic Alexanders': Ashton 2012b: 192–3). So, for example, the Ionian cities of Clazomenae, Colophon, Erythrae, Priene, Smyrna and Teos had all minted substantial issues of silver coins with civic types under Persian rule in the fourth century BC. By the early third century, the only silver coins being struck by these cities were 'civic Alexanders', with unobtrusive local mint-marks and symbols on the reverse (see further below, pp. 51–3).

Why did the late fourth century see so sharp a change in the minting behaviour of the Greek cities of Asia Minor? The problem is bound up with wider questions of the 'vitality' or 'decline' of the Greek *polis* in the early Hellenistic period. We will consider three possible answers: (i) the deliberate suppression of civic coinages by Alexander and his Macedonian successors (Antigonus, Lysimachus and later the Seleucids); (ii) a lack of need for civic coinage in the face of the abundant new royal silver and gold coinage of Alexander; and (iii) wider changes in civic identity and civic self-representation in the early Hellenistic period.

III   Civic coinage and civic autonomy

The first possibility is that the rapid decline in civic coinages in the early Hellenistic period reflects a top-down royal decision to close existing civic mints. On this view, the striking of silver coinage was a symbol of political autonomy, and can only have been undertaken by free cities: when a city came under the control of a Hellenistic king, it lost its right to mint its own coins.

This supposed link between political autonomy and the right to strike coins is very fragile indeed (Martin 1985; Howgego 1995: 39–44; Meadows 2001). As we have seen, this model does not apply at all to the Achaemenid empire (above, p. 46). Furthermore, there are several clear examples of 'subject' cities minting their own distinctive civic coinages throughout the Hellenistic period. So, for example, in the 250s BC the small city of Cyme in Aeolis simultaneously struck Attic-weight royal coins of the Seleucid king Antiochus II and silver coins with civic types on the so-called 'Persic' weight-standard (Figs. 3.3–3.4; see further below, pp. 53–5). The civic and

Figure 3.3. Tetradrachm of Antiochus II, struck at Cyme (*c.* 261–246 BC). The one-handled jug at top left of the reverse type is a common motif on Cymaean coinage; the two monograms below appear in exactly the same form on contemporary 'double-*sigloi*' of Cyme (see Figure 3.4). 17.08 g. CNG 87 (18th May 2011), 619. Courtesy of Classical Numismatic Group.

Figure 3.4. Silver 'double-*siglos*' of Cyme (*c.* 261–246 BC). 10.46 g. BM 1891.10.2.13 (NC 13 [third series], 1892, Pl. I No. 24).

royal issues share various control-marks, and are clearly the product of the same mint (Ashton 2012a). Whatever 'subjection' to the Seleucid kings meant for Cyme, it certainly did not involve any restriction of its right to mint its own silver coins. More importantly, this whole approach assumes that cities can be neatly divided into two legal categories: 'autonomous' and 'subject' *poleis*. This dichotomy simply did not exist. As John Ma insisted in his classic *Antiochos III and the Cities of Western Asia Minor*, most *poleis* were simultaneously self-governing and subordinate to the king. The precise details of a city's status (the payment of tribute, presence or absence of a royal garrison, intervention of the king in local decision-making) were a matter of constant negotiation and local variation (Ma 2002: 150–74). It is of course possible that kings may have limited the rights of individual cities to mint their own coins, though it is hard to see why they would bother. But sweeping changes in civic coinage such as that which occurred *c.* 300 BC certainly cannot be explained in terms of any formal distinction between 'free' and 'subject' cities.

IV The obsolescence of civic coinage?

A second possibility is that cities stopped minting civic coinages (or moved over to striking 'civic Alexanders') because the need for local coins had disappeared. This position was most clearly formulated by Thomas R. Martin, in his influential *Sovereignty and Coinage in Classical Greece*. As Martin writes,

> the large-scale production of Alexander's coins in the mints of 'free' cities of Asia Minor had the indirect effect of making the production of local types largely superfluous. So much money was being produced by Alexander's agents that the cities could close their mints if they wished, saving themselves the trouble of running a municipal operation... this was probably a decision imposed by the nature of the marketplace. (Martin 1985: 128)

This is likely to be basically correct. The rich and diverse monetary ecosystem of fourth-century Asia Minor really did suffer mass extinction between 325 and 300 BC, and it would be perverse not to connect this to the flood of new Alexander-style silver now available.

That said, the supplanting of local coinages by the abundant new Alexander-coinage was a gradual process, rather than a single one-off

Figure 3.5. Silver hemidrachm of Byzantium (late fourth century BC). The obverse carries the abbreviated ethnic B-Y; in the local Greek script of Byzantium (adapted from the Megarian alphabet), the letter *beta* looks like a distorted *pi.* 2.50 g. ANS 1966.75.57.

Figure 3.6. Silver hemidrachm of Cius in Bithynia (late fourth century BC). 2.51 g. ANS 1944.100.42047.

event. Hoards in late fourth- and early third-century BC Asia Minor suggest that the 'trickle-down' of the new Macedonian royal coinages was actually rather slow. In the generation after Alexander's death, hoards which include a mix of Alexander-coinage and local coins are exceptionally rare (Callataÿ 1994a). Two large hoards from Bithynia, in northern Asia Minor, both buried *c.* 310–300 BC, make the point nicely. The first hoard, discovered on the territory of ancient Astacus (near modern İzmit), contained three Alexander drachms and 430 civic hemidrachms minted at Byzantium, Chalcedon and Cius (Figs. 3.5–3.6; *IGCH* 1365); the other (findspot uncertain) consisted of 202+ Alexander drachms, along with three civic hemidrachms of Cius (*IGCH* 1444). There is no sign of Alexander drachms gradually 'driving out' local Bithynian coinages. On the contrary, as late as the end of the fourth century, local civic coinages and the new royal Alexanders seem still to have circulated – or at least been hoarded – almost completely separately from one another.

The epigraphic evidence paints a similar picture of gradual infiltration of civic economies, rather than a sudden glut of new Alexander-style coinage. The key text here is a long inscription from the Ionian city of Colophon, dated *c.* 311–306 BC (Migeotte 1992: 214–23) – that is to say, late in the period of massive production by Alexander's mints in western Asia Minor. This inscription records cash contributions towards the building of a new city wall at Colophon by around 850 individual citizens and foreigners. Most of the contributions are simply listed as being in '*drachmai*' (i.e. silver drachms) or in '*chrysoi*' (i.e. gold staters, probably Alexander's Attic-weight gold didrachms). Just one donation, offered by a Macedonian called Eudemus, is described as being in 'drachms of Alexander' (*drachmai Alexandreioi*).

Eudemus is presumably a veteran of one of the Macedonian royal armies, who has settled at Colophon with a hefty nest-egg of Alexanders to ease his

Figure 3.7. Silver drachm of Colophon (*c.* 375–350 BC). The reverse type carries the abbreviated ethnic of Colophon (Κολοφῶ) and a magistrate's name (Ζηνῆς). 3.54 g. ANS 1977.158.339.

retirement: he promises the enormous sum of 10,000 drachms. But the fact that Eudemus' gift – uniquely in this long document – had to be specified as 'Alexander drachms' shows that Alexanders were still a relatively rare sight at Colophon. Most of the 850-odd private contributions towards the city walls were made in the local silver coins of Colophon itself, which were still being minted in relatively large quantities in the last decades of the fourth century (Fig. 3.7; Kinns 1980: 303–23). As late as *c.* 311–306 BC, Alexanders were still far from driving the local coinage of Colophon out of the market. On the contrary, even at this late date, Alexander drachms and tetradrachms still had the status of a foreign coinage at Colophon, only used by Macedonian settlers like Eudemus (Marcellesi 2004: 34–5).

V 'Civic Alexanders' and civic identity

By the end of the fourth century, very few traditional civic coinages were still being struck in western Asia Minor: Colophon's own civic silver issues came to an end around 300 BC. Nonetheless, the Greek cities of the peninsula did not give up minting coins altogether in the third century. Instead, very many *poleis* moved over to striking coins with uniform types, the 'civic Alexanders'. This need not indicate anything about the cities' relationship to the Macedonian kings. Owing to its sheer abundance, the Alexander-coinage rapidly lost its original ideological meaning as a Macedonian royal issue, and came to be seen as a relatively neutral 'Hellenic' coinage (Meadows 2009b).

The third-century 'civic Alexanders' were genuine civic coinages. It is worth emphasizing the point, since these coins have often been treated – quite wrongly – as a subset of Macedonian royal coinage, rather than as civic issues. The 'Alexanders' struck by the cities of Asia Minor carried distinctive local mint-marks and symbols, making it very clear to any user that these were not Macedonian royal issues (Ashton 2012b: 192–3; see above, Chapter 2, pp. 25–7). So the civic Alexanders of Priene in Ionia (*c.* 280–275 BC) carry the abbreviated ethnic Πρι on the reverse, along with

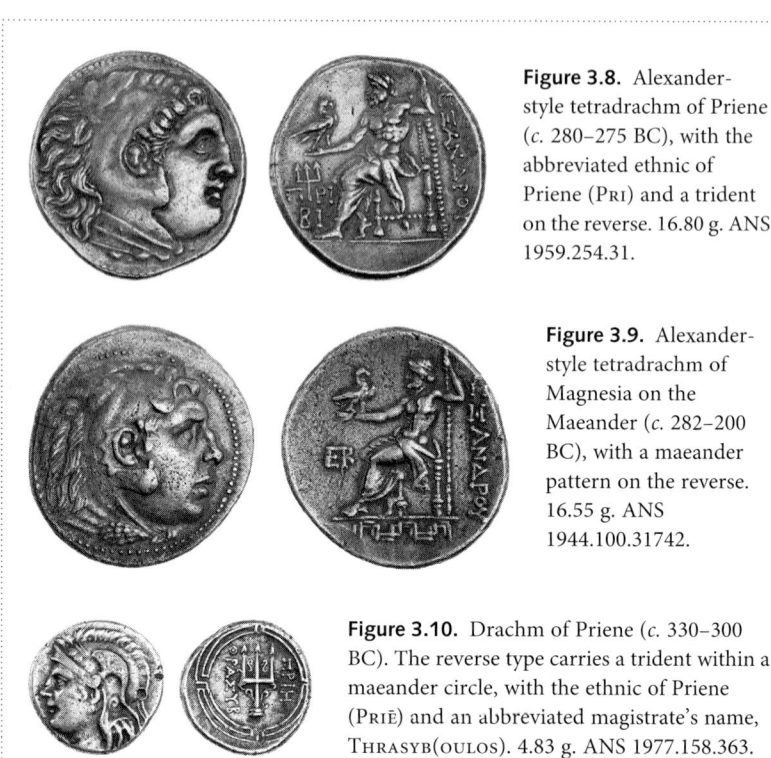

Figure 3.8. Alexander-style tetradrachm of Priene (*c.* 280–275 BC), with the abbreviated ethnic of Priene (Pri) and a trident on the reverse. 16.80 g. ANS 1959.254.31.

Figure 3.9. Alexander-style tetradrachm of Magnesia on the Maeander (*c.* 282–200 BC), with a maeander pattern on the reverse. 16.55 g. ANS 1944.100.31742.

Figure 3.10. Drachm of Priene (*c.* 330–300 BC). The reverse type carries a trident within a maeander circle, with the ethnic of Priene (Priē) and an abbreviated magistrate's name, Thrasyb(oulos). 4.83 g. ANS 1977.158.363.

the local symbol of a trident (very common on the earlier civic coinage of Priene) (Fig. 3.8). Similarly, the city of Magnesia on the Maeander struck civic Alexanders with a maeander pattern on the reverse, recalling the city's location on the north bank of the Maeander river, the greatest river of western Asia Minor (Fig. 3.9; Thonemann 2011: 38–9).

We ought to understand the phenomenon of the 'civic Alexander' as a positive choice by Greek *poleis* in Asia Minor to represent their civic identities in a new way. The Prieneans' or Magnesians' choice to move over to minting civic coins with Alexander-types need not reflect any decline in autonomy or civic pride. For a small city like Priene, striking its own coins was important for two separate reasons: first, because it showed what a special and distinctive place Priene was; second, because it showed that Priene was a proper city just like its big urban neighbours, Miletus and Ephesus. Around 325 BC, what mattered most was Prienean distinctiveness, and so the Prieneans chose to strike coins with distinct civic types (Fig. 3.10).

Around 275 BC, the accent lay on what Priene had in common with its neighbours, and so it chose to strike coins with uniform 'Panhellenic' types. Both are ways of talking about civic identity, but the emphasis has changed.

This new emphasis on the cities' collective identity can also be seen in other aspects of *polis* self-representation in the early Hellenistic period. In the sphere of public communication (inscriptions, papyri and official documents of all kinds), the local Greek dialects of Asia Minor (Ionic, Aeolic, Doric) and the various non-Greek languages of the peninsula (Lycian, Carian, Lydian) were rapidly replaced in the early Hellenistic period by a uniform Panhellenic dialect of Greek, the '*koinē*' or 'common Greek' (Colvin 2011; Briant 2006: 322–7). This is not to say that local languages and dialects died out, but merely that in public life, cities opted to use a dialect which was common to the entire Graeco-Macedonian world. At the same time, the various institutions of the Greek *poleis* – organs of government, magistracies, formal age-classes and so on – became increasingly homogeneous: just as in the modern world, everyone agreed that 'democracy' was the only civilized way to run a state (Carlsson 2010). Even the town plans and public architecture of Greek cities became more uniform in this period, as every respectable Greek *polis* sought to obtain its 'kit' of civic buildings (gymnasium, theatre, bouleuterion, stoas) (Billows 2003).

The decision by many Greek cities *c.* 300 BC to move over from distinctive civic coinages to homogeneous 'civic Alexanders' fits beautifully into this wider shift in patterns of civic self-representation. We ought not to see this as any kind of decline in vitality or local civic pride. Rather, membership of a cultural *koinē* became a central part of *polis* identity in the early Hellenistic period: cities were proud of their local distinctiveness, but they were also proud of being part of a wider world of interconnected *poleis* (Ma 2003b, and see further Chapter 4 below). Striking coins with common international types, but a distinctive local blazon or abbreviated ethnic on the reverse, was a way of indicating their place in a newly globalized Hellenic world.

VI   Civic coinages in the third century

A few distinctive civic coinages did continue to be produced in western Asia Minor during the third century. The abundant civic coinage of Rhodes, one of the great trading powers of the eastern Mediterranean, continued in an

Figure 3.11. Didrachm of Rhodes (*c.* 275–250 BC). The enormous Classical and Hellenistic coinage of Rhodes goes through numerous iconographic variations and changes of weight-standard (Ashton 2001), but the basic types, a portrait of Helios on the obverse and a Rhodian rose on the reverse, remain constant throughout. 6.66 g. ANS 1944.100.48620.

Figure 3.12. Silver '*siglos*' of Miletus (*c.* 260–250 BC), perhaps tariffed as a didrachm. The coin carries a MI monogram at left, with magistrate's name (LEONTISKOS) below. 5.16 g. Oxford (J. G. Milne 1924).

Figure 3.13. Silver 'double-*siglos*' of Phaselis (*c.* 250–225 BC). Like the 'double-*siglos*' of Magnesia (Figure 3.14 below), this coin was perhaps tariffed as a very light-weight tetradrachm. 10.27 g. ANS 1961.179.55.

unbroken sequence throughout the period (Fig. 3.11; Ashton 2001). The mint of Ephesus – an important royal mint for Demetrius Poliorcetes and Lysimachus – also went on producing civic silver on a modest scale, albeit with a long break between 281 and the 240s BC (Kinns 2006: 34–6; Delrieux 2007: 146–8). Starting in around 260 BC, Miletus struck an abundant civic silver series with Apollo on the obverse and a lion and star on the reverse (Fig. 3.12; Ashton and Kinns 2003: 8–20). Smaller civic issues were minted in the early third century at Alexandria Troas, Abydus and Mytilene (Meadows 2004), in the mid-third century at Chios and Cyme (Kinns 2006; Ashton 2012a), and in the late third century at Cos, Calymnus, Iasus and Cnidus (Ashton 2007; Höghammar 2007). A particularly fine series of civic silver was struck in the mid-third century by the Greek city of Phaselis in eastern Lycia, home to one of the great merchant shipping fleets of the eastern Mediterranean, depicting the prow and stern of a warship on the obverse and reverse (Fig. 3.13; Heipp-Tamer 1993).

Perhaps the most surprising feature of these third-century civic silver coinages is that none of them was struck on the Attic weight-standard, the chief international currency standard of the Greek world in the third century BC, used for the royal coinage of the Seleucids, Attalids, Antigonids, and of course for the ubiquitous Alexander-coinage. With the exception of Rhodes, all the civic issues in the preceding paragraph were struck on a distinctive 'Persic' weight-standard of *c.* 5.60 g, perhaps imitating the weight of the defunct fourth-century Persian *siglos* (Ashton 2012b: 195).

It is especially telling that many of the cities took to minting two separate silver coinages alongside one another: local civic coins on the 'Persic' weight-standard and international Attic-weight coinages with Macedonian royal types (Alexanders or Lysimachi). So the third-century silver issues of the small city of Magnesia on the Maeander consisted of an attractive Persic-weight civic coinage, with an armed horseman on the obverse and a butting bull in a Maeander circle on the reverse (Fig. 3.14; Kinns 1989b: 137–43), alongside much larger issues of Attic-weight civic Alexanders (see Fig. 3.9 above; Ashton and Kinns 2004: 71–83). Apparently we are dealing with a pattern of twin-track minting, with Persic-weight civic coinages for 'horizontal' transactions within and between the Greek cities of western Asia Minor, and Attic-weight Alexanders and Lysimachi being used for 'vertical' transactions with the great Hellenistic royal states (such as the payment of tribute). The different patterns of circulation of Miletus' two third-century coinages (Persic-weight and Attic-weight) are particularly striking: the Persic-weight coinage hardly moves outside Miletus' immediate hinterland, while the Attic-weight coinage travels freely across the entire Aegean and Near East (Reger 2011: 378–86). We will come back to this particular example in Chapter 6, in the context of 'open' and 'closed' currency systems in the Hellenistic world.

Figure 3.14. Silver 'double-*siglos*' of Magnesia on the Maeander (*c.* 210–200 BC). 10.89 g. ANS 1976.247.25.

Coins and walls at Teos

The Ionian city of Teos minted no silver coinage at all for most of the third century BC. At some point between *c.* 220 and 190, the city struck two exceptional series of silver coins, a very small issue of Attic-weight civic Alexander tetradrachms (Fig. 3.15) and a rather larger issue of local-weight hemidrachms (*c.* 1.30–1.92 g) with civic types (Fig. 3.16; head of Dionysus and lyre). These were effectively the only silver issues struck by Teos in the entire Hellenistic period (Kinns 1980: 218–23, 519–20, AR Series VI–VII).

As it happens, we know that in the very late third or early second century BC (exactly the period of these two small silver issues) the Teans built an impressive new circuit of walls for their city, today surviving only in ruins (McNicoll 1997: 157–60). An inscription from this period (*c.* 220–190 BC) records the expenditure for increasing the height of a stretch of fortifications:

> Theogeiton, son of Hegetor and grandson of Hegetor, Eucrates son of Eucrates, and Apollodorus son of Apollodorus were the overseers (*epistatai*). Six stone courses were added to the height of this tower and the abutting wall; six courses were added to the next tower along, with four courses added to the abutting wall, and four crenellations. The expenditure came to 3,422 drachms and 5 obols, and 38 drachms and 3 obols of Alexander. (*SEG* 35, 1151)

This last clause shows that the rebuilding of the walls of Teos was mostly paid for in local silver drachms, with 'Alexander drachms' being used only on a smaller scale, probably for imported stone or foreign labour. The coinage of Teos in this period dovetails beautifully with the epigraphic evidence: we can surely assume that the two small silver issues of *c.* 220–190 BC were struck specifically in order to pay for the city's new wall-circuit. It is even possible that the choice of denomination (hemidrachms) for the local silver reflects its intended use – a hemidrachm is a plausible day's pay for an unskilled construction worker (compare Ashton 2001: 92).

VII   The revival of civic types: the second century BC

The last major phase of minting of 'civic Alexanders' came in the period *c.* 225–165 BC, when Alexander tetradrachms were struck by more cities in western and southern Asia Minor than ever before (Price 1991: I, 76–9).

Figure 3.15. Alexander-style tetradrachm of Teos (*c.* 220–190 BC). 16.92 g. Private collection.

Figure 3.16. Civic hemidrachm of Teos (*c.* 204–190 BC). These coins seem to have been struck on a slightly reduced version of the Attic weight-standard. 1.64 g. Oxford (J. G. Milne 1924).

Figure 3.17. 'New Style' wreathed tetradrachm of Athens (*c.* 165 BC). The example illustrated here belongs to the first annual issue of this enormous coin series. 17.00 g. ANS 1944.100.24568.

By contrast, the mid-second century BC (*c.* 165–140 BC) saw a widespread revival in the use of distinctive civic types throughout the Aegean world. This revival seems to have begun in mainland Greece, before spreading to Asia Minor.

After relatively little minting activity in the third century BC (Kroll 2013), Athens initiated a large new series of silver tetradrachms and drachms, probably in the mid-160s BC (Thompson 1961; Lewis 1962; Mørkholm 1984a). Like the traditional Athenian 'owl' coinage, these 'New Style' coins carry a portrait of Athena on the obverse and an owl on the reverse (Fig. 3.17). The owl is now depicted standing on an olive-oil amphora, and the whole reverse type is encircled by a laurel wreath: in antiquity, these coins were known as *stephanēphoroi*, 'wreath-bearers'. (Other aspects

Figure 3.18. Wreathed tetradrachm of Eretria on Euboea (*c.* 165–160 BC), probably modelled on the Athenian New Style coinage. 16.90 g. ANS 1967.152.263.

Figure 3.19. Wreathed tetradrachm of Cyzicus (*c.* 160 BC), with portrait of Kore Soteira on the obverse. The reverse type recalls the royal coinage of Philip V of Macedon, which also features a club in an oak wreath. 15.61 g. ANS 1944.100.42736.

of this important coinage are discussed in Chapter 6, pp. 124–6, and Chapter 7, p. 132.)

These new Athenian 'wreathed' types were widely imitated throughout the Aegean, for instance by the Euboean cities of Eretria and Chalcis, both of which struck civic tetradrachms on the Athenian model in, most probably, the late 160s (Fig. 3.18; Picard 1979: 198–202). But by far the highest concentration of wreathed issues is found in western Asia Minor, where the mid-second century saw a positive explosion of civic tetradrachms of this kind. Wreathed issues were struck by Cyzicus, on the south coast of the Propontis; Abydus in the Troad; the mainland Aeolian cities of Aegae, Cyme and Myrina; and the Ionian cities of Lebedus, Smyrna, Magnesia on the Maeander, and Heraclea under Latmus (Figs. 3.19–3.21; Le Rider 2001b; Meadows and Houghton 2010). Smaller issues of wreathed tetradrachms were struck in the same period by Mytilene on Lesbos and Colophon in Ionia. Most of these civic coinages seem to have been struck during a relatively short period, between about 160 and 140 BC, although a few wreathed issues, such as the coinage of Tenedus, were initiated or revived in the early first century BC (Callataÿ 1998).

Figure 3.20. Wreathed tetradrachm of Myrina in Aeolis (*c.* 160–140 BC). Myrina was a tiny town on the coast of Asia Minor, which struck an unexpectedly large series of wreathed coinage in the mid-second century BC. 14.51 g. ANS 1944.100.44235.

Figure 3.21. Wreathed tetradrachm of Magnesia on the Maeander (*c.* 150–140 BC). Note the little Maeander pattern on the reverse, below Apollo's feet. 15.53 g. ANS 1967.152.445.

It is easy to see why these second-century 'wreathed' tetradrachms are particularly prized by modern coin collectors. The coins are struck from dies of the highest artistic quality, on broad, spread flans, which show off the engravers' art to the best effect. Examples struck from worn dies are very rare, suggesting that the dies tended to be discarded after relatively little use: the cities were concerned that these coins should look as good as possible. Their types are full of dense local allusions: so the wreathed coins of Magnesia on the Maeander depict the city's two chief patron deities, Artemis 'of the white brow' and Apollo Pythius with his oracular tripod, along with the name of a local civic magistrate and a little Maeander pattern (Fig. 3.21; Jones 1979).

One curiosity of the wreathed coinages of Asia Minor is that the size of the various issues seems often to bear little relation to the size and importance of the cities concerned. So the major city of Mytilene on Lesbos struck only a tiny issue of wreathed tetradrachms in the late 160s BC (Mattingly 1993: no. 468), while the beautiful tetradrachms of Myrina (c. 160–140 BC), an insignificant town on the coast of Asia Minor south-west of Pergamum, are among the most abundant of all second-century silver coinages (Fig. 3.20; Sacks 1985). Still more curious, many of the wreathed tetradrachms struck in western Asia Minor at this period seem to have made their way to Seleucid Syria, where they were hoarded in large numbers between about 150 and 120 BC, often in very fresh condition, suggesting that they had hardly circulated before being exported to the East (Psoma 2013). The reasons for this are far from clear: some of these apparently civic coinages may in fact be 'surrogate' royal coinages, minted by the Attalid kings of Pergamum, who are known to have provided military and financial support for the Seleucid pretender Alexander I Balas in Syria in 153/2 BC (Hoover and MacDonald 1999–2000).

Be that as it may, it is impossible to explain the sudden mass revival of civic types between 165 and 140 BC in purely practical terms. Wherever these coins may have ended up, the decision of cities like Myrina and Cyme to move over from 'civic Alexanders' to 'wreathed' types was not just a matter of Attalid geopolitics. Instead, we must be dealing with a more fundamental change in how cities wished to represent their local identity on an international stage.

Once again, the wider cultural and political context is crucial. Between 200 and 188 BC, Roman armies had humbled the two great royal powers of the Aegean world, the Antigonid and Seleucid kingdoms (Derow 2003). In 196 BC, at the Isthmian games at Corinth, the Roman general Flamininus had proclaimed all the Greeks of Asia and Europe to be free, ungarrisoned, free from tribute and subject to their own laws (Polybius 18.44–7; see Chapter 9 below, p. 169). In the course of a generation, the old Macedonian order in the Aegean had been shattered; the *dénouement* came in 168, after Rome's victory over Perseus at Pydna, when the Antigonid kingdom was dismembered and split into four nominally independent republics. New regional powers, like the Attalids of Pergamum, had to treat the Greek cities of their kingdoms with much more sensitivity than their Macedonian predecessors had done (Thonemann 2013a; Chapter 4 below, pp. 77–82).

Eventually, of course, the coming of Rome to the Greek East would prove to be a false dawn for the Greek cities, as was vividly demonstrated in 146 BC, with the sack of Corinth and the crushing of the Achaean League. But during the 160s and 150s – the years of the revival of civic coinages in

Greece and Asia Minor – the free *poleis* of these areas could reasonably have seen themselves as entering a new golden age.

VIII Reasons to be proud: gods and athletes

Not all of the new civic coinages that emerged in the mid-second century followed the Athenian 'wreathed' model. A second distinctive group of coinages was minted by the cities of Thasos and Maroneia in the north Aegean (Chapter 2 above, pp. 29–31; Psoma 2013: 289–92), Odessus in Thrace, Alexandria and Parium in the Troad (Meadows 1998), and Clazomenae in Ionia, along with the *koinon* of Athena Ilias in the Troad (discussed in Chapter 4 below, pp. 82–4).

On the reverse, instead of a wreath, these tetradrachms carry the name of a civic deity, always laid out in two vertical lines, with the ethnic in a horizontal line below. So the rare tetradrachms of Clazomenae (*c.* 160 BC) carry a portrait of Zeus on the obverse, with the name of 'Zeus Saviour Manifest' and the abbreviated ethnic KLAZO framing a standing Amazon on the reverse (Fig. 3.22; Meadows 2009a). Similarly, the coins of Alexandria Troas (from 165/4 BC) bear a bust of Apollo on the obverse and a standing Apollo figure on the reverse; the god is identified as 'Apollo Smintheus', with the abbreviated ethnic ALEXAN and a magistrate's name beneath his feet (Fig. 3.23; Bellinger 1961: 93–102).

These half-dozen cities have nothing much in common with one another, and as with the contemporary 'wreathed' tetradrachms, the similarity of the types is surely a matter of fashion as much as anything. It is striking that the name of the god (Zeus Saviour Manifest at Clazomenae, Heracles Saviour at

Figure 3.22. Tetradrachm of Clazomenae, in the name of Zeus Sōter Epiphanēs ('Saviour Manifest') (*c.* 160 BC). 16.73 g. ANS 2008.30.1.

Figure 3.23. Tetradrachm of Alexandria Troas, in the name of Apollo Smintheus. This is a rare example of a precisely dated Hellenistic coin series: the letters *rho*, *nu* and *gamma* to the right of Apollo represent Year 153 of a local civic era, corresponding to 149/8 BC. 16.97 g. ANS 1967.152.420.

Figure 3.24. Gold stater of Ephesus (*c.* 133–88 BC), with 'Hellenistic' Artemis on the obverse and 'Anatolian' Artemis on the reverse. 8.51 g. Oxford, HCR6789 (Spink 1958).

Thasos, Apollo Smintheus at Alexandria Troas) occupies the same place – two vertical lines, flanking the image of the deity on the reverse – as had traditionally been reserved for the king's name on earlier Macedonian royal coinage. The very layout of the coin legends may be designed to highlight the cities' new-found independence from the Hellenistic monarchs: the only higher authority they now recognize is not Macedonian kings, but the gods.

But we are certainly also dealing with a resurgence of old-fashioned civic pride. From the very beginning, Greek civic coinages had carried images of local gods and heroes. The renewed prominence of local deities on the city coins of the second century BC could perhaps be connected to the remarkable proliferation of civic festivals across the Greek world, particularly in western Asia Minor, in the late third and early second century BC (Chaniotis 1995; Parker 2004). More than ever before, the fame of one's local god, and his or her chief festival, was a sign of a city's prominence in the Greek world more widely.

The second century also saw a trend for the depiction of particular civic cult statues on coinages (Mørkholm 1991: 25–6). From the late second to the early first century BC, Ephesus struck an occasional issue of Attic-weight gold staters with images of the Ephesian Artemis on both faces (Fig. 3.24; Jenkins

Figure 3.25. Wreathed tetradrachm of Mytilene, with portrait of Zeus Ammon on the obverse, and mask of Dionysus on the reverse (*c.* 165–160 BC). 16.74 g. Baldwins, New York Sale XXVII (4 January 2012), no. 498. Courtesy of A. H. Baldwin & Sons Ltd., London.

1980; Callataÿ 1997: 289–90). The obverse carries a fairly standard portrait bust of Artemis in Greek style, but the reverse unmistakably depicts the famous Anatolian cult statue of Artemis Ephesia, with her body covered in mysterious egg-shaped protuberances (Morris 2001).

A still more striking case is the rare 'wreathed' coinage of Mytilene, the largest city on Lesbos, perhaps minted in the 160s BC. These coins depict on the reverse a mask of Dionysus, mounted on a crude triangular block representing his 'body' (Fig. 3.25). This is surely a depiction of the famous olive-wood mask of Dionysus Phallen, said by Pausanias to have been rescued from the sea by fishermen and worshipped as a cult image at the small neighbouring Lesbian city of Methymna (Paus. 10.19.3; Casevitz and Frontisi-Ducroux 1989). To all appearances, the Mytileneans are simply trying it on: a prestigious Methymnaean cult image is depicted as though it were 'really' a Mytilenean cult. No doubt some fierce local rivalry between the two cities underlies this outrageous cultic pilfering.

For a small Hellenistic city without a major cult festival of its own, the surest route to international prestige was an athletic or musical victory at one of the four great festivals of the Greek world, the Olympic, Pythian, Nemean and Isthmian games. These Panhellenic contests were known as 'crowned games' (*stephanitai agōnes*), meaning that victors did not receive cash prizes, but simply a crown of laurel. Nonetheless, victorious athletes could expect to receive lavish material rewards and honours from their home city. The earliest Greek inscription from the Phoenician city of Sidon is an epigram honouring a victorious charioteer at the Nemean games, 'the first of our citizens to bring home an equestrian victory from Greece' (Austin 2006: no. 140). Victory at the Panhellenic games was a particular source of pride for the Sidonians, since it meant that their superficially Hellenized city had been recognized on an international stage as part of the Greek 'club' (Millar 1983).

Such individual victories were sometimes celebrated on civic coinages in the late Hellenistic period. In the mid-second century BC, the wrestler Athenopolis, a native of the small city of Priene in western Asia Minor, won Priene's first ever victory at the venerable Pythian games at Delphi (Ebert 1972: no. 73). A small Prienean issue of silver drachms, probably dating to this period, depicts on the reverse a winged Victory placing a tiny crown on the name Athenopolis (Fig. 3.26; Thonemann 2011: 37, 121). This extraordinary type has no antecedents among Hellenistic civic coinages. Nike figures are occasionally found crowning the names of kings and dynasts – as for instance on coins of Lysimachus (see above, Fig. 1.23) or Philetaerus (see above, Fig. 1.8) – but not private individuals like Athenopolis. It is tempting to see the coinage as minted specifically for the purpose of celebrating Athenopolis' victory.

Similarly, in the early years of the first century BC, the town of Chalcis on Euboea struck bronze coins with an image of a charioteer on the obverse and the name 'Theocles son of Pausanias' on the reverse, surrounded by a laurel wreath (Fig. 3.27). Theocles was a famous Chalcidian

Figure 3.26. Drachm of Priene honouring Athenopolis the wrestler (*c.* 150 BC). The motif of a Nike figure crowning Athenopolis' name is derived from Hellenistic royal coinages. 4.04 g. Gemini Auction III (9 January 2007), 187. Courtesy of Gemini LLC.

Figure 3.27. Bronze coin of Chalcis (*c.* 100 BC). The reverse carries the name THEOKLĒS PAUSANIOU in a laurel wreath. The coin has been countermarked with a tripod symbol on its (very worn) obverse. 6.07 g. ANS 1953.171.219.

athlete, who from his boyhood onwards won a string of athletic victories at Chalcis and elsewhere. Presumably these coins were struck to commemorate a chariot victory won by Theocles at one of the great Panhellenic festivals (Knoepfler 1979; van Bremen 2007: 355–6), just like Athenopolis' commemorative coinage at Priene.

4

Collective identities

I Introduction

The Greek *polis* was famously – and controversially – described by the sociologist W. G. Runciman as an 'evolutionary dead-end' (Runciman 1990). The Greek world in the fourth century BC comprised perhaps as many as a thousand tiny self-contained citizen-states (Hansen and Nielsen 2004: 53–4). As we saw in Chapter 3, the rise of the great Macedonian superstates (and later of Rome) had less of an impact than one might expect on the civic life and corporate identities of the Greek *poleis*. In many respects, life went on much as before; the largest Greek city-states – notably Rhodes and Syracuse – could even still pursue imperialist agendas of their own. Nonetheless, as Runciman rightly saw, the Greek cities' intense ideological commitment to autonomy and independence made it difficult for them to adapt to the changed conditions of the Hellenistic *oikoumenē*. Mutual suspicion and micro-nationalism left the Greek *poleis* helplessly divided in the face of Macedonian and Roman power.

That said, the Hellenistic period did see sustained efforts by the Greek city-states to overcome their long-standing political and social disunity. Inter-*polis* diplomacy flourished, often couched in the language of mythological kinship (*syngeneia*) (Erskine 2002). New networks of social relations emerged, vividly attested by the hundreds of inscribed decrees honouring foreign judges or recognizing the *asylia* ('inviolability') of far-off cities (Ma 2003b). Perhaps most important of all, new or revived leagues of city-states emerged in various parts of the Greek world (Mackil 2013), most notably the second-century Achaean League, which brought almost a hundred different Peloponnesian towns together under a single federal umbrella.

As Fergus Millar has written, coinage in the ancient world was 'the most deliberate of all symbols of public identity' (Millar 1993: 230; cf. Howgego 2005). For this reason, coinage is a superb category of evidence for these new, distinctively Hellenistic patterns of cross-*polis* social and political relations. Just as the modern Euro embodies the federal ideals of a Europe determined on 'ever closer union' (in the words of the 1958 Treaty of

Rome), so the common coinages of the Achaean or Lycian League are poignant testimony to the Greek cities' attempts (unsuccessful though they would ultimately be) to build new solidarities in a newly globalized world of Eurasian empires.

II *Ethnos* and *koinon*

Poleis had never had a monopoly on the striking of coinage in the Greek world. In the fifth and fourth centuries BC, coins had been minted by kings, tyrants, leagues, religious confederacies and even (in a few rare cases) individual generals. Throughout large parts of mainland Greece – Thessaly, Phocis, Locris, Aetolia, Acarnania, Arcadia – the *polis* was in fact relatively unimportant. The inhabitants of these regions instead saw themselves first and foremost as members of large and fluid *ethnē*, 'tribes' or 'nations' (Morgan 2003), and often chose to mint coins in the name of their wider 'ethnic' community rather than their particular home-town (Psoma and Tsangari 2003; Psoma 2012). In many cases, such as in Boeotia, co-operative coinages with common types, struck by several different communities at once, preceded the emergence of formal federal structures (Figs. 4.1–4.2; Mackil and van Alfen 2006).

In the Hellenistic period, several of these large *ethnē* developed into organized federal states. The Greek word for these regional confederacies is *koinon*, literally a 'common thing' (Walbank 1976/7; Mackil 2013). The most important of the mainland Greek *koina* in the third century BC was

Figure 4.1. Early Boeotian 'federal' stater of Tanagra (mid-fifth century BC). The foreparts of the horse on the reverse are a civic symbol of Tanagra. 12.08 g. ANS 1967.152.251.

Figure 4.2. Early Boeotian 'federal' stater of Thebes (mid-fifth century BC). The reverse carries the legend Tʜ-ᴇ, inscribed 'retrograde' (backwards), as in many early Greek inscriptions. 11.93 g. ANS 1944.100.19847.

undoubtedly the *koinon* of the Aetolians. The Aetolians inhabited a mountainous part of central Greece to the west of Delphi. In the fourth and third centuries, the Aetolian League grew from a loose 'ethnic' confederation into one of the great powers of central Greece, eventually incorporating most of their neighbours (Locrians, Dorians, Phocians and others) into a Greater Aetolian state (Scholten 2000). Their prestige in mainland Greece derived above all from the Gallic invasion of that region in 279 BC (Mitchell 2003), when the Aetolians defeated the Gauls in a great battle fought in a snowstorm at the gates of Delphi (Paus. 10.19–23).

Several small bronze and silver issues in the name of the Aetolians are known from the late fourth and early third century. Coin production really took off between 238 and 229, when the League was at war with the Macedonian king Demetrius II. During this period the Aetolians struck large numbers of gold didrachms and silver tetradrachms on the Attic weight-standard (Figs. 4.3–4.4; Scholten 2000: 131–63; Tsangari 2007). The gold coins carry on the obverse a bust of Athena in a Corinthian helmet, while the silver coins bear an image of Heracles in a lion-skin headdress; both types echo the gold and silver coins of Alexander the Great. On the reverse, both the gold and silver issues carry a female personification of Aetolia, seated on a pile of Gallic shields. This probably depicts a famous statue dedicated by the

Figure 4.3. Gold stater of the Aetolians (*c.* 220–205 BC). The reverse depicts a seated personification of Aetolia holding a winged Nike, who is laying a victory wreath on a tiny figure at bottom right, perhaps an Aetolian warrior. 8.45 g. ANS 1944.100.19481.

Figure 4.4. Tetradrachm of the Aetolians (*c.* 238–229 BC). The most prominent shield on the reverse is of a distinctively Macedonian type: compare the Macedonian shield on contemporary coins of Antigonus Gonatas (Figure 8.22 below). 16.95 g. ANS 1944.100.19483.

Figure 4.5. Didrachm of the Aetolians (*c.* 220–205 BC). The types are closely modelled on the royal coinage of Demetrius Poliorcetes (above, Figure 1.24). 10.62 g. ANS 1964.149.1.

Aetolians at Delphi after their defence of the sanctuary in 279 (Paus. 10.18.7). On many of the coins, a single Macedonian shield is ostentatiously added to the shields of the defeated Gauls (Fig. 4.4), encouraging the viewer to see the Macedonians as the new enemy of Greek civilization.

Towards the end of the third century, the Aetolians moved over to minting silver didrachms and drachms on a different weight-standard, based on a drachm of *c.* 5.00 g (Fig. 4.5). Coinages on this so-called 'reduced Aeginetan standard' were very widespread throughout the Peloponnese and mainland Greece in the later Hellenistic period (Mørkholm 1991: 8–9). Several inscriptions from Boeotia and Delphi refer to something called *symmachikon argyrion*, 'allied silver', which is almost certainly a way of referring to this large category of mainland Greek coinages, discussed further in Chapter 7 below, pp. 140–1 (Grandjean 1995; Psoma 2007a; controversial reassessment in Doyen 2012). These new Aetolian coins also imitate earlier Macedonian royal coinage. The didrachms carry a portrait of Apollo Thermius, the chief federal deity of the Aetolian League, based on the early third-century portrait coinage of Demetrius Poliorcetes (Chapter 1 above, p. 21). On the reverse, the hero Aetolus (the eponymous ancestor of the Aetolians) is shown standing with his foot on a rock, in the same pose as Poseidon on earlier coins of Demetrius.

Given the Aetolians' fierce hostility to Macedon, these imitations of Macedonian royal types are very surprising: perhaps mercenaries in Aetolian service were accustomed to being paid in good Macedonian coinage. But no less striking is the way in which the Aetolians co-opted and adapted Macedonian iconography to express a specifically Aetolian ethnic identity. Their proud depictions of Aetolia, the hero Aetolus and Apollo Thermius reminded the viewer that it was now the Aetolians, not the Macedonians, who were the dominant power in the mainland Greek world.

This period saw other mainland Greek *ethnē* using coinage to express their collective identity in new ways. Immediately to the west of Aetolia, beyond the delta of the river Achelous, lived the Acarnanians, whose *koinon* may date back to the fifth century BC. In the fifth and fourth centuries, the coins of the region had consisted almost entirely of local imitations of Corinth's famous Pegasus staters. In the early third century, the Acarnanian *koinon* started minting its own distinctive federal coins, the most abundant of which have an image of the river-god Achelous in the form of a man-faced bull on the obverse, and the chief federal deity, Apollo Actius, on the reverse (Fig. 4.6; Dany 1999: 276–339; BCD Akarnanien 15–35).

North of Acarnania, in the far north-west of mainland Greece, lay the remote district of Epirus. The old Molossian ruling dynasty, best known for Olympias, the mother of Alexander the Great, and the general Pyrrhus, came to an end in 232 BC, to be replaced by a new federal Epirot *koinon* organized on the model of the Aetolian League (Cabanes 1976: 357–83). The earliest coins of this new *koinon* are spectacular silver didrachms, with the two chief deities of Epirus, Zeus of Dodona and Dione, on the obverse, and a charging bull within an oak wreath on the reverse (Fig. 4.7; Franke 1961); later issues carry an image of Zeus alone, with an eagle perched on a thunderbolt (Fig. 4.8).

Figure 4.6. Drachm of the Acarnanians (*c.* 272–167 BC). The obverse carries what appears to be a magistrate's name, Lykourgos, behind the river-god Achelous. However, this name appears on Acarnanian coins throughout the period (*c.* 272–167 BC), and seems to have become a 'fossilized' part of the coins' design: compare the Macedonian Aesillas coinage, Chapter 9 below, pp. 175–6. 5.17 g. ANS 1944.100.19465.

Figure 4.7. Didrachm of the Epirote *koinon* (shortly after 232 BC). 10.13 g. ANS 1967.152.244.

Figure 4.8. Drachm of the Epirote *koinon* (late third century BC). 4.73 g. ANS 1944.100.18826.

Figure 4.9. Didrachm of the Thessalian *koinon* (late second or early first century BC). The reverse carries the names of two officials of the *koinon*, AMYNANDROU and XENOPHANTOS. 6.13 g. ANS 1935.117.163.

Finally, in Thessaly, the north-eastern part of the Greek mainland, *poleis* such as Krannon and Larisa had long rubbed shoulders with myriad smaller non-*polis* communities. Here, a new Thessalian *koinon* was established in 194 BC under Roman patronage (Larsen 1968: 281–94; Graninger 2011). The various coinages of Thessalian *poleis* disappear altogether, and through the second and first centuries BC the *koinon* minted substantial issues of silver didrachms, with images of the two chief Thessalian federal deities, Zeus Eleutherios and Athena Itonia, on the obverse and reverse (Fig. 4.9; Klose 1998; *BCD Thessaly* 330–63).

III   The Achaean League

The most extraordinary success story among the Hellenistic Greek federal states was the Achaean League. In 280 BC, four small towns in the northern Peloponnese (Dyme, Patrae, Pharae and Tritaea) combined to form a new Achaean *koinon*. An Achaean League of some sort had existed in the fifth and fourth centuries, but the new Hellenistic *koinon*, like the Aetolian League, rapidly grew far beyond the traditional 'ethnic' bounds of Achaea. Between 251 and 229, under the leadership of the remarkable Aratus of Sicyon, the Achaean League incorporated the great cities of Corinth, Megalopolis and Argos. By 192, when Sparta was forced into the League, the Achaeans were left as the sole major power in the Peloponnese.

The historian Polybius of Megalopolis, musing on the remarkable growth of the Achaean *koinon*, highlighted the role of common institutions in fostering a collective identity among the members of the League:

> In our own time there has been a startling growth of power and solidarity among the Achaeans... not only have they created an allied and friendly commonwealth (*koinōnia*), but they even use the same laws, weights, measures and coins, as well as the same magistrates, councillors and jurors. And so the organization of virtually the whole Peloponnese differs from that of a single *polis* only in not having a single wall around all its inhabitants. (Polybius 2.37.8–11)

For Polybius, the coinage of the Achaean League was an indication of the new social and political solidarity of the second-century Peloponnese. Most modern scholars have agreed. During the early years of the second century BC, no fewer than nineteen cities, including all the major cities of the Peloponnese (Sparta, Messene, Argos, Corinth, Megara, Sicyon, Megalopolis), struck silver coins with common Achaean League types (Figs. 4.10–4.11; Thompson 1968a: 85–104; BCD Peloponnesos 106–9). These small silver coins (*c.* 2.50 g) were triobols or hemidrachms on the 'allied' or 'reduced Aeginetan' weight-standard (since a drachm was made up of six obols, 'triobol' and 'hemidrachm' are synonyms). The coins carry a bust of Zeus Homarius on the obverse, the god worshipped at the federal shrine (the 'Homarium') of the Achaeans near Aegium in the northern Peloponnese (Walbank 2000). The reverse consists of a monogram of the two letters *alpha* and *chi* (the first two letters of the name 'Achaeans'), surrounded by a wreath. The different mints are variously indicated, usually

Figure 4.10. Silver triobol of the Achaean League, struck at Corinth (*c.* 171–168 BC). The reverse type carries the monogram of the Achaean League (A-CH) and a winged Pegasus, the civic blazon of Corinth. 2.44 g. ANS 1963.31.369.

Figure 4.11. Silver triobol of the Achaean League, struck at Sparta (*c.* 192–188 BC). The reverse type carries the abbreviated Spartan ethnic L-A(ΚΕΔΑΙΜΟΝΙΩΝ) to the left and right of the Achaean monogram. 2.40 g. ANS 1944.100.38875.

with a civic symbol (e.g. a winged Pegasus for Corinth, Fig. 4.10) or an abbreviated ethnic (e.g. L-A for Lacedaemon-Sparta, Fig. 4.11).

The chronology of the Achaean League silver has been very controversial (Warren 1999a). Most of the coins seem to have been struck in two great bursts of activity, *c.* 192–188 BC, when the Achaeans were at war with the Aetolian League and the Seleucid king Antiochus III (the so-called 'Early' group, Fig. 4.11), and *c.* 171–168 BC, during the Third Macedonian War (the 'Late' group, Fig. 4.10). After the cataclysmic Roman defeat of the Achaean League and sack of Corinth in 146 BC, there is a complete break in the series, until the coinage briefly revives under Roman rule, perhaps in the 80s BC (the so-called 'Final' group).

The cities of the Achaean League also produced a large federal bronze coinage (Figs. 4.12–4.13; Warren 2007; 2008). This coinage was apparently struck in a single enormous minting operation, perhaps in the immediate aftermath of the Third Macedonian War, *c.* 167–164, although a date of *c.* 148–146 is also possible (Mattingly 2011). These bronze coins carry on the obverse an image of Zeus Homarius holding in his right hand a small Nike figure, who presents him with a wreath; the reverse depicts a seated personification of Achaea, perhaps imitating the image of Aetolia on the third-century Aetolian League tetradrachms. Most of the coins carry the common Achaean ethnic ('of the Achaeans') side by side with the ethnic of the individual city ('of the Messenians, Sicyonians, Tegeans, etc.').

Figure 4.12. Bronze coin of the Achaean League, struck at Megalopolis (*c.* 167–164 BC). The reverse legend reads Achaiōn Megalopo(litōn) ('of the Achaeans; of the Megalopolitans'), with an abbreviated civic magistrate's name (Aris- Panti-). 5.04 g. ANS 1944.100.40160.

Figure 4.13. Bronze coin of the Achaean League, struck at Pheneus (*c.* 167–164 BC). The obverse carries the name of a civic magistrate Nikaios, and the reverse bears the common Achaean ethnic (Achaiōn, at left) and the ethnic of Pheneus (Pheneōn, at right). 5.27 g. ANS 1944.100.40197.

The scale of this bronze coinage was spectacular. The coins were struck in the names of no fewer than forty-five different cities and villages across the Peloponnese, well over half the seventy-odd known members of the Achaean League, many of which had never minted their own coins before. The most recent study (Warren 2007) suggests that the coins were struck off *c.* 1,600 obverse dies, more than were used for the *entire* abundant series of Athenian New Style tetradrachms between *c.* 164 and the 40s BC (*c.* 1,300 obverse dies; see Chapter 3 above, p. 57).

The purpose of this huge bronze coinage is hard to judge. There seems to have been a general shortage of silver in the Greek world in the mid-160s, due to the closure of the Macedonian gold and silver mines and the removal from circulation of vast quantities of silver coinage as booty to Rome (see below, pp. 77–82, on the contemporary light-weight cistophoric coinage in Asia Minor). This coinage could well be some kind of substitute for the earlier League silver coinage, which it was no longer feasible for the Achaeans to mint. One attractive possibility is that the Achaeans may have minted this coinage specifically in order to 'buy up' the existing silver coins in circulation in the individual cities of the *koinon*, to maximize the silver available for League expenditure (Kroll 2009).

But whatever the immediate aims of these coins may have been, they also indicate the remarkable commitment of the Peloponnesian cities to the federal ideals of the Achaean League. The picture of Achaean 'federalism' which we get from the silver and bronze coins of the Achaean League is strikingly different from the impression given by the coins of Aetolia and other northern Greek *koina*. Aetolian federal coinage, like the Aetolian *koinon* itself, was heavily centralized: no individual cities are named on the coinage, which presents itself as the product of 'the Aetolians' as a single unitary whole.

The Achaean coinage, by contrast, is expressly the product of an alliance of independent cities. The *poleis* of the Achaean League were not simply subsumed in the greater whole, but retained their own local civic identity under a common federal banner. (Think of the contrast between the single, Aetolian-style coinage of the United States and the multiple, Achaean-style coins of the Eurozone countries, with common reverse types but distinctive national iconography on the obverse: Figs. 4.14–4.15.) The presence among the bronze mints of tiny communities like the Arcadian micro-*poleis* of Helisson, Teuthis and Thisoa is particularly telling. Not for nothing did Polybius claim that the Achaeans had always followed 'one single political principle... the freedom of the individual cities and the unity of the Peloponnesians' (2.42.3–6).

Figure 4.14. Modern US dime (1986). The fifty States of the Union all use coins with the same obverse and reverse types, bearing the legend *e pluribus unum* ('one from many'). ANS 1987.153.7.

Figure 4.15. Contemporary one Euro coin of Greece. A common European obverse type (map of Europe) is paired with a distinctive national reverse type (an image of an ancient Athenian 'owl' tetradrachm). ANS 2002.24.111.

Figure 4.16. Lycian silver stater, struck at Pinara in the name of the dynast Kherei (late fifth century BC). The portrait of Athena on the obverse may be modelled on the silver coinage of Athens. 8.48 g. ANS 1989.14.2.

IV   The Lycian League

The Achaean League coinage was the model for another major 'federal' coinage of the second century BC, the silver coinage of the Lycian League. The Lycians were a non-Greek people who inhabited the rocky peninsula between Fethiye and Antalya on the south coast of Asia Minor (Bryce 1986; Keen 1998; Hansen and Nielsen 2004: 1138–43). In the Classical period, various Lycian towns and dynasts had minted their own distinctive silver coins, with legends in the local Lycian script (Fig. 4.16; Mørkholm and Zahle 1972; 1976; Vismara 1989–96). These coinages all came to an end in the mid-fourth century, and for almost two hundred years no coins at all were struck in the region.

By the early second century BC, Lycia had become a Hellenized, but still culturally distinctive region of twenty-odd independent city-states. After a short period of subjection to the island *polis* of Rhodes (188–167 BC), the Lycians were declared free by the Roman senate in 167 BC (Bresson 1999). Shortly afterwards, perhaps in the 150s or 140s (Ashton and Meadows 2008: 131–2), the Lycians started minting their own silver drachms (Fig. 4.17; Troxell 1982: 25–98). These coins carry a portrait of Apollo on the obverse and a *kithara* ('lyre') within a shallow inset square on the reverse; in antiquity the coins were known as *kitharephoroi* or 'lyre-bearers'. Above

Figure 4.17. Drachm of the Lycian League, struck at Rhodiapolis (mid-second century BC). The reverse carries the 'federal' ethnic Lykiōn at the top, with the letters Rh-o below. 2.91 g. ANS 1973.101.7.

Figure 4.18. Plinthophoric drachm of Rhodes (Group A, shortly after 190 BC). The reverse carries the magistrate's name Aristokritos, the abbreviated ethnic R-o, and a Rhodian rose. 2.96 g. ANS 1987.25.31.

the lyre, the coins carry the legend Lykiōn, 'of the Lycians', with the first two letters of some sixteen different Lycian cities (My for Myra, Pa for Patara, etc.) to the left and right of the lyre.

The *kitharephoroi* are very similar in design and weight (*c.* 2.80–2.90 g) to the voluminous Rhodian 'plinthophoric' coinage (*c.* 3.05 g), minted from the 190s down to the early first century BC (Fig. 4.18). The Rhodian *plinthophoroi* carry a head of Helios on the obverse and a rose within an inset square – the eponymous *plinthos* or 'brick' – on the reverse (Jenkins 1989; Ashton 2001). Several cities in the region (Stratonicea, Caunus, Ceramus) struck coins on this Rhodian weight-standard with an inset square on the reverse, and we should see the Lycian League coinage as part of a wider 'Rhodian currency zone' along the south coast of Asia Minor in the mid-second century BC (Ashton 2013: 257–63).

However, other aspects of the coinage's design – common types, with a federal ethnic ('of the Lycians') alongside an abbreviated city name – are clearly modelled on the contemporary coins of the Achaean League. The organization of the second-century Lycian League is very obscure. There was a common League army, common League cults of the goddess Roma and Apollo Alkimos, and international diplomacy seems to have been undertaken in common (Rousset 2010). As in Achaea, the Lycian League was not a true federal state, since the individual Lycian cities retained a high level of internal autonomy. But the League's coinage beautifully shows the paramount importance of 'Lycianness' to the communities of the region: it was their common identity as Lycians, not their separate identity as 'Myrans' or 'Patarans', that they chose to emphasize.

Even some towns that were not formally members of the Lycian League struck coins with these common Lycian types. In the late second century BC, two cities just to the east of Lycia, Phaselis and Olympus, minted their

Figure 4.19. Drachm of Phaselis, imitating the types of the Lycian League coinage (late second century BC). The reverse legend reads Phasēli(tōn), 'of the Phaselites'. 2.33 g. ANS 1984.165.1.

Figure 4.20. Late drachm of the Lycian League (mid-first century BC). The federal ethnic L-Y now appears on the obverse, below Apollo's head, with the letters M-A on the reverse. 2.08 g. ANS 1987.77.20.

own drachms with the same types as the Lycian League coins, though without the common Lycian ethnic (Fig. 4.19). In the earlier second century BC, Phaselis had minted its own silver coinage with local civic types (Heipp-Tamer 1993: 80–3), and so it is very striking to find the Phaselites now voluntarily aligning themselves with the Lycian League in this way.

In the first century BC, perhaps in the 80s BC, the Lycian League coinage underwent a drastic change. The Lycian ethnic moves to the obverse, and the names of individual cities largely disappear, to be replaced by abbreviations for two Lycian mountain ranges, MA for Mt Masicytes in central Lycia and K-R for Mt Cragus in the far west of the peninsula (Fig. 4.20; Troxell 1982: 111–84). The weight-standard drops to *c.* 2.10 g, perhaps for the sake of compatibility with the Roman *quinarius* (Meadows 2002: 127–30). An inscription of the Roman imperial period refers to a financial sub-district (*synteleia*) of the Lycian League 'by Mt Cragus' (*OGIS* 565), and so the two mountain ranges presumably gave their names to federal sub-divisions of some kind. At least in the sphere of coinage, the individual Lycian cities were willing to see their identities completely subsumed into that of the wider Lycian League.

V   The cistophorus: a 'pseudo-federal' coinage

The third major new 'federal' coinage of the second century BC is a very different beast from either the Achaean League or the Lycian League coinage. From around 167 BC down to the principate of Augustus, the main silver coins of western Asia Minor were the so-called *kistophoroi* or 'basket-bearers' (Fig. 4.21; Kleiner and Noe 1977). The name *kistophoros* (usually Latinized to 'cistophorus') comes from the obverse type, which depicts a snake crawling out of a wicker basket (a '*cista*'), encircled by an ivy wreath.

Figure 4.21. Early cistophoric tetradrachm, struck at Pergamum in the 160s or 150s BC. The mint of Per(gamon) is indicated on the reverse, by a monogram at the far left made up of the letters *pi, epsilon* and *rho*. 12.61 g. ANS 1959.254.37.

Figure 4.22. Cistophoric didrachm, struck at Tralles (*c.* 95–90 BC). The mint of Tral(leis) is indicated on the reverse, at bottom left, with an abbreviated magistrate's name (Epai–) above. 6.21 g. ANS 1959.254.57.

On the reverse of the coins, two snakes with forked tongues are shown coiling around a highly decorated bow-case.

Like the third-century civic coinages of western Asia Minor (above, pp. 55), the cistophori were minted on their own distinctive epichoric ('local') weight-standard, with a cistophoric tetradrachm weighing *c.* 12.20 g, around three-quarters of a standard Attic-weight tetradrachm (*c.* 16.80 g in this period). Drachms and didrachms of *c.* 3.05 g and *c.* 6.10 g were also struck, although in much smaller numbers (Fig. 4.22). Their unique weight-standard meant that the cistophori largely stayed in the region where they were minted: the coins are virtually never found in hoards outside western Asia Minor.

In the mid-second century (*c.* 167–133 BC), half a dozen major cities regularly minted coins with cistophoric types: Pergamum, Sardis, Ephesus, Tralles, Laodicea and Apamea in Phrygia. A few small one-off issues were also struck by minor towns such as Adramyttium and Cormasa (Thonemann 2008: 53–8). Just as with the Achaean and Lycian League coinages, the names of the various mints are given in abbreviated form on the reverse, Tral for Tralles, Per for Pergamum and so on. After western Asia Minor became a Roman province in 133 BC, more cistophoric mints popped up, including Synnada, Nysa and Smyrna. Magistrates' names and dates also start to appear on the coins after 133 (Fig. 4.23); eventually the names of the various Greek cities and their local officials came to be replaced with the names of Roman provincial governors (see below, Chapter 9, pp. 177–9).

Figure 4.23. Cistophoric tetradrachm, struck at Laodicea (late second or early first century BC). Like many of the Late Republican cistophori, this coin carries a civic magistrate's name (Apollonius son of Euarchus) on the reverse. 12.32 g. ANS 1944.100.37599.

Figure 4.24. Tetradrachm in the name of Philetaerus, struck under Eumenes I (*c.* 263–241 BC). The first four Attalid rulers (Philetaerus, Eumenes I, Attalus I, Eumenes II) all struck Attic-weight coins with these types. 17.02 g. 1997.9.190.

The cistophori look nothing like any other major Hellenistic coinage; the absence of a royal or divine portrait from the obverse is particularly unusual. With their unusual weight-standard and bizarre images, these coins were clearly meant to look and feel very different from the various 'Alexander-style' royal coinages which had previously been circulating in Asia Minor. Yet despite the apparent 'federal' elements of the coinage – common types, city ethnics and lack of any royal iconography – the cistophori were in fact, at least in their earliest incarnation (*c.* 167–133 BC), the main royal coinage of the last Attalid kings of Pergamum.

The Attalids were relative newcomers to the international stage (Gruen 2000; Kosmetatou 2003). In the third century BC, the Attalids had been one of several minor dynasties on the far north-west fringe of the vast Seleucid kingdom (Chrubasik 2013). Their third-century royal coinage was a fairly standard Hellenistic royal portrait type, with an image of Philetaerus, the founder of the Attalid dynasty (ruled *c.* 282–263), on the obverse (Fig. 4.24; Westermark 1961; Meadows 2013: 154–81). Since Philetaerus never carried the title 'king', he is depicted wearing a wreath rather than a royal diadem; more surprisingly, he is shown as extremely fat, a bit of realism rare in Hellenistic portraits of rulers (Smith 1988: 74–5).

The single most important event in Attalid history was Rome's great victory over the Seleucid king Antiochus III at the battle of Magnesia in 190 BC. Under the terms of the treaty of Apamea in 188 BC, the Roman senate granted vast swathes of the former Seleucid territories in western Asia Minor to their ally, the Attalid king Eumenes II (reigned 197–159 BC). At a stroke, the Attalids were transformed into one of the great powers of the Hellenistic world. For the first twenty years or so after Apamea (c. 188–167), Eumenes continued to mint the traditional Philetaerus coinage. But late in his reign, probably in the mid-160s (Meadows 2013), Eumenes took the radical step of introducing a new, 'cistophoric' coinage on a drastically lightened weight-standard. The Attic-weight Philetaerus coinage continued to be struck along-side the first cistophori, before being phased out in the mid-150s. The cistophorus was effectively the sole silver coinage struck by Eumenes' two successors, Attalus II (159–138 BC) and Attalus III (138–133 BC).

It is far from clear why Eumenes II should have waited twenty years to invent a new coinage for his newly expanded realm. It may be significant that the years immediately before 167 had seen a massive Roman victory over the Macedonian king Perseus (the Third Macedonian War of 171–168 BC), resulting in the closure of the Macedonian gold and silver mines and a flood of Greek silver as booty to Rome (Kay 2013). With his external supplies of silver drying up, Eumenes' introduction of a new – deliberately ugly? – light-weight silver coinage could well have been an attempt to keep as much cash as possible within the bounds of his kingdom (compare pp. 73–4 above, on the bronze coinage of the Achaean League).

But what is really startling about the cistophorus is its complete failure to indicate its Attalid origin. There is no royal iconography, and the coins do not even carry the name of the reigning king. We seem to be dealing with a royal coinage *pretending* to be a federal coinage. As it happens, this fits beautifully with what we know about the ideology of late Attalid rule in Asia Minor (Thonemann 2013a). As a result of the slightly embarrassing way in which Eumenes had won his kingdom (by an *ad hoc* Roman gift), the Attalids could not claim the kind of charismatic and militaristic authority exercised by the other major Hellenistic monarchs over their kingdoms (Austin 1986; Sherwin-White and Kuhrt 1993: 114–40). Instead, Eumenes presented himself as a disinterested champion and benefactor of the Greeks of Asia: his kingdom was conceptualized as a free and equal alliance of independent Greek cities, with the Attalid king simply as a 'first among equals'. The 'quasi-federal' character of the cistophoric coinage is a perfect example of this new, consensual Attalid royal ideology.

In 133 BC, Attalus III bequeathed his kingdom to the Roman people. The Attalid kingdom became the Roman province of Asia, and the cistophorus continued to be the official silver coinage of the province right down to the reign of Augustus. In a tantalizing coda to Attalid history, the years 133–129 saw a pretender to the Attalid throne, Aristonicus, fighting Roman forces in western Asia Minor with the help of a rebel army of former slaves. Aristonicus captured the small cities of Thyatira, Apollonis and Stratonicea, where he minted a small number of cistophori under his assumed royal name 'Eumenes III' ("Ba(sileus) Eu(menēs)": Fig. 4.25; Robinson 1954). These rare rebel coins carry the only mention of an Attalid ruler on any of the cistophoric issues.

Figure 4.25. Cistophorus in the name of Eumenes III, struck at Thyatira in Lydia (132 BC). Thyatira (abbreviated Thya) was never an 'official' Attalid mint. Aristonicus' throne-name Ba(sileus) Eu(menēs) appears within the lower coils of the snakes, with the letter *beta* – 'Year Two' of a short-lived royal era of Aristonicus – tucked inside the bow-case, below the right-hand snake. 12.54 g. ANS 1944.100.37579.

The coinage of a social revolutionary?

The slave rebellion led by Aristonicus is very poorly attested. Our most detailed account comes from the Augustan geographer Strabo:

> Leucae is a small town near Smyrna, which Aristonicus raised in revolt after the death of Attalus III Philometor (133 BC). Aristonicus was thought to be part of the royal family, and he was trying to win the kingdom for himself. He was later defeated by the Ephesians in a naval battle off the territory of Cyme, and was expelled from Leucae. He went deep into inland Asia Minor and quickly gathered a large force of poor men and slaves, won over by the promise of freedom,

whom he called Citizens of the Sun (*Heliopolitai*). He first captured Thyatira, and then the town of Apollonis, and attacked other fortresses. But his successes were brief. The cities of western Asia Minor soon sent an army against him, helped by Nicomedes of Bithynia and the Cappadocian kings. Then five Roman ambassadors arrived in Asia, followed by an army led by the consul Publius Crassus, and Marcus Perperna brought an end to the war soon after. Aristonicus was captured and sent to Rome, where he ended his life in prison. (Strabo 14.1.38)

It is hard to say whether Aristonicus' liberation of the slaves of Asia Minor and foundation of a utopian community of 'Heliopolitans' was a purely cynical move, or whether his uprising genuinely aimed at social revolution. Either way, his coinage gives us a fascinating glimpse of the short-lived successes of this extraordinary Hellenistic slave uprising. (Robinson 1954; Adams 1980; Jones 2004.)

VI 'Festival' coinages

In the years after the treaty of Apamea (*c.* 188–182 BC), another long-standing association of cities in Asia Minor began to strike its own coins for the first time. Since the late fourth century BC, several cities in the far north-west of the peninsula had gathered every year at the small city of Ilium to celebrate a festival in honour of the goddess Athena Ilias. Just as at Athens, the festival was called the 'Panathenaea', the 'All-Athena' festival. A Lesser Panathenaea was held every year, with a particularly grand 'Greater Panathenaea' every fourth year. This was a great gathering of people from all the cities of north-western Asia Minor, with sacrifices, athletic and dramatic contests, and a huge festival market or *panegyris*.

The festival was administered by two boards of representatives from the participating cities, a council (*synedrion*) and a college of five agonothetes ('contest organizers'). Both boards held office for a four-year period, from one Greater Panathenaea to the next. This 'Confederation (*koinon*) of Athena Ilias' was not a political organization like the Achaean League: it had no common army, and so far as we know it developed no common laws or institutions. The only thing that the cities of this confederation had in common was their shared participation at this great annual festival – they

Figure 4.26. Tetradrachm in the name of Athena Ilias (Athēnas Iliados), with images of Athena on both faces (mid-second century BC). This coinage is not a civic issue, and so the ethnic of Ilium (Ilieōn) does not appear. 16.87 g. ANS 1945.33.5.

were simply 'the cities that have a common share in the sanctuary and the *panegyris*' (*I.Ilion* 1, 306 BC).

At some point shortly after 188 BC, the organizers of the festival of Athena Ilias began to strike regular issues of fine Attic-weight tetradrachms, which continued to be minted down to *c.* 31 BC (Fig. 4.26). These coins seem to have been produced on a regular rhythm, once every four years, to coincide with the celebration of the Greater Panathenaea (Knoepfler 2010). The coins carry the name and portrait of the goddess in whose honour the festival was held, Athena Ilias, and the name of the chairman of the college of ago-nothetes. This remarkable coinage was long attributed to the city of Ilion, the host-city of the festival. Only in the 1960s was it finally recognized as a product of the confederation which organized the festival (Robert 1966) – as if today's International Olympic Committee were to start printing its own banknotes.

Why did the festival officials take the extraordinary step of striking their own coins? The *panegyris* of the Greater Panathenaea was a massive market fair, lasting at least sixteen days, which would have seen slaves, livestock, textiles and other goods being bought and sold in vast quantities (Chandezon 2000). According to one recent interpretation, the coinage could have been intended to act as a common currency at this great fair. Buyers and sellers would have had to exchange their various local coinages for Athena Ilias coins, probably in return for a fee (Psoma 2007b; 2008). But it is hard to see how this miniature 'closed-currency' system would work in practice, given that the Athena Ilias coins are on the ordinary international

Attic weight-standard – and, moreover, are of a very large denomination, poorly suited to ordinary market exchange.

Instead, it may well be significant that the coins always carry the name of the presiding agonothete, the 'contest organizer'. The Greater Panathenaea involved both athletic and dramatic contests, including tragic performances. Competitions of this kind did not come cheap: the cost of hiring a professional theatrical troupe for such a festival in the Hellenistic period was well over 6,000 drachms (Slater 2010), and individual star athletes and musicians could command astronomical fees – at the Delian Apollonia festival of 192 BC, the flautist Telemachus was paid an appearance fee of 1,500 drachmas (*I.Délos* 399, A56–7). The festival agonothetes may have struck the Athena Ilias coinage specifically in order to pay the wages and expenses of the competitors, not to mention any cash prizes.

Now, the event managers of the Greater Panathenaea could of course have chosen – as they must have done before 188 – to carry on paying their performers in ordinary Attic-weight coins (Alexanders, Philetaeri, Lysimachi, etc.). By minting their own coinage, the agonothetes did not magically summon up more money to spend on the festival. Instead, their decision to melt down their silver reserves and start striking new coins in the name of the goddess was first and foremost an ideological one. The coinage reflects a decision by the cities of the Troad to use the festival as a stage on which to assert their collective identity as 'the *koinon* of Athena Ilias'.

The case of the *koinon* of Athena Ilias is far from unique. Another non-*polis* association, the guild of Dionysiac Artists in Ionia and the Hellespont, also struck its own coins in the mid-second century BC (Fig. 4.27; Lorber and Hoover 2003). Several such professional guilds of actors and musicians operated across the Hellenistic world; this particular association, based at the Ionian city of Teos, served the cities and sanctuaries of western Asia Minor. We should imagine the Artists as a kind of huge travelling circus, who trundled up and down the Aegean coast performing (for a fee) at dozens of different festivals every year. Their coinage is known from a single unique specimen, on the ordinary Attic weight-standard: it has a portrait of Dionysus on the obverse, and a thyrsus (a giant fennel-staff topped with a pine-cone, a typical attribute of Dionysus) within an ivy wreath on the reverse. The legend reads simply 'of the Artists of Dionysus'.

Just as with the coins of the *koinon* of Athena Ilias, the 'point' of this coinage is essentially to express collective identity. It displays the Artists' independence from any one *polis* or royal court, and presents them as a

Figure 4.27. Tetradrachm in the name of the Dionysiac Artists, with the legend TŌN PERI TON DIONYSON TECHNITŌN (*c.* 160–150 BC). Only a single example of this tetradrachm is known, suggesting that the original issue was fairly small. 16.87 g (Lorber and Hoover 2003). By permission of Freeman & Sear.

distinct and self-governing society in their own right. In the Hellenistic period, the various semi-nomadic guilds of Dionysiac Artists started to behave like independent *poleis* in other ways, electing annual magistrates, passing their own honorific decrees and entering into bilateral treaties (and disputes) with other cities and kings. Minting their own coins was one way of expressing this sense of belonging to their own, albeit unusually rootless, community.

Several other coinages in the name of deities are known from the third and second centuries BC, most of which should probably be connected with great international festivals like the Ilian Panathenaea. Two particularly striking examples come from late Attalid Pergamum. In 181 BC, a Pergamene festival in honour of Athena Nicephorus ('bringer of victory'), the Nicephoria, was reorganized as a sumptuous four-yearly athletic and musical contest (Rigsby 1996: 363–77; Jones 2000). Three specimens survive of an Attic-weight tetradrachm issue in the name of Athena Nicephorus (Fig. 4.28; Mørkholm 1984b: 187–92; Marcellesi 2012: 125–7). These coins seem to be a one-off issue, perhaps struck to mark the first celebration of the Nicephoria. The Pergamene mint also struck a large number of small bronze coins in the name of Athena Nicephorus, along with a few silver hemidrachms on the cistophoric weight-standard, which were presumably linked in some way with the four-yearly celebrations of the Pergamene Nicephoria (Fig. 4.29; Westermark 1995; Marcellesi 2012: 121–2, 127–8).

Finally, at some point in the 140s BC, the Pergamene mint produced an issue of Attic-weight tetradrachms in the name of the Divine Syrian Cabeiri

Figure 4.28. Tetradrachm in the name of Athena Nicephorus, struck at Pergamum, perhaps to mark the first celebration of the Nicephoria festival in 181 BC. 16.08 g. BM 1975–02–08–1 (Photograph © A. Meadows).

Figure 4.29. Bronze coin in the name of Athena Nicephorus, struck at Pergamum (second century BC). 3.57 g. ANS 1944.100.43276.

Figure 4.30. Tetradrachm in the name of the Divine Syrian Cabeiri, struck at Pergamum (c. 145–140 BC). 16.67 g. ANS 1978.34.1.

(Fig. 4.30). These coins carry a portrait of the goddess Demeter on the obverse and the Cabeiri (an obscure pair of young male deities, sometimes identified with the brothers Castor and Pollux) standing within a wreath on the reverse. Long attributed to the Cycladic island of Syros, these coins have now been firmly linked to the important Pergamene mystery cult of the Cabeiri (Meadows 2013: 184–6). Little is known about the Pergamene Cabeiria festival, but it was clearly an important event in the city's festival calendar (Wörrle 2000: 557–8), and these coins presumably played a role similar to that of the slightly earlier coinage of Athena Nicephorus.

5

Hellenizing identities

I Introduction

What is Hellenization? This question lies at the heart of most recent work on the societies along the fringes of the Hellenistic world, both to the east (Parthia, Armenia, the Indo-Greeks) and west (Carthage, Italy, Spain). Without doubt, certain aspects of Greek culture – the use of coined money, the Greek language, naturalistic sculpture, urbanism – were very widely adopted by the non-Greek neighbours of the major Graeco-Macedonian royal states. But in what sense, if any, is it helpful to conceive of these societies as 'Hellenized'?

The adoption and adaptation of Greek culture was certainly not a matter of a triumphant Greece or Macedon imposing its values on a vanquished barbarian periphery. On the contrary, Hellenization is often most visible where Graeco-Macedonian colonial power was at its weakest. So in Parthia, as we will see later in this chapter, Greek iconography on coinage and the royal title 'Philhellene' emerged at precisely the moment when the Parthians defeated and supplanted the Graeco-Macedonian Seleucid dynasty in Mesopotamia. Hellenizing cultural traits were not adopted by the Parthians to proclaim a self-consciously 'Greek' or 'hybrid' identity: rather, Greek culture became a means of asserting Parthian power and distinctiveness. Foreign cultural motifs were used by the Parthians 'within a nevertheless culturally distinct package of self-definition' (Curti, Dench, and Patterson 1996: 181–5).

The problems of 'Romanization' as a conceptual framework for describing cultural change in the Roman world have been widely discussed (Woolf 1998; Keay and Terrenato 2001; Mattingly 2011: 203–45). With a few notable exceptions (Rajak 1990; Hornblower 1996 [2003]; Wallace-Hadrill 2008: 14–28), Hellenization has not enjoyed the same kind of sustained theoretical reflection. Some scholars have wanted to ditch the (modern) terms 'Hellenization' and 'Romanization' altogether, in favour of more apparently neutral concepts like 'creolization', 'hybridization' or 'discrepant experience'. This is unnecessary: what was distinctive about the Hellenistic period was precisely the fact that it was Hellenic culture that was appropriated by so wide a range of different peoples (Mullen 2013: 3–19). This chapter will show how coinage can help us understand the bewildering variety of Hellenizing identities adopted in different parts of the Hellenistic world.

II   Hellenistic Iran

Persis, the centre of the old Persian empire of the Achaemenids in modern south-western Iran, is one of the most obscure corners of the Hellenistic world (Callieri 2007). Like the rest of Iran and central Asia, Persis was certainly part of the successor kingdom of Seleucus I (reigned 312–281 BC), but we have no idea when or why Seleucid rule came to an end in this region. A Seleucid satrap is still attested in Persis in the late 220s (Polybius 5.41.1), and Persian troops may still have formed part of the Seleucid army in the early second century, but these could easily be mercenaries rather than Seleucid subjects. The problem forms part of a wider debate about the strength or weakness of the Seleucid kingdom in the third and early second century BC (Sherwin-White and Kuhrt 1993; Engels 2013).

Coinage provides virtually our only evidence for the breakdown of Seleucid rule in Persis. At some point between the early third and the early second century BC, a native Iranian dynasty emerged in the region. The members of this dynasty carried the title of *frataraka* or 'forerunner', an old Achaemenid title for a local official operating below the chief provincial governor, the satrap. The *fratarakā* (pl.) minted a series of coins in their own name, perhaps at Istakhr, just to the north of the old Achaemenid royal palace complex at Persepolis (Klose and Müseler 2008: 15–40). Neither the Achaemenids nor the Seleucids seem to have minted coins in Persis proper, and so these issues (silver tetradrachms, drachms and obols) are perhaps the earliest coins ever struck in south-western Iran. Many of the *fratarakā* tetradrachms are overstruck on early third-century silver tetradrachms of Seleucus I, Antiochus I and Demetrius Poliorcetes (Hoover 2008b: 213–15; *NAC* Auction 59, Lot 653).

The character of this native Persian dynasty is far from clear. They have traditionally been regarded as an independent quasi-royal Persian house, although they could equally well have been Seleucid vassals, operating as the local enforcers of a Seleucid satrap (Engels 2013). This uncertainty also extends to the dating of the *fratarakā* coinages. The fact that so many of the coins are overstruck on early third-century Seleucid issues suggests a date in

Figure 5.1. Tetradrachm minted by Wādfradād (perhaps late third century BC). The irregular shape of the coin results from overstriking on an earlier tetradrachm. 15.65 g. Oxford (Baldwin donation 1939).

Figure 5.2. Drachm minted by Wahbarz (perhaps mid-third century BC). The reverse, depicting a Persian royal figure slaying a kneeling Macedonian, carries the legend 'Wahbarz, the commander, was victorious'. 4.24 g. Private collection (Klose and Müseler 2008: 36, Kat. 2/16).

the mid-third century BC, but a case has also been made for a 'low' chronology in the first half of the second century BC (Shayegan 2011: 168–78; Wiesehöfer 2011).

The coins were struck in the names of four dynasts, Ardaxšir, Wahbarz, Baydād and Wādfradād (their sequence remains controversial). The tetradrachms of Ardaxšir, Wahbarz and Wādfradād all carry on the obverse a portrait of a bearded and moustached male figure, wearing a Persian headdress (the so-called *kyrbasia*) bound with a diadem (Fig. 5.1). On the reverse, this Persian man – probably a generic 'Iranian ruler figure' – is depicted standing before a large building crowned with three fire altars, perhaps depicting one of the great Achaemenid-era buildings in Persis, the Ka'ba at Naqsh-e Rustam or the Zendan at Pasargadae (Potts 2007). The coins carry a legend in the Persian language, written in Aramaic script, reading 'Ardaxšir/ Wahbarz/Wādfradād, *fratarakā* by grace of the gods, son of Persis'.

Only one of these four dynasts, Wahbarz, is known from written sources. He is very likely to be the 'Oborzos' mentioned in a late Greek source as having murdered three thousand settlers (presumably Greeks or Macedonians) in Persis at an uncertain date (Polyaenus 7.40). Along with his standard dynastic tetradrachm-types, Wahbarz also introduced an extraordinary new image on the reverse of his silver drachms (Fig. 5.2). This shows a Persian man, in the royal dress worn by the Great King in

Figure 5.3. Tetradrachm minted by Baydād (perhaps mid-third century BC). The legend on the reverse reads 'Baydād, *frataraka* by grace of the gods, son of Bagawart'. 16.79 g. ANS 1968.244.40.

pre-Hellenistic Iranian art, about to slay a kneeling Macedonian soldier. The coin legend describes Wahbarz as *karanos*, 'commander' (Shayegan 2011: 170–1).

Despite a recent attempt to interpret Wahbarz as a loyal Seleucid vassal (Engels 2013), this remarkable coin-type is best taken as a pointed declaration of Persian independence from Macedonian rule. The image of the Persian king slaying a kneeling enemy has a long history on Achaemenid seals and funerary reliefs from Achaemenid-era Lycia (Klose and Müseler 2008: 28–9). Wahbarz seems to have been presenting himself as a local Iranian successor to the great Achaemenid monarchs of the past.

Perhaps the most distinctive coin-type struck by the *fratarakā* dynasts is a tetradrachm minted by Baydād (Fig. 5.3). The obverse carries a highly distinctive portrait – probably an image of Baydād himself – showing the *frataraka* sporting an elaborate headdress, with long ear-flaps tucked below a broad band; he also wears a diadem and hoop earrings, along with a splendid beard and moustache. On the reverse, Baydād is shown seated on a throne, wielding a sceptre, in front of a Persian military standard. The king's pose is identical to that of Zeus on the silver coins of Alexander the Great.

What kind of picture does this amazing coin series give us of Persian cultural identity in the Hellenistic period? From one perspective, the *fratarakā* coinage is clearly part of the wider Graeco-Macedonian numismatic *koine*. Earlier Macedonian royal coinages provide the model for the weight-standard (Attic) and denominations (drachm, tetradrachm), as well as for the right-facing diademed ruler portrait, the Zeus-like seated figure on Baydād's coinage, and even the borders of dots on the obverse and reverse. The exotic portrait of Baydād, for all its superficially Persian attributes (headdress, earrings, twirly moustache), is in stylistic terms unambiguously a portrait *à la grecque*: note in particular the highly individualized features, the long neck with pronounced tendon and deep-set eyes.

Nonetheless, from another perspective, these coins offer a vivid picture of a cultural group asserting itself in opposition to Graeco-Macedonian culture. The *fratarakā*'s titulature is entirely Persian in form, and is given in the Persian language and the old Aramaic script. Ardaxšir's coins depict a scene of distinctively Persian religious ritual, with fire altars on the roof of a Persian cult building, and the Achaemenid-style king crushing a hapless Macedonian on Wahbarz's coinage is a powerful statement of Iranian nationalism. The mix of cultural signifiers is a very complex one: the coins are Greek in style and form, but combatively Persian in content and meaning.

III   The Parthians and their neighbours

Similarly ambivalent styles of self-representation are found elsewhere on the eastern periphery of the Hellenistic world. Third-century Parthia was a remote backwater of the Seleucid kingdom, in the far north-east of the Iranian plateau. Around 245–238 BC, the Seleucid satrap of Parthia, a certain Andragoras, struck a small series of gold staters and silver tetradrachms in his own name, usually seen as marking a revolt against Seleucid rule (Lerner 1999: 13–31). These coins could have been minted pretty much anywhere in the Hellenistic world: the gold staters depict a heavily bearded male figure (probably Zeus) on the obverse, with a winged Nike figure driving a four-horse chariot on the reverse (Fig. 5.4).

Andragoras' independence, if such it was, was short-lived. In around 238 BC, Parthia was overrun by a nomadic people known in Greek sources as the Parni, led by a certain Arsaces (Strabo 11.9.2–3; Justin 41.4–5). As with the Persian *fratarakā*, the early history of the Arsacids is deeply obscure; it is

Figure 5.4. Gold stater of Andragoras of Parthia (*c.* 245–238 BC). The identity of the diademed figure on the obverse is uncertain. 8.50 g. CNG Triton XVI (8 January 2013), 550. Courtesy of Classical Numismatic Group.

Figure 5.5. Silver hemidrachm of an early Arsacid Parthian ruler (late third century BC). 1.99 g. CNG Triton XIII (4 January 2010), 501. Courtesy of Classical Numismatic Group.

Figure 5.6. Silver stater of Tarkumuwa, struck at Tarsus (*c.* 375 BC). Tarkumuwa is known only from his coinage; he seems to have been a Persian satrap of Cilicia (Casabonne 2004: 174–81). 9.84 g. ANS 1944.100.54387.

even possible that they were originally semi-independent Seleucid vassals. The first coins minted by the Arsacids were a series of silver drachms and hemidrachms on a light Attic weight-standard (*c.* 4.00 g), probably to be dated to the late third century BC (Sellwood 1980; Sinisi 2012). These coins carry a very un-Greek portrait of a clean-shaven king wearing a soft pointed tiara with earflaps and neckguard (Curtis 1998). On the reverse, an archer sits on a throne, also wearing a soft hat, dressed in a tight-fitting rider's suit with a long-sleeved coat slung over his shoulders (Fig. 5.5). The legend, in Greek, reads 'of Arsaces *autokrator*'. The term *autokrator* ('independent ruler') may be meant to distinguish the Iranian Arsacids from the Graeco-Macedonian 'kings' (*basileis*) in western Asia.

Like the *fratarakā* coins, the early Arsacid Parthian drachms are a complex mixture of Greek and Iranian elements (Dąbrowa 2008). The language of the coin legend is Greek, albeit with an unusual royal title (*autokrator*), and the general layout of the coins, with portrait-bust on the obverse and a seated figure on the reverse, is clearly modelled on contemporary Seleucid coinage. But the seated archer echoes an old Achaemenid motif, as found for instance on the fourth-century coinage of the satrap Tarkumuwa at Tarsus in Cilicia (Fig. 5.6; Curtis 2007: 414–17; Erickson and Wright 2011). The image of the seated archer, plucking at his bow, may have had a wider significance in Parthian royal ideology. The Roman author Cassius Dio gives a vivid account of the Parthian king Phraates IV receiving a group of Roman ambassadors in 36 BC, 'seated on a golden chair and twanging his bow-string', as if the king were acting out the iconography of the Parthian royal coinage (Dio 49.27.4; Fowler 2005: 147–9).

During the reign of Mithradates I (*c.* 171–138 BC), the Parthians extended their rule across the whole western part of the Iranian plateau. Between 141 and 138 BC, they overran Mesopotamia, bringing an end to Seleucid rule east of Syria (Boiy 2004: 166–71; Gaslain 2010). As the Parthians moved west, Mithradates' coinage took on more and more Hellenizing elements. Late in his reign, the king struck a spectacular series of silver tetradrachms at the former Seleucid royal capital of Seleucia on the Tigris (Le Rider 1965: 363–9). The Iranian elements of the early Parthian coinage have disappeared. Aside from his tremendous beard, Mithradates is depicted in conventional Graeco-Macedonian royal style, with bare head, diadem and thick wavy hair, paired with a nude standing Heracles on the reverse (Fig. 5.7). He would, I'm sure, be incandescent to be told that 'his beard, long hair, and dour expression are those of an Oriental absolute monarch' (Smith 1988: 118) – on the contrary, Mithradates' image is that of a king in the familiar Macedonian mould. The coins still carry the name of Arsaces, the official 'throne name' of all the Parthian kings, but the distinctive royal title *autokrator* has now been replaced by the titles *basileus megas* ('Great King') and 'Philhellene' – that is to say, not a Greek, but a friendly neighbour to the Greeks (Ferrary 1988: 497–526; Wiesehöfer 1996).

Mithradates' Hellenizing style was continued by his successor, Phraates II (*c.* 138–127 BC). Phraates' tetradrachms carry the legend 'of Great King Arsaces, Bringer of Victory (*nikēphoros*)', and depict a seated deity being crowned by a winged Nike figure (Fig. 5.8). The body of this god/goddess belongs to a young woman, with breasts and elegantly folded legs, but the face is that of a man with a heavy beard (Curtis 2007: 420–1). This bearded goddess seems to be a deliberate blurring of two quite different visual languages: the artist has chosen to invest the Parthian king, beard and all, with the iconography of the Greek goddess Tyche.

Figure 5.7. Tetradrachm of Mithradates I, struck at Seleucia on the Tigris (*c.* 141–138 BC). 14.81 g. ANS 1944.100.82040.

Figure 5.8. Tetradrachm of Phraates II, struck at Seleucia on the Tigris (*c.* 138–127 BC). Note Phraates' thoroughly Greek-style facial hair: compare the neat curly beards of the Antigonid kings Philip V and Perseus (Figures 8.24–8.25 below). 16.42 g. ANS 1967.152.703.

Figure 5.9. Drachm of Mithradates II, struck at Rhagae (*c.* 121–91 BC). The coin legend – still in Greek, but in an ever less legible script – describes Mithradates as 'Great King of Kings, (God) Manifest' (BASILEŌS BASILEŌN MEGALOU EPIPHANOUS). 4.17 g. ANS 1944.100.82449.

As the hybrid coinage of Phraates II indicates, it is very difficult to judge how deep the cultural Hellenism of the second-century Parthian kings really went. Fine Greek-style sculpture and metalwork have been found at the early Arsacid site of Nisa in modern Turkmenistan, and Greek cultural practices survived in the old Seleucid cities of Mesopotamia deep into the Parthian period (Invernizzi 2007; Hauser 2012). But the Hellenizing coin iconography of Mithradates I and Phraates II was gradually abandoned by their successors (Dąbrowa 2010). Mithradates II (*c.* 121–91 BC) dropped the plain Greek-style diadem in favour of a spectacular jewelled tiara (Fig. 5.9). By the mid-first century BC, the Parthian royal coinage had left its Greek models far behind: the highly stylized ruler portraits of Phraates IV (*c.* 38–2 BC) show an Iranian king with heavy braided hair, a broad diadem pulled low over his forehead and a magnificent royal robe slung over his shoulders (Fig. 5.10; Assar 2006; Sellwood and Simonetta 2006).

In the wake of the Seleucid collapse in the East, several small Near Eastern Seleucid 'successor states' emerged on the fringes of the new Parthian empire. The region of Elymais, modern Khuzestan in south-western Iran,

Figure 5.10. Tetradrachm of Phraates IV, struck at Seleucia on the Tigris (May 34 BC). This is a rare example of a Hellenistic royal coin series precisely dated to the year and month (see Chapter 6 below, p. 114): this particular example is dated to the month Daesius, year 278 of the Seleucid era. 11.71 g. ANS 1944.100.82806.

Figure 5.11. Tetradrachm of Kamniskires I Nicephorus, struck at Susa (*c.* 147–140 BC). The image on the reverse, showing Apollo seated on an *omphalos* ('navel-stone'), is a standard Seleucid type (cf. Figure 1.26). 16.32 g. ANS 1968.183.10.

Figure 5.12. Drachm of Kamniskires II and Anzaze (*c.* 83–72 BC). The reverse legend reads Basileōs Kamnaskirou kai Basilissēs Anzazēs, 'of King Kamnaskires and Queen Anzaze'. 3.86 g. ANS 1944.100.84892.

broke away from the Seleucids in about 147 BC (Le Rider 1965: 349–61; Potts 1999: 384–91). During a brief period of independence, Kamniskires I Nikephoros (*c.* 147–140 BC) minted silver tetradrachms imitating the contemporary Seleucid royal coinage of Demetrius II (Fig. 5.11; Haaff 2007). The Elymaeans were soon incorporated into the Parthian kingdom, and seem not to have minted coins again until the early first century BC. The royal portraits on the coins of Kamniskires II and Queen Anzaze, struck between 83 and 72 BC (Assar 2006: 79), have a far more Iranian appearance, reflecting Parthian dominance in the region (Fig. 5.12).

Figure 5.13. 'Seleucid-style' tetradrachm of Hyspaosines of Characene, dated to Year 187 of the Seleucid era (126/5 BC). 15.91 g. CNG 75 (23 May 2007), 603. Courtesy of Classical Numismatic Group.

Figure 5.14. Tetradrachm of Tigranes II of Armenia, struck at Antioch (*c.* 75–69 BC). 15.81 g. ANS 1967.152.647.

Immediately to the west of Elymais was Characene, at the head of the Persian gulf (Cohen 2013: 109–27; Kosmin 2013). A former Seleucid official, one Hyspaosines (ruled *c.* 141–124 BC), struck royal tetradrachms in the Seleucid style with a seated Heracles on the reverse (Fig. 5.13; Schuol 2000: 218–20, 291–300); this region, too, became a Parthian vassal state in the late second century BC. Finally, in the southern Caucasus, Armenia had already become independent of Seleucid rule by 189 BC (Strabo 11.14.15). The first of the Artaxiad kings of Armenia to mint a substantial coinage was Tigranes II (ruled *c.* 95–56 BC), who briefly transformed his small upland kingdom into the greatest power of the Near East. Tigranes' tetradrachms, mostly struck at Antioch after his conquest of Syria *c.* 75 BC, show the king wearing a splendid Armenian five-pointed pearled tiara, decorated with a star between two eagles; the reverse type, however, is a thoroughly Greek-style personification of the Tyche ('fortune') of Antioch (Fig. 5.14; Nercessian 2006; Hoover 2007: 296–8).

IV   Bactrians and 'Indo-Greeks'

Imagine a forty- or fifty-page history of Franklin D. Roosevelt's presidency based solely on the iconography of the US dime, or a biography of Queen

Elizabeth II based on the £5 and £10 note. That gives a fair idea of the modern historiography of the Hellenistic kingdoms of the Far East, the Graeco-Bactrian kingdom of northern Afghanistan (*c.* 245–130 BC) and the Indo-Greek kingdom(s) in the far north-west of the Indian subcontinent (*c.* 200 BC–AD 10). These exotic kingdoms, entirely cut off from the rest of the Greek-speaking world, have exercised a powerful fascination on generations of scholars. Yet with the exception of the marvellous site of Ai Khanoum in eastern Bactria (Hiebert and Cambon 2008), the archaeological and written evidence for the Hellenistic Far East is wretchedly poor (Mairs 2011). The history of the Graeco-Bactrian and Indo-Greek dynasties has to be written almost entirely from their beautiful and fascinating royal coin issues.

Unfortunately, coins are a very poor source for traditional political history. Some forty-two different Bactrian and Indo-Greek kings are known from coin legends, only eight of whom (at most) are mentioned elsewhere (Seldeslachts 2004). It is far from clear that we have got these kings in the right order; some of them may not even have existed (Demetrius II and a shadowy 'Demetrius III' could well be the same man). If a king is known to have minted large numbers of different coin-types, he is generally assigned a long reign and a large kingdom, and whole dynasties have been reconstructed from the stylistic resemblances between coin-types (Guillaume 1990). Even very recent monographs (Widemann 2009) give elaborate accounts of the 'personalities' and 'policies' of kings who are effectively known only from coin portraits. The Bactrians and Indo-Greeks are, in fact, a salutary illustration of the kinds of things numismatic evidence *cannot* be made to tell us (Holt 2012).

The basic outline of Graeco-Bactrian history is clear enough. Around 245 BC, the Seleucid satrap of Bactria, Diodotus I, broke away from the Seleucids (Lerner 1999: 13–31; Holt 1999) and established an independent kingdom in the valley of the Oxus, the modern Amu Darya, which divides Afghanistan from the central Asian republics (Turkmenistan, Uzbekistan and Tajikistan). Diodotus' coins, like those of his near-contemporary Andragoras in Parthia (above, p. 91), are in the conventional Macedonian royal style, with diademed royal portrait on the obverse and an image of Zeus wielding a thunderbolt on the reverse (Fig. 5.15).

At some point in the early second century BC, large parts of north-west India seem to have been incorporated into the Graeco-Bactrian kingdom (Widemann 2009: 60–9; Holt 2012: 154–8). Demetrius I of Bactria, who reigned around the turn of the second century, adopted an elephant-skin

Figure 5.15. Gold stater of Diodotus I of Bactria (*c.* 245–230 BC). 8.45 g. ANS 1980.109.108.

Figure 5.16. Tetradrachm of Demetrius I of Bactria (*c.* 200–190 BC). The dour portrait of Demetrius – thick neck, square jaw, grim expression – makes a sharp contrast with the youthful, idealized portraits of contemporary Seleucid kings. 16.41 g. ANS 1997.9.67.

headdress for his coin portrait, probably in commemoration of a successful Indian campaign (Fig. 5.16). This portrait type echoes the elephant-skin headdress worn by Alexander the Great on the early satrapal coinage of Ptolemy I (see above, pp. 18–20).

The largest and most varied Graeco-Bactrian coinages are those of Agathocles and Eucratides I. The coinage of Agathocles (*c.* 190–180 BC) includes a particularly striking set of 'heritage' tetradrachms (Holt 1984). The obverse types of these coins depict half a dozen earlier rulers of Bactria, including Alexander the Great, Diodotus I, Demetrius I, and a mysterious 'Antiochus Nicator', either the Seleucid Antiochus II or an otherwise unknown Bactrian king (Figs. 5.17–5.18; Jakobsson 2010). The portraits are based on these various rulers' own coin-types; the alleged portrait of Alexander is in fact the Heracles portrait from Alexander's silver tetra-drachms (an easy mistake to make: see pp. 147–8 below).

The large coinage of Eucratides (*c.* 170–145 BC) includes two distinctive new royal portrait types. The first depicts Eucratides, a dour middle-aged man, wearing a cavalry helmet; in the second type, the viewer looks at Eucratides from behind his heavily muscled shoulders, as he brandishes a spear (Figs. 5.19–5.20; Smith 1988: 113–14). These unusual militaristic portraits may reflect the repeated invasions of the Graeco-Bactrian

Figure 5.17. 'Heritage' tetradrachm of Agathocles (*c.* 190–180 BC). The obverse carries the Heracles portrait from Alexander's silver coinage, with the legend ALEXANDROU TOU PHILIPPOU, 'of Alexander son of Philip'. 16.69 g. Oxford (Senior).

Figure 5.18. 'Heritage' tetradrachm of Agathocles (*c.* 190–180 BC). The obverse depicts a predecessor of Agathocles, identified as ANTIOCHOS NIKATŌR. His portrait, with receding hair and furrowed brow, bears no resemblance to the coin portraits of the Seleucid kings Antiochus I and II. 16.30 g. ANS 1966.150.2.

Figure 5.19. Tetradrachm of Eucratides (*c.* 170–145 BC). The obverse depicts the king in middle age, wearing a Macedonian cavalry helmet. 17.02 g. ANS 1970.203.1.

kingdom during Eucratides' reign, first by Mithradates I of Parthia, then by successive waves of nomadic Saka and Yuezhi from the central Asian steppe (Rapin 2007: 47–50; Hiebert and Cambon 2008; Holt 2012: 190–202). The Bactrian kingdom seems finally to have collapsed *c.* 120 BC.

Figure 5.20. Tetradrachm of Eucratides (*c.* 170–145 BC). The heroic portrait on the obverse vividly evokes the king's physical strength and martial prowess, while still observing (more or less) the ordinary conventions of ruler portraiture on coins. 16.95 g. ANS 1997.9.68.

Figure 5.21. 'Greek-style' tetradrachm of Agathocles (*c.* 190–180 BC). Stylistically there is little to distinguish this coin from contemporary Seleucid royal issues. 16.51 g. ANS 1997.9.188.

If the basic outlines of the history of Bactria are more or less clear, the same cannot be said of the Indo-Greek kings. As one specialist on south Asian coinage recently put it, 'in English there is nothing that could really be recommended above Wikipedia. This is not a compliment for Wikipedia… In such a field, where most conclusions are guesswork and often draw on secondary sources simply because primary ones do not give answers, the mashing together of secondary material on Wikipedia is as good as any' (Bracey 2011: 51).

The first Indo-Greek coinages were struck by the Graeco-Bactrian king Agathocles (*c.* 190–180 BC) in the wake of the conquest of India. Alongside his Greek-style royal tetradrachms (Fig. 5.21), Agathocles also struck square bronze and silver coins, with the legend 'of King Agathocles', rendered in Greek on one face (BASILEŌS AGATHOKLEOUS), and in the Brahmi script on the other (RAJANE AGATHUKLAYASA) (Figs. 5.22–5.23; Audouin and Bernard 1974). These are the first bilingual coins known from any part of

Figure 5.22. Silver drachm of Agathocles (*c.* 190–180 BC), with Greek and Brahmi legends on obverse and reverse. 3.22 g. CNG Triton VIII (10 January 2005), 632. Courtesy of Classical Numismatic Group.

Figure 5.23. Bronze coin of Agathocles (*c.* 190–180 BC). The dancing goddess on the obverse has no close parallels in Greek coin iconography. 10.49 g. ANS 1944.100.74404.

Figure 5.24. Drachm of Apollodotus I (*c.* 175–165 BC). To a Greek viewer, the exotic elephant was a kind of visual shorthand for Greek rule in India; to an Indian viewer, the humped bull evoked traditional Gandharan religion (MacDowell 2007: 246–7). 2.41 g. ANS 1944.100.74510.

the Hellenistic world. The silver issues depict Indian Vedic deities, perhaps Vasudeva and Sankarshana, on the obverse and reverse, while the bronzes depict a lotus-bearing goddess (perhaps Lakshmi) and a standing lion.

Agathocles' successors in India continued to strike 'bilingual' coins of this kind, usually with legends in the Greek and Kharoshthi scripts, in a range of different metals and formats (Bopearachchi 1991; 1998). Apollodotus I (perhaps *c.* 175–165) struck a large issue of square drachms on a distinctive Indian weight-standard (*c.* 2.45 g), with an elephant on the obverse and hump-backed bull on the reverse, with the legend 'of King Apollodotus the Saviour' in Greek and Kharoshthi (Fig. 5.24). Menander (perhaps *c.* 155–130 BC) minted enormous numbers of round Indian-weight drachms with a 'shoulder portrait' of the king on the obverse (imitating the contemporary portraits of Eucratides in Bactria) and a standing Athena on the reverse, again with Greek and Kharoshthi legends on the two faces (Fig. 5.25).

What does this remarkable series of coins tell us about the character of the 'Indo-Greek' kings? Without doubt, we are seeing two different

Figure 5.25. Drachm of Menander (c. 155–130 BC). The legend reads 'of King Menander the Saviour', in Greek and Kharoshthi. 2.49 g. ANS 1944.100.74561.

Figure 5.26. Indian *karshapana*, with aniconic punch-marks on a roughly rectangular flan (third century BC). 2.50 g. ANS 1991.8.2.

Figure 5.27. Tetradrachm of Archebius (c. 80–60 BC). Like most Indo-Greek kings, 'King Archebius the Just, Bringer of Victory' (Basileōs Archebiou Dikaiou Nikēphorou) is known only from his coins. 9.44 g. ANS 1995.51.210.

numismatic traditions coming into contact. The rectangular shape of some of the coins and the Indian weight-standard of *c*. 2.45 g both derive from a local monetary tradition of punch-marked silver coins called *karshapana*, widely used in north-east India before the coming of the Greeks (Fig. 5.26; Gupta and Hardaker 1985; Cribb 2007: 340–1). But the use of written legends and divine images on coins has no Indian precursors: even an image of Lakshmi, accompanied by a legend in Brahmi, would have had strong Hellenizing overtones for an Indian viewer, simply by dint of being a coin image with a legend attached to it.

We also have no way of telling how 'Greek' the later Indo-Greek kings may have been. Although a figure like Archebius (perhaps *c*. 80–60 BC) is usually seen as a Greek 'survivor' in India, he could equally well be a local Indian king appropriating Greek cultural motifs (his personal name, the Greek script, a Eucratides-style portrait) in the sphere of monetary production (Fig. 5.27). As Shailendra Bhandare has recently emphasized in the context of the so-called Porus coinage of Alexander the Great (Bhandare 2007), much modern scholarly work on the Indo-Greek coinage is still underpinned by a covert set of Hellenocentric and orientalizing

Figure 5.28. Siculo-Punic tetradrachm (*c.* 410 BC). The two faces both carry Punic legends, QRTḤDŠT ('Carthage') on the obverse and MḤNT ('the camp') on the reverse. 18.12 g. ANS 1944.100.79692.

Figure 5.29. Tetradrachm of Syracuse (*c.* 415–405 BC). Both the obverse and reverse types of this abundant coinage were imitated – on separate occasions – by Carthaginian mints in Sicily. 17.15 g. ANS 1997.9.43.

assumptions. The picture of Indo-Greek coinage as the work of ethnically 'Greek' kings, gradually accommodating themselves to the cultural norms of a native subject population, may owe more to modern colonial preconceptions than to the realities of Hellenistic India.

V   Carthage and the west

In the western Mediterranean, non-Greek peoples had begun to adopt Hellenizing motifs on their coinage long before the conquests of Alexander. In the last decade of the fifth century BC, the Carthaginians began striking coinage in western Sicily, perhaps at Entella, initially to pay Campanian mercenary soldiers (Lee 2000). The earliest of these 'Siculo-Punic' coin issues were Attic-weight silver tetradrachms, with the forepart of a horse being crowned by a flying Nike figure on the obverse and a palm-tree on the reverse (Fig. 5.28; Jenkins 1974).

Many aspects of these coins were modelled on the contemporary Greek coinages of eastern Sicily. Most obviously, the Nike figure crowning a horse echoes the contemporary coinage of Syracuse, which depicts a winged Nike crowning a four-horse charioteer (Fig. 5.29). The palm-tree had a distinct symbolic significance in Carthaginian culture (Prag 2006: 26–8), but a Greek viewer could equally well have read the image as a visual pun on the Carthaginians' Phoenician identity (the Greek word for palm-tree is

Figure 5.30. Siculo-Punic tetradrachm (*c.* 320–310 BC). The legend on the reverse reads 'MMḤNT' ('people of the camp'). The horse may be a symbol of the Carthaginian deity Ba'al Hammon. 17.26 g. ANS 1967.152.696.

Figure 5.31. Siculo-Punic tetradrachm (*c.* 300–290 BC), with Heracles-Melqart bust on the obverse, and reverse legend 'MMḤNT' ('people of the camp'). 16.65 g. ANS 1944.100.79789.

phoinix). It is tempting to see the palm-tree as a true 'bilingual' type, bearing one meaning for a Carthaginian viewer and another for a Greek.

The Carthaginian mint in Sicily continued to produce large Hellenizing silver issues throughout the fourth century, all characterized by this kind of iconographic bilingualism. Coins of the mid-fourth century show a female head wearing a necklace and triple-pendant earring, with four dolphins swimming around her (Fig. 5.30; Jenkins 1977). This type derives from the nymph Arethusa on Syracusan coinage; to a Carthaginian viewer, it would naturally have evoked the Punic goddess Tanit. Finally, around 300–290 BC, the Carthaginians minted tetradrachms echoing the Heracles portrait on the silver coinage of Alexander the Great (Fig. 5.31; Jenkins 1978). A Carthaginian would no doubt have taken this as an image of the Punic god Melqart, while a Greek viewer could have read it as a Carthaginian claim to Mediterranean great-power status alongside the Macedonians. Both interpretations would have been equally correct (Yarrow 2013: 354–9).

Carthaginian imperialism in Sicily made the island a fertile zone of contact between Greek and Punic culture in the fourth and early third century BC (Prag 2010) – a miniature Hellenistic world *avant la lettre*. The Siculo-Punic coin-types beautifully illustrate the paradoxical character of Hellenizing identities at the edge of the Greek-speaking world. The fourth-century Carthaginians certainly did not aspire to become more Greek, and yet the various elements of Siculo-Punic coinage were all Greek in origin.

Nor was this iconography solely for use within Sicily: when the Carthaginians began striking their own bronze and precious metal coinage in North Africa in the late fourth century BC, they used the same Hellenizing types as had been pioneered in Sicily (Visona 1998). Greek monetary culture, here as in Parthia, was firmly appropriated for the Carthaginians' own ends.

One of the most extraordinary coinages of the Carthaginian world was struck during the Mercenary War (241–237 BC) between the Carthaginians and their disgruntled mercenaries, who had been left unpaid after the Roman victory in the First Punic War (264–241 BC) (Hoyos 2007). The rebel mercenary army struck a large silver and bronze coinage in several denominations, much of it overstruck on earlier Carthaginian issues (Crawford 1985: 135–8). The silver was heavily debased, although the addition of arsenical copper made the coins appear to be of better quality than they actually were (Carradice and La Niece 1988). The largest denomination, the double-shekel, carries a bust of Zeus on the obverse, with a charging bull on the reverse; the shekel bears a head of Heracles-Melqart and a prowling lion (Fig. 5.32; Yarrow 2013: 359–64). What is really remarkable about these coins is their legend: LIBYŌN, 'of the Libyans', written in Greek.

How did this rag-tag mercenary army come to identify themselves as Libyans? The term clearly cannot have any real ethnic content, since the rebels were a mix of Africans, Greeks, Celts, Iberians and others (Polybius 1.67.7). Instead, the use of the common term 'Libyans' must indicate the rebels' desire to create an autonomous political community of their own (Zimmermann 2001). The mercenaries were not just looking for revenge against Carthage; they wanted a permanent home on North African soil. This also helps explain why they chose to use Greek (rather than Punic) on their coins – quite simply, they wanted their coinage to look like that of a self-governing Greek *polis*. The Hellenizing motifs here serve a purpose

Figure 5.32. Debased silver shekel of the 'Libyans'. The portrait of Heracles-Melqart on the obverse may be a conscious echo of the silver coins of Alexander the Great. 7.86 g. Oxford, SNG Ashmolean II 2192.

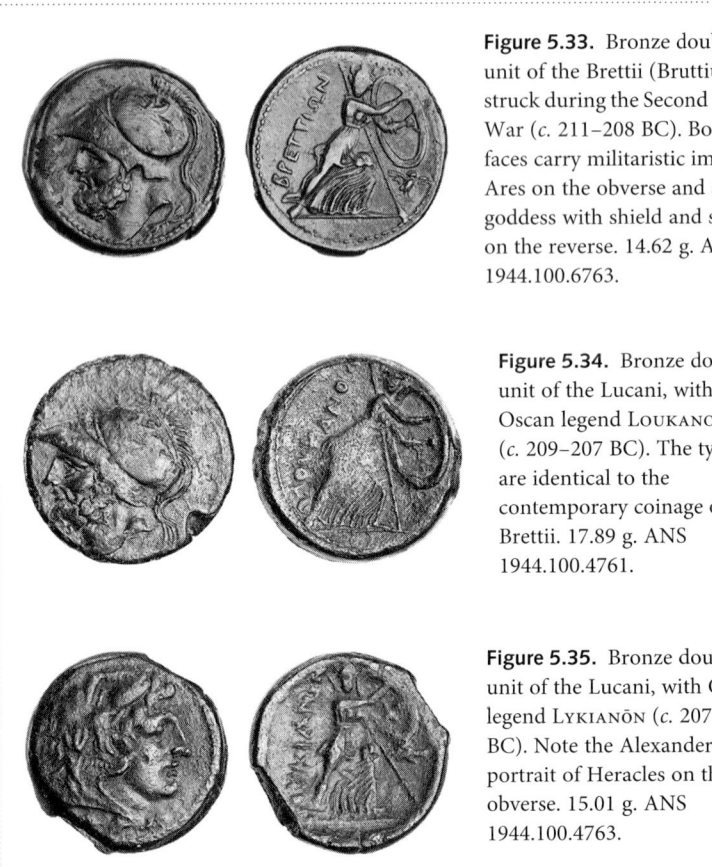

Figure 5.33. Bronze double-unit of the Brettii (Bruttium), struck during the Second Punic War (*c.* 211–208 BC). Both faces carry militaristic images: Ares on the obverse and a goddess with shield and spear on the reverse. 14.62 g. ANS 1944.100.6763.

Figure 5.34. Bronze double-unit of the Lucani, with Oscan legend Loukanom (*c.* 209–207 BC). The types are identical to the contemporary coinage of the Brettii. 17.89 g. ANS 1944.100.4761.

Figure 5.35. Bronze double-unit of the Lucani, with Greek legend Lykianōn (*c.* 207–204 BC). Note the Alexander-style portrait of Heracles on the obverse. 15.01 g. ANS 1944.100.4763.

completely different from the fourth-century Siculo-Punic coinage. The striking of coins in the Greek style was a way for this ethnically mixed community to assert their political solidarity and independence.

The Mercenary War was not the only occasion on which warfare was a stimulus to communal representation on coinage in the western Mediterranean. Growing Roman control over the Italian peninsula had brought an end to the civic coinages of the Greek cities of southern Italy by the mid-third century. A brief period of renewed independence from Rome during the Second Punic War (218–201 BC) saw an explosion of coin issues throughout the region (Crawford 1985: 52–74). The Italic communities of Bruttium, in the far south of the peninsula, struck a large issue of gold, silver and bronze (*c.* 216–203 BC) with Greek-style iconography and the Greek coin

Figure 5.36. Silver didrachm of the Sicels (*c.* 214–213 BC). 6.86 g. ANS 1997.9.217.

Figure 5.37. Tetradrachm in the name of Queen Philistis of Syracuse (*c.* 240–215 BC). 13.60 g. ANS 1964.79.53.

legend BRETTIŌN, 'of the Brettii' (Fig. 5.33; Rutter 2001: 157–61; Fronda 2010: 149–59). Further to the north, two small issues of silver and bronze were struck in the name of the Lucanians of the central Appennines (*c.* 209–204 BC). Their coinage carried a legend in the Greek script, first in the Oscan language (LOUKANOM, 'of the Lucani') and subsequently in Greek (LYKIANŌN) (Figs. 5.34–5.35; Rutter 2001: 129–30; Isayev 2007: 24–5). Both the Brettii and Lucani were Oscan-speaking Italic peoples, fighting alongside the Carthaginians under Hannibal. Their decision to mint Greek-style coins with Greek legends in this period was a sign not so much of cultural Hellenization, as of the adoption of a common and widely understood symbolic language of local autonomy.

Something similar can be seen in Sicily at the same period. A fine series of gold and silver coins in the name of the 'Sicels' (SIKELIŌTAN) was minted at Morgantina in eastern Sicily (*c.* 214–213 BC), shortly before the Roman reconquest of the island in 212–211 (Erim 1989: 31–4; Prag 2012). The main silver type depicts a veiled head of Persephone on the obverse, with Nike driving a four-horse chariot on the reverse (Fig. 5.36). The types mirror the contemporary coinage of Hieron II at the Greek city of Syracuse in eastern Sicily (Fig. 5.37, itself modelled on Ptolemaic coinage: see below, Chapter 8, pp. 161–3), but the legend refers to the native non-Greek inhabitants of the island, the Sicels. Once again, Hellenizing coinage serves as a vehicle for asserting a distinctive local identity under the shadow of Roman and Carthaginian power.

Part III

Political economy

6

Currency systems

I   Why mint coins?

Why did Hellenistic kings and cities mint coins? An easy question to pose, but not so easy to answer. In the modern world, most states operate with 'fiat money' (Latin *fiat*, 'let it be so'), where governments and central banks can increase the amount of money in an economy simply by printing more money (or more complex variants such as quantitative easing). Governments can pursue reasonably sophisticated monetary policies by manipulating the money supply, thereby controlling interest rates and inflation. Few of these measures were available to ancient states. Money in the ancient world mostly took the form of 'commodity money', coins which were worth their weight in scarce commodities such as gold or silver. Increasing the money supply meant either digging more gold or silver out of the ground or, more straightforwardly, invading another state and annexing its precious metal reserves, as was done by Alexander the Great between 334 and 330 BC (see Chapter 1 above) and on an even more massive scale by Rome in the second and first centuries BC (Kay 2013; 2014: 21–42).

   Without doubt, the main reason why ancient states minted coins was in order to make state payments: paying armies, subsidizing the food supply, funding public works and so forth. In a classic essay, Chris Howgego showed that this can seldom have been the whole story (Howgego 1990). States were aware of the need for a steady supply of coin for day-to-day exchange; they periodically renewed worn coins, and could strike coins for purely ideological reasons (advertising the accession of a new ruler, or proclaiming a city's independence). The problem for us is to judge how far these various 'secondary' motives drove minting behaviour in the Hellenistic world. Our answer will have wide-ranging consequences for our understanding of the Hellenistic economy. Did kings and cities have anything resembling a 'monetary policy'? Were they aware of phenomena such as inflation and liquidity, and did they try to control them through the coin supply?

By way of example, let us take a look at one recent approach to Hellenistic royal coin production. In his studies of the Seleucid royal economy, Makis Aperghis has argued that the Seleucid royal silver coinage was (at least in peacetime) a 'replacement' coinage (Aperghis 2001: 92–5; 2004: 228–46). The amount of silver coinage in circulation in the Seleucid world would naturally have shrunk by *c.* 1–2 per cent per annum, as a result of coins leaving the kingdom, hoards being buried and not recovered, and so forth. Aperghis argues that the Seleucids minted silver at a rate intended to keep the total money supply roughly stable: 'the supply of tetradrachms in the market was to be "topped-up" by Seleukid issues whenever it fell below the level required by the economy' (Aperghis 2004: 230). The number of Seleucid royal coins in the 'circulation pool' gradually rose from about 10 per cent at the death of Seleucus I (281 BC) to 70 per cent at the death of Antiochus VII (129 BC), a rate consistent with the idea that the Seleucids were deliberately topping-up the money supply in their kingdom throughout this period.

But this picture of a sophisticated Seleucid monetary policy runs into various conceptual problems (Bresson 2005: 56–9). How could the Seleucids possibly have known how much money was in circulation in their vast kingdom? And, so long as they had enough cash in hand to meet their immediate state expenses, why should they care one way or the other? Furthermore, Aperghis assumes that whenever the Seleucid kings struck coins, they were *adding* to the total money supply of their kingdom. This seems intuitively obvious, but need not be the case. Let us imagine that 60 million Alexander tetradrachms were minted over the period 333–290 BC, and that in the latter half of this period (311–290 BC), 3 million Seleucid tetradrachms were produced. How much silver was in circulation by 290 BC? It could, in theory, be anywhere between 60 million and 63 million tetradrachms (without allowing for natural shrinkage): it all depends where the Seleucids got their silver from. If the Seleucids had taken 3 million worn Alexander tetradrachms, melted them down and restruck them as Seleucid coins, the total money supply would remain exactly the same.

This kind of re-use of existing coined silver is widely attested in the Classical and Hellenistic world. Numerous Cretan silver coin issues of the Classical and Hellenistic periods are overstruck on earlier Cretan and Cyrenaic coins (Fig. 6.1; Le Rider 1966), and in the Seleucid world, an entire issue of tetradrachms struck in 161 BC by the Seleucid king Demetrius I (reigned 162–150 BC) was overstruck on coins of an unsuccessful Seleucid pretender, Timarchus (Fig. 6.2; Hoover 2008b). In the mid-330s BC, the Delphic Amphictyony produced a large new silver coinage by

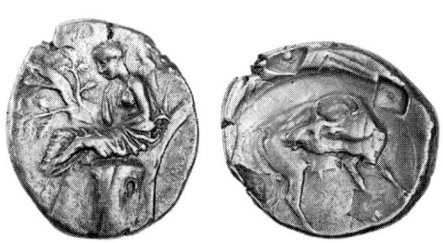

Figure 6.1. Silver stater of Gortyn (*c.* 360–322 BC), overstruck on a coin of Cnossus (Le Rider 1966: 59, no. 15b). The new Gortynian types show Europa seated in a tree on the obverse, and a bull on the reverse. On the reverse, at upper right, one can make out traces of the original undertype (a rectangular labyrinth pattern). 11.77 g. ANS 1961.63.3.

Figure 6.2. Tetradrachm of Demetrius I and Laodice, overstruck on a coin of the pretender Timarchus (161 BC). If you rotate this image ninety degrees counter-clockwise, it is easy to make out the nose, lips and chin of Timarchus' portrait, just below the necks of Demetrius and Laodice. The reverse type has been rather carelessly double-struck. 16.44 g. ANS 1967.130.1.

melting down a range of old coins (Kinns 1983): we simply have no way of knowing how common this kind of melting down and restriking may have been in the Hellenistic world.

There are, in fact, strong reasons to think that Hellenistic states did not pursue 'monetary policies' as such, but instead struck coins mainly in response to immediate practical needs. Seleucid royal mints closed and re-opened erratically through the third century BC, often in tandem with the presence of royal armies, suggesting an absence of long-term monetary planning (Houghton 2004: 53–4). But the key test-case is the royal coinage of Mithradates VI of Pontus (reigned *c.* 120–63 BC; see further Chapter 8 below, pp. 166–8). Unusually, Mithradates' silver tetradrachms carry dates giving the year and month in which they were struck (Fig. 6.3). Between 95

Figure 6.3. Tetradrachm of Mithradates VI of Pontus (March 75 BC). The date is indicated on the reverse, with the year behind the stag's rump (BKS, Year 222 of a local Pontic era) and the month at the base of the wreath (the Greek letter *stigma*, indicating Month 6). In the spring of 75 BC, Mithradates suddenly started minting vast quantities of silver coins, in preparation for the Third Mithradatic War. 16.89 g. ANS 1972.184.14.

Figure 6.4. Tetradrachm of Phraates IV, struck at Seleucia on the Tigris (November 26 BC). The lowest line of the Greek reverse legend reads ZPS, Apel(laiou) – that is, Year 286 of the Seleucid era (26/5 BC), in the month Apellaeus (November). 9.91 g. ANS 1979.189.15

and 64 BC, the coins were struck to a very irregular rhythm, with huge 'bulges' of production between 89 and 85 BC (the period of the First Mithradatic War with Rome) and again in 75–74 BC (the build-up to the Third Mithradatic War). A particularly intense phase of minting took place in May and June 89 BC, when Mithradates was massing an army for his invasion of Cappadocia in the summer of that year, sparking the First Mithradatic War. To all appearances, Mithradates' silver coinage was struck solely in order to meet the king's immediate military expenses (Callataÿ 2000). A similar case can be made for the large issues of Phraates IV of Parthia (*c.* 38–2 BC), also dated by both year and month, where minting again seems to cluster in the years immediately before and after major campaigns (Fig. 6.4; Callataÿ 1994b: 62). If we can generalize from these two cases – and that is a big 'if' – then the size and make-up of the Hellenistic money supply at any given time would largely be determined by the scale of recent royal warfare: a kind of inadvertent 'military Keynesianism'.

At any rate, these sporadic wartime 'bulges' of coin production could have dramatic unintended consequences. The clearest example comes from early Hellenistic Babylon. The so-called Babylonian Astronomical Diaries are cuneiform documents listing day-by-day observations of celestial, climatic and economic phenomena at Babylon, including silver price equivalents for six staple goods (barley, dates, wool and others). The years after Alexander's death (*c.* 323–300 BC) saw dramatic increases in commodity prices at Babylon: prices for all kinds of goods rose threefold, with the average price of barley skyrocketing to four or five times its level before the Macedonian conquest. This was surely a byproduct of the massive production of silver coin by Alexander's Babylonian mint in the 320s and 310s (see Chapter 1 above). The sudden glut of cash, intended for the payment of Macedonian and allied troops, led to a period of runaway inflation in the local Babylonian economy (Temin 2013: 53–65; Pirngruber, forthcoming). Hellenistic states simply did not have the conceptual tools at their disposal to control or avoid short-term monetary crises of this kind.

That said, kings and cities clearly did make sophisticated choices about what kinds of coin to mint and when: that is shown, apart from anything else, by the careful use of varying weight-standards over time, as we shall see shortly. In this chapter I will focus on the most important choice facing Hellenistic states, between an 'open' or 'epichoric' monetary system (sections II and III), and the eventual collapse of this distinction in the later Hellenistic period (section IV). The changes undergone by Hellenistic currency systems in the wake of Rome's conquest of the Greek East will be treated separately in Chapter 9.

II   'Open' currency systems: the Seleucids

As we saw in Chapter 1, the numismatic landscape of the early Hellenistic period was dominated by the huge silver and gold coin issues struck in the name of Alexander the Great between 325 and 290 BC. This vast mass of Alexander coinage, all struck on the Attic weight-standard (based on a drachm of *c.* 4.30 g), rapidly became the main international currency of the Greek-speaking world. It is easy to see why states – particularly ones employing large numbers of mercenary soldiers, who had become used to receiving their pay in Attic-weight coin – might have chosen to operate an

Pseudo-Aristotle on Hellenistic economies

The only surviving ancient account of the place of coinage in the Hellenistic economy is a curious little pamphlet, preserved in Book 2 of the *Economics* attributed to Aristotle (hence 'pseudo-Aristotle'). This text consists of a short description of four types of 'economies', royal, satrapal, city and household (2.1.1–8), followed by a rather miscellaneous historical compendium of money-making schemes (2.2.1–41). The pamphlet is usually dated to the early Hellenistic period, and the description of 'royal' and 'satrapal' economies may well have been written with the Seleucid kingdom in mind.

Pseudo-Aristotle begins by describing the royal economy:

> This exercises power over the whole and has four aspects, relating to coinage, to exports, to imports, and to expenditure. Let us take each of these separately. As concerns coinage, I mean when and what to mint, whether of large or small denomination. As concerns exports and imports, I mean which of them, having been received from the satraps in their provinces, are to be profitably disposed of on the king's behalf, and when. As concerns expenditure, I mean what cuts are to be made and when, and whether expenses should be met with coinage or with goods in place of coinage.

And that is pretty much it on the royal economy. The following section, on the satrapal economy, is a bare list of the different kinds of taxes and tolls levied on subject populations (land taxes, customs dues and so forth). Despite recent attempts to wring some historical insights from this text (Aperghis 2004: 117–35), Moses Finley was surely right to describe it as 'six short paragraphs of excruciating banality' (Finley 1970: 15). As far as economic analysis goes, a bright twelve-year-old could do better.

'open' currency system which allowed both Alexanders and other Attic-weight coinages to circulate freely.

This was the path taken by the Antigonids of Macedon, Lysimachus in Thrace, the Attalids of Pergamum (at least down to the 160s BC) and, above all, by the powerful Seleucid kings of Mesopotamia and Syria. The original core of

Figure 6.5. Tetradrachm of Antiochus III, struck at Antioch (*c.* 211/10 BC). 16.88 g. ANS 1944.100.75151.

Seleucid power was Babylon, which Seleucus I governed as satrap from 320 to 316 BC, and again from 312 BC onwards. Seleucus gradually incorporated all the eastern provinces of Alexander's short-lived empire, and by 281 BC, the Seleucid realm stretched from the coast of the Aegean to the foothills of the Himalayas (Sherwin-White and Kuhrt 1993; Bosworth 2002: 210–45). It was not just the vast scale of the Seleucid kingdom that favoured the adoption of an 'open' currency system. The western Seleucid territories, in Asia Minor and the Levant, had long been closely integrated into wider Aegean and east Mediterranean networks of exchange: the easy movement of money across the Seleucid coastal interface could only benefit the royal economy.

Hoards from the Seleucid world abundantly confirm this picture of free circulation of Attic-weight coins, whatever their mint of origin. A large hoard of 752 Attic-weight tetradrachms from Mektepini in central Phrygia (*IGCH* 1410), buried during the last years of Seleucid rule in Asia Minor (*c.* 195 BC), included a mere 96 royal Seleucid coins, 34 of them struck by the reigning king, Antiochus III (Fig. 6.5). The bulk of the hoard consisted of tetradrachms in the name of Alexander (490, mostly posthumous 'civic Alexanders') and Lysimachus (112, again mostly posthumous 'civic' issues). The hoard also included several Attic-weight coins struck by rival dynasties, the Antigonids of Macedon (22 tetradrachms) and the Attalids of Pergamum (14 tetradrachms). It appears that even after almost a century of Seleucid rule in Asia Minor, Seleucid royal issues still made up only a relatively small proportion of the Attic-weight coinage circulating in the region (Le Rider and Callataÿ 2006: 71–99, 114–28).

As a result of this 'open' circulation pool, royal coin issues could be remarkably small in absolute terms. A recent study of Antigonid royal coinage has shown that the silver and gold coinages of the third-century Antigonid kings were far too small even to have paid for Antigonid military activity in the period, let alone any other royal expenses (Panagopoulou 2001). People in the Antigonid or Seleucid kingdoms must have been accustomed to making and receiving payments in a mish-mash of different Attic-weight currencies. At Arcesine on the Aegean island of Amorgos in the early third century BC, a cash loan to the city by a certain Alexandros was to be repaid 'in Attic, or Alexandrian, or Demetrian coin, in whole coins, approved, uncut, uncountermarked, free of all taxes' (*IG* XII 7, 69). Alexandros wanted to be reimbursed in full Attic-weight coin, and the coins had to be in decent condition, but he was happy with any of the three main Attic-weight coinages circulating on Amorgos at the time (coins of Athens, Alexander and Demetrius Poliorcetes).

That is not to say that all varieties of Attic-weight coinage were treated indiscriminately in the Seleucid world. Fresh coins of the reigning king seem often to have circulated slightly above their intrinsic value, or at least to have been preferred in transactions (not quite the same thing). In sales contracts from Uruk in Mesopotamia, coins of the reigning king are often specified as the sole acceptable currency (Le Rider and Callataÿ 2006: 114–16). Similarly, when Laodice III (the wife of the Seleucid king Antiochus III) offered a gift of 10,000 *medimnoi* of wheat to the small Carian city of Iasus, she stipulated that the proceeds from the sale of the wheat should be used to provide dowries for poor Iasian women, to a maximum of '300 drachms of Antiochus' per head (Fig. 6.5; Ma 2002: 329–35, no. 26). If Antiochus III's coinage was slightly overvalued at Iasus, that would make it well worth specifying which particular variety of Attic-weight drachms was meant.

This preferral or overvaluation of 'official' royal coins may help explain two curious episodes in the 180s and 170s BC. Between the 220s and 180s, a group of mints in Pamphylia (Perge, Side, Aspendus and Phaselis) struck large quantities of civic tetradrachms on the Attic weight-standard. Very many of these coins subsequently had royal countermarks applied to them, first by the Attalid kings of Pergamum (mid-180s BC) and subsequently by the Seleucids (170s–160s BC) (Figs. 6.6–6.7; Meadows 2013: 170–3; Hoover 2008a). Since both kingdoms were operating an 'open' Attic-weight currency system at the time, these little royal stamps cannot have made a significant difference to the exchange value of the coins. Instead, the countermarks probably signalled that Pamphylian tetradrachms were to circulate as 'royal money', with the appropriate value-added premium. The Attalid and Seleucid kings thus neatly avoided the trouble and expense of melting down this civic coinage and restriking it with royal types.

Figure 6.6. Civic tetradrachm of Side in Pamphylia (*c.* 205–190 BC). The obverse carries an Attalid countermark (*c.* 188–180 BC), with a bow in case and the letters Sar, indicating that the coin was countermarked at (or for) the city of Sardis in Lydia. 16.33 g. ANS 1984.5.106.

Figure 6.7. Civic tetradrachm of Side in Pamphylia (*c.* 205–190 BC). The anchor countermark on Athena's helmet was applied in Seleucid Syria in the 170s or 160s BC. 16.56 g. ANS 1944.100.50920.

III 'Epichoric' currency systems

As in the Classical period, a few Hellenistic Greek states chose to operate a 'closed' or epichoric ('local') currency system, in which all internal transactions had to be made in the state's own coins, usually (but not always) on a distinctive local weight-standard. An epichoric currency system had many advantages (Kroll 2011: 229–31). A state could over-value its own coins, assigning them a value higher than their real bullion content; it could also charge a premium for the exchange or reminting of foreign currency. So, for example, in the mid-fourth century BC, the city of Olbia on the north coast of the Black Sea passed a law requiring that all sales and purchases taking place in the city should be carried out only in Olbian bronze or silver coins (Dubois 1996: no. 15; Osborne 2008: 339–42). People bringing foreign currency into Olbia were obliged to 'sell' their coins for Olbian legal tender. Even if the Olbian state did not levy a tax on these sales, it is not difficult to see how the Olbians could have made a tidy profit from this arrangement.

Figure 6.8. Civic tetradrachm of Byzantium (*c.* 240–220 BC). The obverse carries a veiled portrait of Demeter, perhaps imitating contemporary Ptolemaic coins with portraits of Arsinoe II and Berenice II (Figures 8.11–8.12 below). 13.00 g. ANS 1966.75.60.

Figure 6.9. Alexander-style tetradrachm in the name of King Seleucus, struck at Antioch (*c.* 300–281 BC). The reverse bears a countermark applied at Byzantium (*c.* 240–220 BC), with the letters B-Y (in the local Greek script) and a ship's prow (Le Rider 1999: 24, no. 21). 16.94 g. ANS 1944.100.15612.

A few Hellenistic Greek cities seem to have operated a strict 'epichoric' currency system of this kind. In north-west Asia Minor, the cities of Byzantium and Chalcedon, on the two shores of the Bosporus straits, ran a joint epichoric currency system from the 240s to the 220s BC. During this period, both cities minted civic tetradrachms on a distinctive local weight-standard of *c.* 13.2 g (Fig. 6.8). Attic-weight (and Ptolemaic-weight) coinage continued to circulate in the region, but only after it had been counter-marked by one or the other city (Fig. 6.9; Thompson 1954; Marinescu 2000). These countermarks served to validate foreign tetradrachms for use within the local 'Bosporan' currency system, perhaps by re-tariffing them as five-drachm pieces.

Nonetheless, this short-lived Bosporan currency system is a somewhat unusual case – and its brief life-span indicates how difficult it must have been to sustain strictly 'closed' systems of this kind. Instead, most Greek cities seem to have worked with a flexible mix of 'open' and 'epichoric' elements. As we saw in Chapter 3 (pp. 53–6), many *poleis* in western Asia Minor simultaneously struck coins on two different weight-standards, Attic and local. This gave a city like Miletus the best of both worlds. The Milesians could over-value their own local silver coins as much as they liked: the third-century civic coinage of Miletus seems to have been based on a drachm of *c.* 2.80 g, a mere 65 per cent of an Attic-weight drachm. Of course, these heavily over-valued coins would not be accepted at their face value anywhere outside Miletus – but who cared? The Milesians also had their own coinage of good Attic weight for 'international' transactions (a series of 'civic Alexanders'), and foreign Attic-weight coinage was allowed to circulate freely at Miletus alongside the light-weight civic coinage. If one could get away with putting 35 per cent less silver in one's drachms for local use, why not do so?

The plethora of different weight-standards and local currency systems which thus characterized the third-century Greek world might seem like a recipe for muddle. In fact, it need not have been anything of the sort. If a foreign coinage was not accepted at its nominal face-value, it could always simply be exchanged at its bullion weight. A list of donations to the sanctuary of Apollo at Didyma near Miletus, dating to 177/6 BC, includes a silver bowl described as weighing '100 Rhodian drachms, or 62 drachms of Alexander' (*SEG* 29, 1091). The bowl must have weighed around 270 g, the equivalent of 100 Rhodian drachms at *c.* 2.70 g or 62 Attic-weight 'drachms of Alexander' at *c.* 4.36 g. Hellenistic money-changers (*trapezitai*) must have been very used to making this kind of *ad hoc* conversion between the bullion values of dozens of different local civic currencies (Chandezon 2000).

A few of the large Hellenistic kingdoms chose to roll out a 'closed' epichoric currency system across their entire realm. The best-known example is the Ptolemaic dynasty of Egypt. Ptolemy I Soter, appointed as satrap of Egypt in 323 BC, initially struck silver tetradrachms on the common international Attic weight-standard (17.25 g), as we saw in Chapter 1 (pp. 18–20). But after Ptolemy's acclamation as king in 306 or 305 BC, the weight of the Ptolemaic tetradrachm dropped sharply, first to around 15.70 g (*c.* 305 BC), and subsequently to around 14.27 g (*c.* 294 BC, Fig. 6.10), where it stabilized for the rest of the Hellenistic period (Lorber 2012a). Around the same time as the final weight reduction of his silver, Ptolemy also introduced a new gold denomination, the *trichryson*, a large gold coin weighing around 17.80 g (five drachms on the new Ptolemaic weight-standard: Fig. 6.11). The gold *trichryson* was valued at 60 silver drachms, implying a distinctive Egyptian gold-to-silver ratio of 1:12, rather than the 1:10 which was standard elsewhere in the Greek world at this period. Unlike most other Hellenistic dynasties, the Ptolemies also struck a large

Figure 6.10. Tetradrachm of Ptolemy III, struck at Alexandria (*c.* 246–221 BC). The types are identical to the lifetime tetradrachms of Ptolemy I; the little cornucopia-mint-mark on the reverse is the only indication that this coin was in fact struck half a century later. 14.22 g. ANS 1935.117.1092.

Figure 6.11. Gold *trichryson* ('triple gold stater') of Ptolemy I (*c.* 294–285 BC). 17.86 g. ANS 1944.100.75736.

Figure 6.12. Ptolemaic bronze drachm of the late third century BC. At the time of their introduction by Ptolemy II (*c.* 261/60 BC), these huge bronzes were the highest-denomination token coins ever produced in the Greek world. 74.07 g. ANS 1944.100.77240.

fiduciary bronze coinage – large both in quantity and in the physical size of the coins – which circulated widely in rural Egypt throughout the Hellenistic period (Fig. 6.12; von Reden 2007: 58–78).

The precise workings of the Ptolemaic closed currency system are still controversial, but the basic picture is clear enough. Within Egypt, and in the Ptolemaic possessions overseas (Cyrene, Syria and Phoenicia, Cyprus, and – at least in the third century – parts of the Aegean and coastal Asia Minor), Ptolemy's own royal coins were the sole legal tender. Ptolemaic bronze, silver and gold coins did not circulate outside of the Ptolemies' zone of control, and Attic-weight coins (including 'Alexanders') are all but absent from Ptolemaic hoards. A papyrus dating to 258 BC shows that the exchange of foreign coins for Ptolemaic gold coinage was strictly controlled by royal officials (Austin 2006: no. 299), and it is likely enough that the Ptolemies charged a hefty premium on such exchanges.

Why was it the Ptolemies, rather than any other of the major early Hellenistic dynasties, who chose to 'close' their currency system in this way? Some scholars have suggested that the Ptolemies had a distinctively 'mercantilist' economic policy, striving to promote exports through currency controls and tight exchange regulations, but this is fantasy: ancient states simply did not think in these terms (Manning 2010: 117–64). Geography may have been more important. Egypt has no native sources of silver; if the Ptolemies wished to maintain a silver-based monetary economy, they had to find a means of stopping silver coin from leaving the kingdom. And Egypt has always been something of a world unto itself. The Nile valley, the heart of the Ptolemaic kingdom, is hemmed in by desert to east and west, and the great harbour-city of Alexandria was effectively the sole Mediterranean 'gateway' to Ptolemaic Egypt (Thompson and Buraselis 2013). This relative seclusion may have encouraged Ptolemy to run his kingdom – and, by extension, his entire east Mediterranean empire – as though it were a single, enormous Greek *polis*, with its own 'civic' currency system.

As we saw in Chapter 4 (pp. 77–82 above), the Attalids of Pergamum also established an epichoric currency system of their own in western Asia Minor. The Attalid cistophoric coinage, first struck in around 167 BC and retained by the Romans after the end of the Attalid dynasty, was based on a very light drachm of *c.* 3.05 g (Fig. 6.13). This weight-standard was probably chosen for its compatibility with the largest epichoric civic coinage then being struck in the eastern Aegean, the so-called 'plinthophoric' coinage of Rhodes, also based on a drachm of *c.* 3.05 g (Fig. 6.14; Ashton 2013). Just as for the Ptolemies, the Attalids' main reason for moving over to an epichoric currency system was surely to stop silver from leaving the kingdom (p. 80 above): a cistophoric tetradrachm, weighing slightly less than a tridrachm on

Figure 6.13. Early cistophoric tetradrachm, struck at Pergamum (*c.* 160–150 BC). Attalid cistophori were struck very thin, so that the flan is around the same diameter as an Attic-weight tetradrachm. 12.58 g. ANS 1951.5.13.

Figure 6.14. Plinthophoric drachm of Rhodes (Group B, mid-second century BC). The reverse carries the magistrate's name Artemōn and a Rhodian rose. 3.04 g. ANS 1944.100.48764.

the Attic weight-standard (*c.* 12.20 g), would lose a quarter of its nominal value on leaving Attalid territory.

The undesirability of exporting cistophori emerges very clearly from several letters of Cicero dating to the 50s and 40s BC. His brother Quintus was governor of the Roman province of Asia from 61 to 58 BC, and received his official allowance in cistophori, the main currency of the province. In the spring of 59 BC, Cicero wrote to the urban quaestors to ask if Quintus might instead draw his allowance in denarii (*Att.* 2.6.2; 2.16.4). Quintus is clearly desperate not to be left with a residue of cistophoric silver at the end of his period of office, which would lose 25 per cent of its purchasing power the moment he took the coins outside the province. Similarly, a decade later, we learn that Cicero himself has assets in Asia worth 2.2 million sestertii, in the form of cistophori deposited with tax-farmers at Ephesus; Cicero is only able to make use of these assets outside Asia through an obscure credit instrument known as *permutatio* (*Att.* 11.1.2; Hollander 2007: 40–4). These two episodes beautifully illustrate the advantages of an epichoric currency system for the state concerned: silver stays where it is struck.

IV The end of the Attic-weight 'koinē'

In the late second century BC, the Delphic Amphictyony, the league which ran the sanctuary and festivals of Apollo at Delphi, passed an enigmatic decree concerning the 'New Style' wreathed coinage of Athens. This coinage was minted by the Athenians in large quantities from the mid-160s down to the 40s BC (Chapter 3 above, pp. 57–8). The decree requires that 'all the Greeks' should accept the Athenian New Style tetradrachm at the value of four drachms of silver. Hefty punishments are laid down for anyone who does not obey the decree, including civic and festival magistrates and 'the money-changers (*trapezitai*) who operate in the cities and at festivals' (Austin 2006: no. 125; Sosin 2004; Bresson 2006).

This seems, at first sight, a peculiar thing to have to impose by decree, given that a tetradrachm is by definition a four-drachm coin! But this inscription has to be read in the context of the huge change in the character of Attic-weight silver coinage in the mid-second century BC. Throughout the third century, most Attic-weight coinage took the form of the ubiquitous royal and civic 'Alexander' tetradrachms, with smaller numbers of Lysimachi and other Seleucid, Antigonid and Attalid royal coinages. As we saw in Chapter 3 (pp. 56–61), Alexander tetradrachms largely ceased to be minted in the second quarter of the second century, to be replaced with a huge variety of civic tetradrachms (the 'wreathed' coinages, coins in the name of deities and so forth). It is easy to see why people might have treated these new varieties of Attic-weight coin with suspicion. One knew where one was with an Alexander tetradrachm; Athenian New Style coins simply did not 'look right'.

The coins' weight-standard may also be significant. Throughout the third century BC, the real weight of 'Attic-weight' tetradrachms (whether Athenian 'owls', civic Alexanders or other royal coinages) remained remarkably stable at around 17.20 g. However, by the early second century BC, many of the Alexanders in circulation had been kicking around for more than a hundred years: simply through ordinary wear and tear, much of the 'Attic-weight' coin in circulation would in fact have weighed in at rather less than 17.20 g (Davesne and Le Rider 1989: 243–68). As a result, from the 170s and 160s onwards, several cities and kings reduced the weight of their fresh silver tetradrachms by 2–3 per cent to match the weight of the worn Alexanders which made up a large part of the circulation pool. Athenian New Style tetradrachms are among the earliest examples of this phenomenon. Although clearly intended to circulate as full Attic-weight tetradrachms, the coins were in fact struck on a fractionally 'sub-Attic' standard of *c.* 16.75–16.80 g.

In the early years of this shift to a 'sub-Attic' weight-standard, some cities could well have refused to accept the Athenian New Style tetradrachms as

Figure 6.15. 'New Style' wreathed tetradrachm of Athens (144/3 BC), with countermark of Tralles. 16.29 g. ANS 1944.100.85073.

bona fide four-drachm pieces. The coins may hence have been circulating at their intrinsic precious metal value, that is to say, a little below four drachms. A New Style tetradrachm struck in 144/3 BC was subsequently countermarked at Tralles in western Asia Minor, suggesting that Athenian coins had to be 'validated' in order to be used at Tralles (Fig. 6.15; Thompson 1961: 81). On this interpretation, the Amphictyonic decree might have been an attempt to ensure that the fractionally light-weight Athenian 'New Style' coinage could circulate freely everywhere at its full nominal face-value of four drachms.

At any event, the Amphictyonic decree heralds the beginning of the collapse of the international Attic-weight currency system of the third and early second century BC. Throughout the Greek world, from the 170s onwards, coinages nominally struck on the Attic standard saw their weights gradually drifting downwards. These 'light-weight' Attic coins continued, of course, to be perfectly acceptable within the states that minted them; but the 'open' circulation pool of the third century (vividly represented in mixed hoards like the Mektepini hoard: above, p. 117) became harder and harder to sustain. The Delphic decree seems to be an attempt – with uncertain success – to reimpose an international 'open' currency system based on the new light-weight Athenian tetradrachm of *c.* 16.75–16.80 g.

The process is particularly clear in the Seleucid kingdom. As we have seen, the third- and early second-century Seleucid kings did very well out of their 'open' attitude to foreign Attic-weight coin. But after the loss of the Seleucid territories in Asia Minor in 188 BC, the weight-standard of the Seleucid royal coinage began a slow decline. In the 170s BC, the weight of Seleucid tetra-drachms from the royal mint at Antioch suddenly dropped from *c.* 17.05 g to

Figure 6.16. Tetradrachm of Antiochus IV, struck at Antioch (*c.* 173/2–169/8 BC). Coins of this type were struck to an average weight of around 16.65 g; this particular example weighs 16.33 g. ANS 1977.158.660.

Figure 6.17. Tetradrachm of Philip I Philadelphus, struck at Antioch (after 88/7 BC). The average weight of these coins was a mere 15.65 g; this example weighs 15.92 g. ANS 1977.158.722.

c. 16.65 g, and by the end of the Seleucid dynasty in 64 BC, the average weight had declined still further, to around 15.40 g (Figs. 6.16–6.17; Houghton 2004: 59–62; Hoover and Iossif 2008). The result was that the 'open' Seleucid monetary system eventually turned into a 'closed' system, in which only light-weight Seleucid royal coins could circulate: hoards from late Seleucid Syria and Phoenicia include little or no foreign coinage.

The late second and first century BC thus saw a gradual return to 'epichoric' currency systems throughout the Greek world. This was, of course, also the period in which Rome became mistress of the Greek East: Macedonia became a Roman province in 146 BC, western Asia Minor followed in 129 (*provincia Asia*), and much of inland Asia Minor and the Levant was incorporated by Pompey in the mid-60s BC. It is very striking that the Roman conquest was not accompanied by any unification of local currencies and weight-standards – quite the contrary. Indeed, as we will see in Chapter 9, there is reason to think that Roman magistrates and generals in the East may positively have encouraged the diversification of currency systems in the Greek world. The age of the global Attic-weight '*koinē*' (*c.* 325–175 BC) was gone for good.

7

Bronze and silver

I   From silver to bronze

So far, this book has concentrated on big, flashy precious-metal coinages: silver tetradrachms, gold staters and other large-denomination issues. But this gives a very misleading impression of how coinage was actually used on a day-to-day basis in ordinary Hellenistic towns and villages. Tetradrachms and staters were the equivalent of £50 notes or $100 bills – handy for making large payments, but not so useful for buying a loaf of bread. Most low-level exchange was instead conducted with bronze coins.

Token bronze coins – that is to say, coins made of cheap metal, assigned a 'token' value by the issuing authority – were first introduced on a large scale in the Greek world in the late fifth and early fourth century BC (Ashton 2006; Konuk 2011; Grandjean and Moustaka 2013). In a culture which assumed that money should be worth its weight in precious metal, this splendid innovation was at first met with suspicion. During the last years of the Peloponnesian War, in the face of a desperate silver shortage, Athens struck a token bronze coinage with a thin silver plating (Fig. 7.1). In his play *Frogs*, Aristophanes gives vivid expression to the Athenians' disgust at being reduced to this 'wretched bronze' (*ponēra chalkia*), 'the vilest coinage ever' (*Frogs* 718–33; Kroll 1976). Nonetheless, by the mid-fourth century BC, bronze coins were in widespread use throughout the Greek world for small, everyday transactions. By the later Hellenistic period, many cities were operating with four or even five different denominations of bronze coinage (Ashton 2012b: 201–2).

An inscription from the small city of Gortyn on Crete illustrates how a community might go about introducing a bronze coinage for the first time. Around 250 BC, the Gortynians decided to stop using small-denomination silver coins (silver obols, worth one-sixth of a drachm) and moved over to a token bronze coinage, apparently with the same face-value as the earlier obols (Figs. 7.2–7.3; Jackson 1971). The use of

Figure 7.1. Athenian bronze coin, with a thin silver plating (*c.* 405 BC). These coins were produced by the Athenian mint in the face of acute financial crisis during the last years of the Peloponnesian War. The silver plating has cracked off in various places, particularly on the reverse. 13.35 g. ANS 0000.999.53695.

Figure 7.2. Silver obol of Gortyn (*c.* 300–250 BC), with head of Europa on obverse and bull on reverse. 0.88 g. Oxford (J. G. Milne 1938).

Figure 7.3. Bronze coin of Gortyn (*c.* 250 BC), with the legend Gorty(niōn). The types – Europa seated in a tree on the obverse, bull carrying Europa on the reverse – are very similar to the late Classical and early Hellenistic silver coinage of Gortyn (above, Figure 6.1). 4.96 g. ANS 1941.131.736.

these new bronze coins was imposed by law, and the old silver obol was forcibly 'demonetized':

> Gods. This was decided by the *polis* after a vote, with 300 men being present. People must use the bronze coinage issued by the *polis*, and no one is to accept the silver obols. If anyone accepts silver obols, or refuses to accept the bronze coinage, or sells anything in exchange for grain, he will be fined five silver staters. (Austin 2006: no. 123)

It is worth noting that the law also discourages people from selling 'in exchange for grain': plenty of low-level exchange in the Hellenistic period clearly still took place without the use of coined money at all.

This chapter will look at the roles played by small-denomination coinage in Greek cities during the Hellenistic period. We shall consider, first, the aims and practicalities of minting bronze and silver coins (section II); second, the patterns of circulation of token bronze coinage within and between cities (section III); and, finally, the different things which bronze

Figure 7.4. Bronze coin of Sestus (*c.* 130 BC). This may well be the very bronze issue mentioned in the honorific decree for Menas; however, his name does not appear on the reverse, which carries only the abbreviated ethnic SĒ. 5.00 g. ANS 1944.100.16621.

and silver coins were used for in Greek *poleis*, with an extended case-study from late Hellenistic Thebes (section IV).

II   The minting of coins

Around 130 BC, the city of Sestus, on the European shore of the Hellespont, decided to strike its own civic bronze coinage for the first time in many decades (Fig. 7.4). One of the two magistrates appointed to oversee the minting process was a certain Menas, honoured a few years later with a long decree recounting the main events of his career in public service. In a few brief (and much-studied) clauses, this decree provides us with our only contemporary account of any Hellenistic city's reasons for minting its own coinage.

> When the city decided to use its own bronze coinage – in order that the city's emblem should be current, and in order that the *dēmos* should receive the profit from this source of revenue – and appointed men who would safeguard this position of trust piously and justly, Menas was appointed, and together with his colleague in office showed suitable care; as a result of this, thanks to the justice and emulation of these men, the *dēmos* has the use of its own coinage. (Austin 2006: no. 252)

Here, in a nutshell, is the Hellenistic state's perspective on the striking of bronze coinage. For the Sestians, the single most important factor is civic prestige. Like any self-respecting *polis*, they want to use coins which carry their own civic 'badge', rather than making do with bronze coins with another city's types (Robert 1973). The profit motive follows as a close second: by minting a fiduciary coinage, the city could expect to benefit financially, since the coinage's face-value was higher than the intrinsic value of the metal.

Prestige was always an important motive for the minting of bronze and silver coins (see Chapter 3 above), for individuals like Menas as much as for the *polis* as a whole. In sharp contrast to the Classical period, when coins seldom carry any writing other than the name of the minting city, Hellenistic civic coinages often carry the names of civic officials on the reverse. These officials are conventionally described as 'mint-magistrates', although in fact there is usually no way of telling what precise role they had in the production of the coinage (Robert 1966: 83–93; Ashton 2012b: 202). No doubt the increasing prominence of mint-magistrates in part reflects the growing interest of Hellenistic *poleis* in the public accountability of their officials (Fröhlich 2004). But from the magistrate's own perspective, the presence of his name on a large coin issue served as a magnificent advertisement for his patriotism and civic-spiritedness, particularly if he was known to have helped pay for the coin issue through a monetary liturgy of some kind.

Individuals named on coins often turn out to be well-known members of their city's political class. To take just one example, Olympius, one of a dozen magistrates to appear on the mid-second-century wreathed tetradrachms of Cyme in Aeolis (Fig. 7.5; Chapter 3 above, pp. 58–61), belonged to the city's wealthiest family. Around the time that Olympius' coins were minted, his sister Archippe funded the construction of a new council house for Cyme, and Olympius himself paid for a colossal statue-group of his family to be erected in front of the building (van Bremen 2008). Having coins struck in their name was clearly just one element of this rich family's blizzard of self-advertisement at Cyme in this period.

Once one local bigwig has had his name immortalized on coins, everyone else wants to do it too: the Hellenistic bronze coinage of Cyme

Figure 7.5. 'Wreathed' tetradrachm of Cyme in Aeolis (*c.* 155–150 BC), with bust of Cyme the Amazon on the obverse, and the name Olympios on the reverse. Aside from the wreath, the types are very similar to the third-century civic coins of Cyme (above, Figure 3.4). 16.07 g. ANS 1954.203.178.

Figure 7.6. 'New Style' wreathed tetradrachm of Athens (*c.* 160 BC), with two monograms and a club symbol flanking the owl on the reverse. 16.96 g. ANS 1954.203.114.

Figure 7.7. 'New Style' wreathed tetradrachm of Athens (115/14 BC), with cacophony of magistrates' names on the reverse. The letter *beta* on the amphora indicates that the coin was struck during the second month of the year. 16.54 g. ANS 1944.100.24716.

provides us with the names of no fewer than 104 different individuals (Masson 1986). Perhaps the most extraordinary example of competitive 'grade inflation' among mint-magistrates is the Athenian New Style coinage of the second and first centuries BC, already discussed several times in this book (Chapter 3, p. 57; Chapter 6, pp. 124–6). The very earliest New Style tetradrachms, dating to the mid-160s BC, carry fairly discreet monograms to the left and right of the owl on the reverse (Fig. 7.6). But these monograms are soon replaced by up to three different magistrates' names spelled out in full, usually accompanied by one or more mint-symbols (Thompson 1961: 546–607; Mattingly 2004: 85–99). The result is that the – originally rather elegant – reverse type of the New Style coinage becomes increasingly cluttered. Fig. 7.7 illustrates an issue dating to 115/14 BC, with the abbreviation ATHE for Athens followed by the three names MĒTRODŌROS, MILTIADĒS and HERMOGENĒS, along with a bunch of grapes as a mint-mark and the letters PE (of uncertain meaning) at the bottom. The whole thing is, frankly, a barely legible mess.

Figure 7.8. Bronze coin of Apamea (early first century BC). Like the coins of the huge 1991 Apamea bronze hoard, this coin was struck in the name of the magistrate Antiphon son of Menecles. 7.46 g. ANS 1944.100.49946.

Profit, the second motive given by the Sestians for striking their own bronze coinage, is fairly self-explanatory. Bronze coins were token coins, with a face-value unrelated to their metal content, and so a city could tariff them as high as the market would stomach: as we will see shortly, some late Hellenistic bronze coins may have had the same face-value as a silver drachm. For similar reasons, the weight of bronze coins – unlike that of silver – was allowed to fluctuate widely. In the early first century BC, the city of Apamea in Phrygia struck a very large series of token bronze and brass coinage in four different denominations (Fig. 7.8; Thonemann 2011: 47, 105–7; Ashton, forthcoming). A huge hoard of 5,946 Apamean bronzes, all in the largest denomination, and all struck from the same pair of dies, was discovered by chance at the site of Apamea in 1991. These coins seem never to have entered circulation – perhaps rejected by the mint for some reason – but their weights nonetheless show enormous variation, from 5.99 g to 10.95 g (Arslan and Devecioğlu 2011).

The profits to be made from striking civic silver and bronze coins were large enough for counterfeiting to be a widespread problem, especially in the form of silver-plated coins with a bronze or lead core. Of the 129 stray Athenian silver coins of the sixth to the first century BC excavated in the Athenian Agora, no fewer than 22 were ancient forgeries made of silver-plated bronze (Kroll 1993: 4–5). Of course, this tells us little about the total proportion of counterfeits in circulation, since worthless fake coins were far more likely to be discarded by their owners. But it is telling that the Athenians felt the need, in 375/4 BC, to draw up detailed legislation on the use of imitative and counterfeit coin (Rhodes and Osborne 2003: no. 25; Ober 2008: 220–45).

Forgery of silver coins continued in the Hellenistic period. An early second-century decree of the city of Dyme in Achaea imposes the death penalty on a group of at least six counterfeiters (two of whom seem to have had false identities!) for producing silver-plated bronze coins:

Figure 7.9. Bronze coin of Pergamum, in the name of Athena Nicephorus (second century BC). 4.27 g. 1944.100.43273.

When Philocles was priest, Damocritus was registrar, and Cleon was boularch (president of the council). The city condemned the following men to death, for stealing sacred property and striking bronze plated coins: Thraecion, whose real name may be Antiochus; Cyllis the goldsmith; Cyllanius, whose real name may be Pantaleon or something else; and Moscholaus son of Moscholaus. When –phanes was boularch, –pillas son of Phileas (was also condemned); when Phileas was boularch, –ias son of Olympichus (was also condemned). (Austin 2006: no. 124; Rizakis 2008: 40–3.)

Producing fake silver-plated coins was clearly a profitable business, but we might have thought that it would hardly be worth bothering to counterfeit bronze coinage. However, a fascinating find from the city of Pergamum in Asia Minor suggests otherwise. In the second and first centuries BC, the Pergamene mint struck an abundant series of bronze coins in the name of Athena Nicephorus (Fig. 7.9; Marcellesi 2012: 127–8). In one of the subterranean vaults supporting the foundations of the theatre at Pergamum, the excavators found a small cache of bronze coins, consisting of two very poor imitations of Athena Nicephorus bronzes, along with twenty-five rough bronze coin-blanks (Voegtli 1990: 48–50; *CH* IX 502). These are almost certainly the remains of a clandestine bronze forger's workshop.

III   The circulation of bronze coinage

Our best evidence for the circulation of bronze and low-denomination silver coins comes not from hoards, but from 'stray' excavation finds. Small change is not normally worth hoarding: the average Hellenistic hoard tends to be made up of big, valuable silver coins, and represents someone's life savings, not the contents of their purse. By contrast, stray coin-finds from a site will usually be coins that people have dropped accidentally while going about their day-to-day business. A recent sample of 1,000 stray coins picked up on the streets of Melbourne during early morning walks in 2006–8 reflects the actual range of coins circulating in Australia remarkably well (Frazer and van der Touw 2010). As we would expect, physically small coins (easy to drop) are slightly over-represented, and high-denomination coins are slightly under-represented (more likely to be picked up). Nonetheless, this should encourage us to take patterns of site finds seriously, as our best indication of the coins actually being used in the average Hellenistic market-town.

Low-denomination coins seldom travel far from their mint, and so most of the bronze coins circulating within cities tended to be of local origin (Knapp 2005: 36–49). That is not to say that Milesian bronze coins were the only token coinage accepted at Miletus (say). In fact, Hellenistic bronze coins – unlike modern coinages – seem often to have retained some or all of their exchange value across state boundaries. Some five thousand bronze coins of the fourth and third centuries BC have been excavated in the Athenian Agora, of which a good 20 per cent were of non-Athenian origin. For comparison, the percentage of foreign coins found on Melbourne streets (including a popular tourist district) in 2006–8 was a mere 1.7 per cent. We can therefore be pretty certain that foreign bronze coins were widely used for small-scale exchange in Athenian markets (Kroll 1993: 166–70). In the second and first centuries BC, the proportion of non-Athenian bronzes in the Agora drops sharply to 2–7 per cent. It is possible that Athenian tradesmen started to reject non-Athenian bronzes in the later Hellenistic period, but this could equally well simply reflect a drop in the number of foreign visitors to Athens, particularly after much Athenian commercial activity shifted to Delos from 167 BC onwards (Habicht 1997: 246–63).

In the few cases where excavators have mapped the precise find-spots of different kinds of coins *within* sites, revealing patterns emerge. For example, in the stadium at the great Panhellenic sanctuary of Nemea, bronzes from particular mints seem to be concentrated in different parts of the stadium seating. We can identify four distinct zones, dominated by bronze coins of Cleonae, Argos, Phlious and Sicyon. These must reflect the seating blocks traditionally taken by these four groups of *polis*-supporters at the biennial Nemean games: Argive spectators were more likely to drop Argive bronzes down the back of their seat (Knapp 2005: 27–30).

A particularly clear picture of local coin circulation comes from the small Hellenistic *polis* of Priene in western Asia Minor. Sensitively excavated by Theodor Wiegand between 1895 and 1898, Priene offers a vivid picture of life in an ordinary small Greek town of the Hellenistic period (Rumscheid and Koenigs 1998). Around 853 Greek coins were found during the excavations in the town (excluding hoards), the overwhelming majority of which (more than 95 per cent) were small-denomination bronze coins. Only around two-thirds of the total coin-finds (564 coins, 66 per cent of the total) were bronze and silver coins of Priene itself – a small enough percentage to make it clear that, as at Athens, foreign coins could circulate freely at Hellenistic Priene. Most of the remainder (178 coins, 21 percent of the total) were struck at the mints of Priene's three immediate neighbours, Magnesia (50), Miletus (85) and Ephesus (43). Another fifty-odd mints are represented in the coin-finds from Priene, but few contribute more than one or two coins to the total (Regling 1927: 169–201). The general picture is one of an 'open' bronze currency system, which in practice was also a highly 'local' currency zone, extending only a day or two's walk from Priene.

One very striking feature of the Priene coin-finds is the near-total absence of royal silver or bronze coinage. Throughout the Hellenistic period, Priene lay within the orbit of one or other major royal power: first Alexander, then Antigonus and Lysimachus, and eventually, for much of the third century, the Seleucids (Sherwin-White 1985). Yet this had virtually no impact on the circulation of everyday bronze coins at Priene: the site has turned up a mere handful of bronzes of Alexander, Philip V, and the Attalid and Seleucid kings. Indeed, throughout coastal Asia Minor, royal coins make up a tiny percentage of excavation finds. Cities further inland seem to have made much more use of royal coinages: some 75 per cent of foreign coins circulating at Sardis were struck by Macedonian, Seleucid or Attalid royal mints (Çizmeli-Öğün and Marcellesi 2011). Breaking down and explaining these kinds of micro-variations in local coin circulation and use is currently one of the major tasks facing Hellenistic numismatics.

Site finds do not usually allow us to say how long bronze coins may have stayed in circulation – a coin could have been lost within weeks of minting, or years later. For a snapshot of an ordinary Hellenistic traveller's purse, we can turn to a small cache of eighty-eight bronze coins, discovered next to the Sacred Way from Miletus to the great sanctuary of Apollo at Didyma (Baldus 1996). This hoard seems to represent the lost money-bag of a pilgrim making his way to Didyma some time in the late second or first century BC, and gives a good sense of the variety of small change circulating in south-west Asia Minor in the late Hellenistic period. The first surprise is the extreme age of some of the coins: a few date as far back as the fourth century BC, as if colonial halfpennies of King George III were still circulating in today's United States! The range of mints is also striking: the

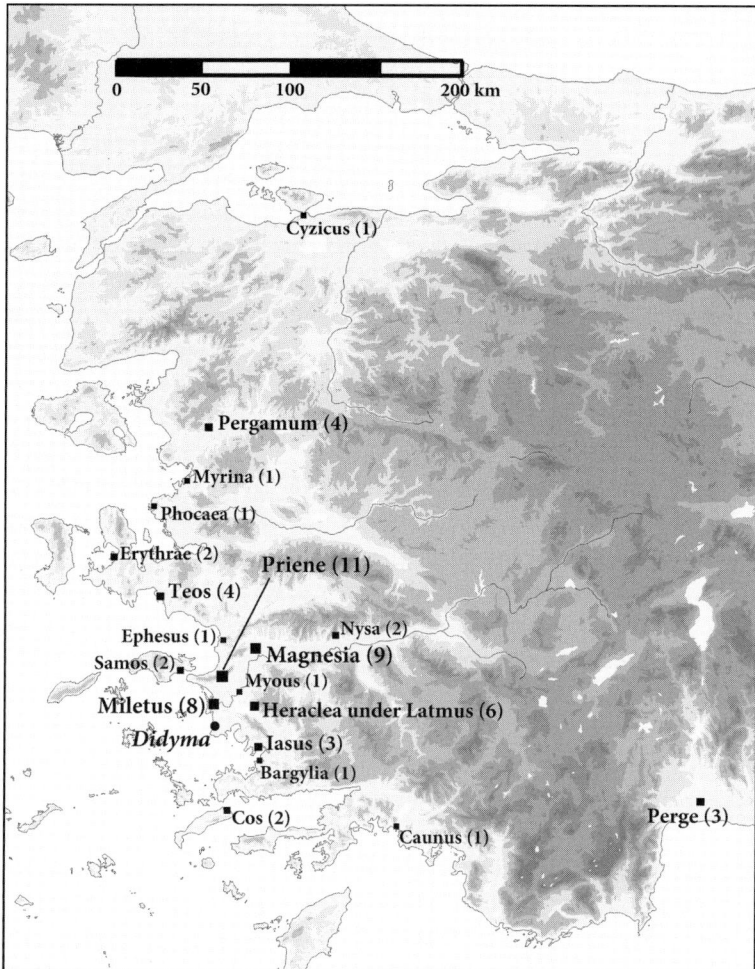

Figure 7.10. Distribution of bronze coins from a late Hellenistic coin hoard, found on the Sacred Way near Didyma.

sixty-three identifiable coins were struck by no fewer than nineteen different cities (Fig. 7.10). However, like the Priene site finds, the majority of coins had not travelled far from their place of minting: 54 per cent were struck by one of the four Greek cities clustered around the mouth of the Maeander river (Priene [eleven], Magnesia [nine], Miletus [eight] and Heraclea under Latmus [six]), and almost all of the rest come from cities in south-western Asia Minor.

Equally striking is a hoard of forty-six bronze coins and one small silver coin discovered in the excavations of a private house at Ascalon, in southern Israel (Gitler and Kahanov 2002). This hoard dates to around 100 BC, and apparently belonged to a merchant sailor: the coins come from a diverse series of coastal mints strung along the main shipping route from western Asia Minor to the Levant (Teos, Samos, Cos, Rhodes, Side, Tyre). This sailor had collected an amazing range of ancient coins. More than half of the coins (twenty-six out of forty-six) were more than a century old at the time they were buried, and the oldest coin (a small Samian bronze) dates back to the late fifth century BC.

As will be clear, small change is a big problem for ancient historians. The patterns of coin-finds at a Hellenistic city like Priene make it impossible to think that the Prieneans operated a genuine 'closed' currency system, at least at the level of small change: there is just too much foreign bronze coinage kicking around. But there are two quite different ways of interpreting this apparent 'openness'. It is possible that the civic authorities at Priene deliberately imposed and regulated a sophisticated fiduciary bronze economy, in which the state licensed certain foreign bronze coinages for circulation (Miletus yes, Pergamum no). Alternatively, we could be dealing with a completely *ad hoc* small change environment, governed simply by what your average Prienean fishmonger was prepared to accept. If the fishmonger's cousin's brother-in-law from Miletus turned up at his stall, and offered two Prienean and four Milesian bronzes for his sea-bass, that was one thing; if a complete stranger turned up and tried to pay for his fish with six Pergamene bronzes, that was something else altogether.

In both economic and social terms, the disappearance of fractional silver (small change worth its weight in precious metal) and the rise of bronze token coinage (small change of purely fiduciary value) in the late Classical and Hellenistic period is a profoundly significant moment in Greek monetary history. In the Archaic Greek world, small change took the form of fractional silver (Kim 2002; Kim and Kroll 2008). A fishmonger did not have to worry all that much about who was buying his fish, since a silver fraction was always worth its weight in silver. But once fractional silver came to be replaced with fiduciary bronze, the whole shape of civic economies changed: small-scale exchange began to depend on trust, custom and personal acquaintance. Here, then, is another answer to the old question of the 'vitality' of the *polis* in the Hellenistic world (above, p. 45). It was the social network of the *polis* – the *polis* as a group of men and women who *knew and trusted one another* – which served to regulate the day-to-day workings of local civic economies in the Hellenistic period.

IV   Silver and bronze at Hellenistic Thebes

I conclude this chapter with one of our most illuminating sources for the day-to-day use of silver and bronze money in a Hellenistic *polis*. This is an inscription from Thebes in Boeotia, probably dating to the mid-second century BC (Grandjean 1995; *SEG* 45, 447). The inscription gives the annual accounts of a Theban by the name of Pompidas, who has a small cavalry squadron under his command. Pompidas lists his revenues and expenses for the year, all of which were received and paid out in the form of either silver drachms – variously described as Boeotian or 'symmachic' ('allied') silver – or 'drachms of bronze'. The complete text reads as follows:

When Miccus was archon: the accounts of the cavalry-commander Pompidas.

- Income from the city: 2,100 drachms of Boeotian (silver). Income from the sale of horses: for Philleas' horse, purchased by Herpondes, 85 drachms of bronze; for Phryniscus' horse, purchased by Euanoridas, 86 drachms of bronze. Further income, from a sale to Caphisodorus, 110 drachms of symmachic (silver).
- Total income: 2,381 drachms, of which 2,210 silver and 171 bronze.
- Expenditure: to Cleon son of Proxenus, 280 drachms of symmachic silver; to Aeschron, 210 drachms of symmachic silver; to Hermaeus son of Charicles, 140 drachms of symmachic silver; to Hypatodorus son of Agasion, 175 drachms of symmachic silver; to Philleas, 280 drachms of symmachic silver; to Phryniscus, 280 drachms of symmachic silver; to Mnesitheus, 245 drachms of symmachic silver. Other expenditure: to Asopodorus for the *stēlē* (i.e. the cost of the inscription), 7 drachms 4 obols (of bronze); to Heraclides for the slaughter of the ox, 5 drachms (of bronze); to Caphisodorus, for 110 drachms of symmachic silver, 137 drachms 3 obols of bronze.
- Total expenditure: 1,760 drachms, of which 1,610 silver and 150 bronze.
- Surplus: 621 drachms, of which 600 silver and 21 bronze. The cavalrymen divided it between them.

The basic picture is clear enough. The cavalry commander Pompidas receives a total 'pay packet' of 2,100 silver drachms per year from the city of Thebes, out of which he has to pay the wages of his seven cavalrymen.

These seven men are each paid between 140 and 280 silver drachms, probably reflecting a daily wage ranging from two-fifths of a drachm to four-fifths of a drachm, calculated over a year of 350 days. Pompidas has also sold two of his cavalrymen's horses for a further 171 'drachms of bronze' – presumably these two horses were getting too old for cavalry warfare. The squadron's expenses also include two minor items, the cost of the inscription itself and the butchering of an ox (presumably for an annual sacrifice), both of which Pompidas pays for in drachms of bronze.

Two different kinds of silver drachm are mentioned in the text, Boeotian silver (the 2,100 drachms which Pompidas receives from Thebes) and symmachic or 'allied' silver (everywhere else in the inscription). Theban silver coins of this period – which carry the legend Boiōtōn, 'of the Boeotians', on the reverse – were struck on the so-called 'reduced Aeginetan standard' of *c*. 5.00 g, in widespread use throughout mainland Greece in this period (Fig. 7.11). The easiest assumption is that 'symmachic silver' (like 'Attic-weight silver') is simply a way of referring to coins struck on this particular weight-standard (Chapter 4, p. 69). When Thebes made state payments to its cavalry, these payments were made in Boeotian drachms; when Pompidas came to pay his cavalrymen their salary, any silver drachms on the 'symmachic' weight-standard would do.

The phrase 'drachm of bronze' looks at first sight to be a contradiction in terms, like 'nickel dollar' or 'copper pound'. In fact, this does not mean that bronze token coins at Thebes were valued at a full drachm: the largest denomination bronze coins in circulation at Thebes at this point were probably worth the same as a silver hemiobol (twelve to the drachm) (Fig. 7.12).

Figure 7.11. Silver drachm of Thebes, on the 'symmachic' weight-standard (early second century BC). The types depict the god Poseidon and a standing Nike figure. 5.07 g. ANS 1944.100.20220.

Figure 7.12. Bronze coin of Thebes (second century BC). The obverse carries a portrait of Athena in a Corinthian helmet, with a military trophy and the legend Boiōtōn ('of the Boeotians') on the reverse. 6.01 g. ANS 1944.100.20194.

'Five drachms of bronze' is really shorthand for 'five drachms' worth of token bronze coins'. To judge from Pompidas' expenditure, small bronze coins were mostly used for ordinary daily expenses in second-century Thebes (selling livestock, paying a stonemason, hiring a butcher), while large state payments such as the salaries of the civic cavalry were always met with good silver coin.

Finally, and most interestingly, we read that Pompidas has 'bought' 110 drachms of symmachic silver from a money-changer by the name of Caphisodorus. These 110 silver drachms 'cost' Pompidas 137 drachms 3 obols of bronze – that is to say, although a silver drachm and (say) twelve bronze coins had the same purchasing power, they could not be exchanged *for one another* on a 1:1 basis. Presumably the fact that bronze coins could not confidently be used outside the city of Thebes (above, pp. 134–8) made them less desirable than 'real' silver drachms. Hence when Pompidas tried to change his bronze coins into silver drachms at the money-changer Caphisodorus, he was charged an eye-watering 25 per cent commission (110 silver drachms for 137.5 drachms' worth of bronze).

The accounts of Pompidas neatly illustrate many of the themes of the last two chapters. The city of Thebes minted two different coinages in this period: silver drachms on a widely accepted regional weight-standard (the 'symmachic silver' of our inscription), and token bronze coins assigned an arbitrary value for circulation within Thebes. Thebes' silver coins were struck, at least in part, in order to allow the city to make state payments to its employees, such as the cavalry unit of Pompidas. In practice, once these silver drachms filtered out into Theban society, they circulated freely with other silver coins on the 'symmachic' weight-standard. Within the city of Thebes itself, most low-level exchanges (up to and including the sale of a horse) were conducted in bronze coinage. These bronze coins were fiduciary coins, of little intrinsic value, and one could never be certain of realizing their full nominal worth once they were taken outside the city. Hence anyone trying to exchange bronze coins for silver with the city's money-changers had to pay an outrageous 25 per cent commission. These were the kinds of norms and constraints that shaped the day-to-day uses of money in the Hellenistic city.

Part IV

Ideology

8

Kings

I Fancy dress and royal ideology

After a hard day's work conquering Persians, a frat party in fancy dress. Here is the historian Ephippus of Olynthus, an eye-witness to Alexander the Great's last years, on the king's unexpected *penchant* for cross-dressing:

> Alexander used to dress up in sacred costumes at banquets. Sometimes he wore Ammon's purple robe, slippers, and a pair of horns like the god; sometimes he dressed up in the garb of Artemis (which he often wore on his chariot), with a Persian robe and a bow and quiver hanging from his shoulders. On occasion he put on the costume of Hermes: his daily clothing was a purple cloak, an off-white tunic and a Macedonian hat with a royal diadem, but at parties he used to wear sandals, a traveller's hat, and carried a herald's staff in his hand; he also often sported a lion-skin and a club like Heracles. (*FGrHist* 126F5)

Demetrius Poliorcetes, too, was notorious for his over-the-top clothing, as Plutarch tells us in his gloriously rococo *Life of Demetrius*:

> There was in fact much of the tragic actor about Demetrius. He not only wore the most extravagant clothing and head-gear, Macedonian hats with double diadems and purple robes with golden decoration, but also slippers of rich purple felt with gold embroidery. He also had an amazing cloak, long in the making, with the universe and stars woven into it; this was left half-finished when he suffered his reversal of fortune, and none of the later kings of Macedon dared to use it, although they were hardly modest in their own lifestyles. (Plut. *Dem.* 41)

We need not take these stories too literally. Ephippus, in particular, is a notorious source of scurrilous nonsense. But like most gossip, these anecdotes do capture an essential truth: Hellenistic royal portraiture really does have a hint of fancy dress to it. Alexander *was* depicted wearing the ram's horns of Ammon, and there *is* something theatrical about the coin portrait of

Figure 8.1. Tetradrachm of Demetrius Poliorcetes, struck in Macedon (*c.* 292–290 BC). The reverse type shows Poseidon seated in a pose very similar to that of Zeus on the tetradrachm coinage of Alexander the Great. 16.99 g. ANS 1980.109.44.

Demetrius Poliorcetes, with his immaculate Alexander-style mane of hair, improbably handsome youthful features and shining bull's horns (Fig. 8.1). All that Ephippus and Plutarch have done is to take these fantasy royal images, created for mass public consumption, and pretend that this is how the kings actually behaved in real life (Smith 1988: 38–9).

Coinage does not just offer magnificent evidence for royal ideology in the Hellenistic period (though it certainly does do that). Coins were also one of the chief media through which royal ideology was communicated in the first place (Clark 2007: 137–61; Noreña 2011). In an age before the mechanical reproduction of images or texts, a royal statute or a royal edict would only ever have been seen or heard by a minuscule proportion of a king's subjects. Royal coin-types, by contrast, were struck by the hundreds of thousands. For most people in the Hellenistic world, images and words on royal coins were their most direct contact with their far-off ruler in Babylon or Alexandria.

What do we actually mean when we talk about 'Hellenistic royal ideology'? It certainly has nothing much to do with a king's actual constitutional powers. Royal ideology is, instead, a set of widespread popular beliefs about a king's status and role: his quasi-divine nature, his generosity as a benefactor, his charismatic authority and personal courage in warfare. 'Doesn't the Queen work awfully hard?' and 'BABY JOY FOR KATE AND WILLS!' are classic expressions of royal ideology. Their truth or untruth is beside the point: they illustrate the values perceived to characterize the modern British monarchy (a strong work ethic, exemplary domesticity), and so serve to reconcile a very wide range of people to the royal family's privileged status (Cannadine 1983; Thonemann 2013a: 38–44).

The dominant ideologies of Hellenistic kingship have been widely studied in recent years (Sherwin-White and Kuhrt 1993: 114–40; Ma 2003a), and we now have a much richer understanding of how royal images could communicate these values than we did a generation ago (Smith 1988; Kropp 2013). What looks to us like fancy dress in fact carries a rich set of symbolic meanings. As we will see later in this chapter, the ram's and bull's horns of Alexander and Demetrius were a highly economical artistic means of indicating the king's divinity (Kroll 2007). Other elements of coin iconography – elephant-scalp headdresses, winged diadems, solar rays, right down to the king's age and hairstyle – all carried their own particular ideological charge.

Nonetheless, before we plunge into details, a brief cautionary tale. Around 310–300 BC, the client-king Abdalonymus of Sidon decorated his sarcophagus with what he clearly intended as a portrait of Alexander riding into battle (Stewart 1993: 294–306). The figure of Alexander is depicted in right-facing profile, wearing a lion-skin headdress, precisely as Heracles is depicted on Alexander's royal silver coins, large numbers of which were struck at Sidon in this period (Figs. 8.2–8.3). Abdalonymus seems to have misread the coin image of Heracles as a portrait of Alexander himself. This was an easy mistake to make: the explosion of royal portraiture on early Hellenistic coinage made it plausible (though certainly wrong) to read the portrait of Heracles on Alexander's coinage as an image of Alexander. It is useful to be reminded quite how ambiguous these images could be. If one of Alexander's own client-kings could get royal coin iconography so spectacularly wrong, what chance did your average ancient viewer have?

Figure 8.2. Tetradrachm in the name of Alexander, struck at Sidon (313/12 BC). Unusually, the Alexander tetradrachms of Sidon can be precisely dated. The Greek letter *phi* on the reverse, in the left field, represents Year 21 of a local era beginning with the Macedonian conquest of 333 BC (Wheatley 2003). 17.09 g. ANS 1944.100.35229.

Figure 8.3. Portrait of 'Alexander', from the sarcophagus of Abdalonymus of Sidon (*c.* 310 BC). This figure forms part of a larger scene of battle between Greeks and Persians, perhaps depicting the battle of Issus (333 BC). Istanbul Archaeological Museum (photograph © L. Yarrow).

II Kings and dynasties

What, then, were the core elements of royal ideology communicated through Hellenistic royal coinages? Here I will single out three key traits: charismatic individualism; dynastic continuity and familial solidarity; and generic similarity between dynasties.

From the early third century onwards, several dynasties chose to depict the reigning king on their coinage. So, for instance, Seleucid silver coins (from Antiochus I onwards) invariably carry an image of the reigning king on the obverse, providing us with a complete portrait gallery of Seleucid monarchs (Le Rider and Callataÿ 2006: 44–8). These royal coin portraits are, for the most part, strongly individualized: no one could mistake the coin portrait of Antiochus I, with his deep-set eyes, slightly sagging jowls and weak chin, for a portrait of Antiochus III, with his receding hairline, high cheekbones and hawk-like features (Figs. 8.4–8.5).

Today, we all expect portraits to look like their subjects. But in the Near East of the third century BC, this individualizing style of royal portraiture was a startling novelty. Egyptian and Near Eastern monarchs, including the

Figure 8.4. Tetradrachm of Antiochus I, struck at Seleucia on the Tigris (*c.* 281–261 BC). 17.11 g. ANS 1944.100.45794.

Figure 8.5. Tetradrachm of Antiochus III, struck at Antioch (*c.* 204–197 BC). Note that the reverse legend (Basileōs Antiochou) is identical to that of Antiochus I: homonymous Seleucid kings were distinguished from one another on coinage primarily by their coin portraits. 17.16 g. ANS 1944.100.75171.

Achaemenid kings of Persia, were always depicted as generic, ageless rulers, with no particularized features (Root 1979). The choice to represent the Seleucid state as embodied in a single charismatic individual – the king as an idiosyncratic personality, rather than a timeless archetype – was something radically new, arising from the messy and violent origins of the new Hellenistic kingdoms. Between 323 and 301 BC, Seleucus I Nicator, Ptolemy I Soter and Antigonus the One-Eyed won their troops' loyalty by dint of their personal success as military predators, rather than through any constitutional or inherited legitimacy (Austin 1986; Ma 2003a). This charismatic, aggressively militaristic ideology of kingship persisted throughout the Hellenistic period (Chaniotis 2005: 57–77) – and we may be grateful that not all kings paraded their military credentials in quite so butch a fashion as Eucratides I of Bactria (Fig. 8.6).

However, not every dynasty opted to change coin portraits with each new king. A single portrait of Ptolemy I Soter – admittedly with variations over time – graces Ptolemaic silver coinage for more than two and a half centuries (Figs. 8.7–8.8; Lorber 2012a). Reigning Ptolemaic kings were

Figure 8.6. Tetradrachm of Eucratides of Bactria (*c.* 170–145 BC). The depiction of Eucratides is the most explicitly martial of all Hellenistic royal coin portraits. 16.53 g. ANS 1995.51.78.

Figure 8.7. Tetradrachm of Ptolemy I, struck at Alexandria (*c.* 294–285 BC). This highly individualized portrait of Ptolemy, with scruffy Alexander-style hair, royal diadem and goat-skin aegis, continued to be used on Ptolemaic silver coinage (with variations) for almost 250 years. 14.25 g. ANS 1944.100.73309.

Figure 8.8. Tetradrachm of Ptolemy VI, with the types of Ptolemy I (*c.* 180–145 BC). The eagle now has feathered legs, and Ptolemy's portrait has taken on a slightly cartoon-like quality. 14.16 g. ANS 1944.100.78717.

depicted only on special issues, like the magnificent gold portrait coins of Ptolemy III (below, p. 156). Likewise, a single coin portrait of the Attalid dynast Philetaerus was used by his successors for more than a hundred years after his death (Chapter 1, p. 11). Royal ideology, then, was not just about the virtues of the reigning king: Hellenistic kings could also choose to emphasize the dynastic continuity of the ruling house.

One particularly striking novelty of the Ptolemaic dynasty was their production of coinage in the name of queens. Ptolemy II Philadelphus married his full sister Arsinoe II in around 275 BC, the first in a long series of incestuous Ptolemaic unions (Ager 2005). After the deification of Ptolemy and Arsinoe as 'sibling gods' (*theoi adelphoi*) in 272/1 BC, Ptolemy II struck a spectacular series of gold coins with twin portraits of himself and Arsinoe on the obverse, and their parents, Ptolemy I and Berenice I, on the reverse (Fig. 8.9; Olivier and Lorber 2013). These coins highlight – and perhaps overplay, who can tell? – the physical similarities between the various members of the family, in order to emphasize their multiple blood-links and familial solidarity. This 'jugate' portrait type was later imitated by several other dynasties, as for instance on the Seleucid coinage of Cleopatra Thea, herself a descendant of the Ptolemaic royal family, and her son Antiochus VIII (Fig. 8.10; Houghton, Lorber and Hoover 2008: I, 469–81).

Figure 8.9. Gold octadrachm (*mnaieion*) of Ptolemy II (*c.* 270 BC), with jugate portraits of two pairs of 'sibling gods', Ptolemy II and Arsinoe II (obverse, with legend Adelphōn, 'siblings') and Ptolemy I and Berenice I (reverse, with legend Theōn, 'gods'). 27.81 g. ANS 1977.158.112.

Figure 8.10. Tetradrachm of Cleopatra Thea and Antiochus VIII, struck at Antioch (*c.* 122–121 BC). Both the image and the reverse legend ('of Queen Cleopatra Thea and King Antiochus') highlight the queen's senior position. 16.61 g. ANS 1944.100.76788.

Figure 8.11. Silver decadrachm in the name of Arsinoe Philadelphus (*c.* 270–241 BC). The ram's horn behind Arsinoe's ear echoes the coin-portraits of Alexander the Great. 35.52 g. ANS 1957.172.1617.

Figure 8.12. Silver Attic-weight pentadrachm in the name of Queen Berenice (*c.* 241–221 BC). Remarkably, while Ptolemy III struck a plentiful coinage with his wife's image, his own portrait only appears on Egyptian coinage after his death (Figure 8.19 below). 19.26 g. ANS 1967.152.626.

After Arsinoe's death in *c.* 270–268 BC, Ptolemy II struck a large issue of silver decadrachms (and, later, gold mnaieia) in the late queen's name, with a magnificent portrait of Arsinoe on the obverse (Fig. 8.11; Carney 2013: 120–4). Arsinoe is shown with a large, rounded eye, and wears a veil and royal crown (*stephanē*) with an unobtrusive ram's horn of Amun behind her ear, indicating her god-like status. His successor, Ptolemy III, similarly struck coins in the name of his own deified wife, Berenice II, this time during her lifetime (Fig. 8.12). Both issues should be connected to the enthusiastic promotion of the cults of Arsinoe and Berenice by Ptolemy II and III respectively (Hölbl 2001: 101–5).

These were not quite the earliest coins in the name of female rulers. Around 300 BC, a certain Amastris, an independent female dynast in coastal Paphlagonia, had struck an issue of silver coins in her own name

Figure 8.13. Silver stater in the name of Queen Amastris (*c.* 300 BC). The obverse depicts a youthful bust in a Phrygian bonnet wreathed in laurel, perhaps the god Mithra; the reverse shows Aphrodite seated on a throne, in a pose reminiscent of the tetradrachms of Alexander the Great and Lysimachus. 9.17 g. ANS 1968.57.76.

(AMASTRIOS BASILISSĒS, 'of Queen Amastris') (Fig. 8.13; Callataÿ 2004). However, the character and context of these coins are very different from the coins of Arsinoe II and Berenice II: they do not carry the queen's portrait, and have none of the divinizing overtones of the Ptolemaic portrait coins.

A final key element of royal ideology is the generic similarity of one dynasty to another. As we have seen time and again throughout this book, Hellenistic royal coinages followed a set of clear iconographic rules. The obverse generally carried a right-facing royal portrait bust (whether the reigning king, the founder of the dynasty or Alexander), usually with a full-length portrait of a deity, flanked by a legend running top to bottom, on the reverse. Hellenistic kings are generally shown as beardless, in their twenties or thirties (whatever their real age), with curly dishevelled hair of medium length, wearing a diadem bound around the head just above the ear (Smith 1988: 46–8). Just as all Hellenistic royal correspondence – Seleucid, Attalid, Ptolemaic – shares a single generic language and diction (Welles 1934; Ceccarelli 2013: 297–330), so Hellenistic royal coinages, for all their various local quirks, ultimately served to express a single common style and ideology of kingship.

On a trivial level, this common style reflects the common descent of the Hellenistic kingdoms from the short-lived empire of Alexander the Great. Direct emulation of Alexander is particularly clear in the case of the Seleucid pretender Alexander I Balas (reigned 152–146 BC), whose portrait coins depict a man with a suspiciously close resemblance to his famous namesake (Figs. 8.14–8.15). But deliberate similarity of style could also be used to express mutual recognition or even alliances between dynasties. Fig. 8.14 shows a coin of Alexander Balas from Phoenician Tyre, struck on

Figure 8.14. Tetradrachm of Alexander I Balas, struck at Tyre (148/7 BC). The reverse type imitates that of contemporary Ptolemaic tetradrachms. The coin issue is precisely dated to Year 165 of the Seleucid era (the three letters behind the eagle's shoulder). 14.05 g. ANS 1944.100.77689.

Figure 8.15. Tetradrachm of Alexander I Balas and Cleopatra Thea, struck at Ptolemaïs-Ake (c. 150 BC). The wedding of Alexander and Cleopatra cemented a short-lived alliance between the Seleucid and Ptolemaic royal houses. 17.30 g. ANS 1959.124.2.

the light Ptolemaic weight-standard of *c.* 14.27 g (Chapter 6 above, p. 121), with a reverse type directly imitating the eagle-on-thunderbolt of the main Ptolemaic royal coinage. Alexander Balas had come to power with the aid of Ptolemy VI, and in 150 BC married Ptolemy's eldest daughter, Cleopatra Thea (Fig. 8.15; Houghton, Lorber and Hoover 2008: I, 209–13). The adoption of aspects of Ptolemaic coin iconography by the Seleucid king was a neat way of signalling this short-lived alliance between the two dynasties.

III Looking like a god

As we have seen, much of the rich iconographic repertoire of Hellenistic royal coin portraits was meant to indicate the king's divinity (Kroll 2007). Ruler cults created delicate problems for Hellenistic portrait artists. Kings were gods, but they were not gods in the same way that Apollo and Zeus were (Price 1984: 1–40; Chaniotis 2003). The standard attributes of the Olympian deities (thunderbolts, tridents and so forth) are actually rather

Figure 8.16. Silver decadrachm of Alexander the Great, perhaps struck at Susa (*c.* 325 BC). The divinizing portrait of Alexander wielding a thunderbolt has no parallels on later Hellenistic royal coinage. 38.71 g. ANS 1959.254.86.

sparingly used, and seldom as an integral element of royal portraits (Smith 1988: 38–45).

For a vivid indication of the road not taken – full identification of kings with the Olympian gods – we can turn to a notorious coinage from the very beginning of the period, the so-called 'Porus' decadrachms of Alexander the Great (Fig. 8.16; Lane Fox 1996; Holt 2003; Bhandare 2007). Almost everything about these coins is fiercely disputed (date, place of minting, significance), but most scholars agree that they were struck somewhere in Mesopotamia in the immediate aftermath of Alexander's victory over the Indian king Porus at the Hydaspes river in 326 BC. The obverse type carries an idealized image of single combat between Alexander on his horse Bucephalus and Porus on his elephant. The reverse bears a full-length portrait of Alexander, wearing full Macedonian military dress and wielding a Zeus-style thunderbolt in his right hand; a Nike figure is flying in from the top left to lay a wreath on Alexander's head. The precise theological meaning of this image has been hotly debated, but the crucial thing from our perspective is its complete isolation in Hellenistic coin art. Kings just did not throw thunderbolts: royal divinity had to be represented in a more allusive, less literalistic manner.

As we have seen, the royal coinage of Lysimachus indicated Alexander's divinity in a very different manner, depicting him with a prominent ram's horn curling over his diadem (Fig. 8.17). The viewer is no doubt meant to think of Alexander's descent from the god Zeus in his Libyan incarnation, Zeus Ammon. Ammon was often depicted in Greek art with ram's horns, as on fourth-century coins of the Greek city of Aphytis on the Chalcidice peninsula (Fig. 8.18). However, no other major Greek deity seems ever to be

Figure 8.17. Tetradrachm of Lysimachus, struck at Lampsacus (*c.* 297–281 BC). Alexander's distinctive quiff ('*anastolē*') is particularly clear on this example. 16.96 g. ANS 1997.9.70.

Figure 8.18. Bronze coin of Aphytis (*c.* 400–350 BC). The bust of Zeus Ammon with ram's horn on the obverse may have directly influenced Lysimachus' coin portrait of Alexander the Great. 7.84 g. ANS 1944.100.10360.

portrayed in quite this way: animal horns were not really part of the iconography of the Olympian gods. The ram's horn was thus a doubly useful visual motif for indicating Alexander's divinity. It evoked his particular claim to divinity, through descent from Ammon, but did not trespass too aggressively on the standard iconography of the Greek gods. The bull's horns of Demetrius Poliorcetes and Seleucus I (Chapter 1 above, pp. 21–2) and the ram's horn of Arsinoe II (above, p. 152) tell a similar story.

The accumulation of divine attributes in royal coin portraiture reached its *ne plus ultra* in a gloriously over-the-top image of Ptolemy III Euergetes (reigned 246–221 BC), which appears on gold octadrachms struck by his successor, Ptolemy IV (reigned 221–204 BC). A rather pudgy Ptolemy III is depicted with Zeus' aegis (a scaly goat-skin breastplate: Lorber 2011) slung around his shoulders; Poseidon's trident, topped with a lotus-bud, can be seen poking out behind his shoulder, and the rays of the sun-god Helios flash upwards from his royal diadem (Fig. 8.19; Johnson 1999; Olivier and Lorber 2013). There is no reason to think that Ptolemy is strictly being 'identified' with any or all of these three deities; rather, the point may be to indicate Ptolemy's godlike dominance over the land, sea and heavens.

The diadem with solar rays, usually called a 'radiate crown', was adopted by several later Ptolemaic and Seleucid monarchs (Bergmann 1998; Iossif and Lorber 2012). The rays were sometimes depicted as shooting out directly from the king's hair, rather than being attached to the diadem, as

Figure 8.19. Gold octadrachm (*mnaieion*) struck by Ptolemy IV (*c.* 217–204 BC), with portrait of the deceased Ptolemy III. These coins were probably struck to celebrate the great Ptolemaic victory over Antiochus III at the battle of Raphia in 217 BC. 27.75 g. ANS 1997.9.178.

Figure 8.20. Silver drachm of Antiochus VI, struck at Apamea in Syria (145/4 BC). His coin portrait conceals the fact that Antiochus was only around four years old at the time these coins were struck. 4.15 g. ANS 1944.100.76553.

Figure 8.21. 'Billon' (silver-alloy) tetradrachm of Tiberius, struck at Alexandria (AD 20/1). The reverse type depicts the deified Augustus (Theos Sebastos) wearing a radiate crown. 13.62 g. ANS 1944.100.69590.

for instance on the silver coins of the Seleucid king Antiochus VI (reigned 144–142 BC: Fig. 8.20). The exact meaning of these solar rays is rather fuzzy, and that was surely the point. They serve to evoke the king's radiance and godlike nature, without making any specific metaphysical claims of the form 'King Ptolemy III is the incarnation of Helios'.

The use of the radiate crown or solar rays to represent a ruler's godlike nature was taken over by the early Roman emperors (Bardill 2012: 28–57). Already in the last years of the Republic, Julius Caesar seems to have been granted the honour of wearing a radiate crown (Florus 2.13.91: *distincta radiis corona*; Weinstock 1971: 381–4). Its widespread use on Roman imperial coinage begins with the reign of Tiberius (AD 14–37), who regularly depicted his deified predecessor Augustus wearing a fine Hellenistic-style radiate crown (Fig. 8.21).

Around AD 30, the radiate crown played a prominent symbolic role in the execution of an obscure Jewish rebel against the Roman order. At the end of Jesus' trial before the governor Pontius Pilate, the governor's soldiers dressed him in a purple robe, put a reed-sceptre in his hand and placed a crown of thorns on his head (Matthew 27:28–29; John 19:2–5). This 'crown of thorns' was not the plaited cluster of spiny twigs familiar from later western art, but a band of cloth with single long thorns projecting out from it, imitating the Hellenistic and Roman radiate crown (Coleman 1990: 47; Amedick 2005). Jesus' crown of thorns, like the rest of his mock-royal regalia, was a way of parodying his alleged status as King of the Jews. The people of Jerusalem would only have needed to pick a coin from their purse to grasp the symbolism without any difficulty.

IV Stories about power: Macedon, Sparta, Syracuse

A few dynasties followed a self-consciously different path on their royal coinages. Perhaps the most striking case is the Antigonid dynasty of Macedon. After Demetrius Poliorcetes' series of divinizing portrait coins (above, p. 146), none of the third-century Antigonid monarchs featured ruler portraits on their coins (Panagopoulou 2001; Kremydi 2011: 171–4). Two distinct series of royal tetradrachms were struck by Macedonian mints during the long reign of Antigonus Gonatas (277–239 BC). The first series, struck from around 267 BC, bears a miniature Macedonian shield on the obverse (an ingenious use of the slightly convex shape produced by ancient punch-and-anvil minting techniques), with a bust of Pan at the centre (Fig. 8.22). Perhaps around 246 BC, Gonatas introduced a new tetradrachm coinage, depicting the god Poseidon wearing a tremendous beard, with his hair wreathed with a diadem-like string of kelp (Fig. 8.23). This image recalls the formal conventions of ruler portraiture (right-facing bust, quasi-diadem), while making it absolutely clear that a god, not Gonatas himself, is being shown. His two successors, Demetrius II (reigned 239–229) and Antigonus Doson (reigned 229–221), continued striking coins with these same two types.

The last two Antigonid monarchs, Philip V and Perseus, did mint their own portrait coins, but unlike virtually all other Hellenistic kings (Parthians aside: Chapter 5, pp. 91–4), the two men carry neatly groomed full beards (Figs. 8.24–8.25). Both kings were probably trying to highlight their connections to the great (bearded) Macedonian ruler Philip II, a figure of little significance to the other Hellenistic dynasties, but a key figure in

Figure 8.22. Tetradrachm of Antigonus Gonatas (*c.* 246–229 BC). The reverse type, a striding Athena Alcidemus (also used by Philip V, Figure 8.24 below), is remarkably reminiscent of the Egyptian satrapal coinage of Ptolemy (above, Figure 1.20). 17.08 g. ANS 1944.100.13851.

Figure 8.23. Tetradrachm of Antigonus Gonatas, second series (*c.* 246–229 BC). The maritime iconography on both obverse and reverse may reflect Antigonus' great victory over the Ptolemaic fleet at the battle of Andros (*c.* 246 BC). 17.11 g. ANS 1964.79.6.

Figure 8.24. Tetradrachm of Philip V (*c.* 221–179 BC). 16.94 g. ANS 1967.152.211.

Figure 8.25. Tetradrachm of Perseus (*c.* 179–168 BC). 17.00 g. ANS 1957.172.711.

Figure 8.26. Tetradrachm in the name of 'King Areus' (Basileos Areos) with the types of Alexander the Great (*c.* 267–265 BC). These were the first coins of any kind ever struck at Sparta. 16.75 g. ANS 1962.140.8.

Macedonian history (Worthington 2008). The absence of any divinizing attributes on the two coin portraits is also striking. There seems to have been no official, state-sponsored ruler cult in Hellenistic Macedon, and the evidence for private and civic cult is very limited (Mari 2008). Philip V and Perseus may well have been deliberately underlining the differences between their 'national' monarchy in Macedonia and the 'personal' monarchies of their dynastic rivals in the East.

Throughout the Hellenistic world, coinage served as a medium for local tyrants and dynasts to stake out their claims to Hellenistic Great Power status. Even the kings of Sparta – a rare city which had never minted coins at all in the Archaic and Classical periods – could not resist striking small 'royal' coin issues in their own name. The very first Spartan coins were in fact tetradrachms in the name of King Areus (reigned 309–265 BC; Cartledge and Spawforth 2002: 34–5). Like many other local dynasts in the early Hellenistic period (King Audoleon of Paeonia, King Monounios of Illyria, the Celtic chieftain Kavaros: Chapter 2, pp. 31–2), Areus struck a coinage closely modelled on the tetradrachms of Alexander the Great, with the legend 'of King Areus' the only indication of its Spartan origin (Fig. 8.26). Later in the

Figure 8.27. Tetradrachm of Sparta (*c.* 227–222 BC), with the letters *lambda* and *alpha* on the reverse (the first two letters of LAKEDAIMŌN). The ruler portrait on the obverse is apparently a portrait of Cleomenes III. 16.33 g. ANS 1944.100.38863.

Figure 8.28. Gold stater of Agathocles of Syracuse (*c.* 310–307 BC), with reverse legend AGATHOKLEIOS, 'of Agathocles'. The goddess on the reverse seems to be a composite of the striding Athena on the satrapal coinage of Ptolemy (Figure 1.20), and the winged Nike on the gold distaters of Alexander the Great (Figure 1.9). 8.54 g. ANS 1997.9.63.

third and second centuries, other Spartan kings went so far as to strike coins with their own portraits on the obverse (Palagia 2006). The example illustrated here is a portrait coin of King Cleomenes III (reigned 235–222), minted in the wake of his revolutionary *coup d'état* in 227, which effectively replaced the traditional Spartan dual kingship with Macedonian-style personal autocracy (Fig. 8.27; Cartledge and Spawforth 2002: 49–58). The interest of these coins lies in the extent to which even Spartan kings – survivors of a much older Greek model of kingship – eventually moved over to Hellenistic modes of royal representation.

Still more striking instances are offered by the early Hellenistic rulers of Syracuse. The tyrant Agathocles of Syracuse (ruled 316–289 BC) struck several issues of gold, silver and bronze coins, many of which imitate contemporary Macedonian types. The best known are an extraordinary series of Attic-weight gold staters (Fig. 8.28), with an obverse type imitating the portrait of Alexander on the contemporary Egyptian satrapal coinage of Ptolemy son of Lagus (Chapter 1 above, p. 19). These coins were minted in the wake of Agathocles' dramatic invasion of Libya and attack on Carthage

Figure 8.29. Gold 'double decadrachm' of Agathocles of Syracuse (*c.* 295–289 BC), with reverse legend Basileos Agathokleos, 'of King Agathocles'. The obverse is a direct copy of the gold staters of Alexander the Great. 5.73 g. ANS 1957.172.1919.

Figure 8.30. Bronze coin of Hieron II of Syracuse (*c.* 240–215 BC). The left-facing portrait on the obverse is unusual for Hellenistic royal coin portraits, and reflects a long-standing preference for left-facing portraits on Syracusan coinage. 17.00 g. ANS 1944.100.57134.

in 310 (Diod. Sic. 20.3–18). For a brief moment, until the collapse of his Carthaginian expedition in 307, it must have seemed as though Agathocles was on the brink of becoming a 'western Alexander' (Stewart 1993: 266–9). After Agathocles' return to Sicily and assumption of the title 'king' (*c.* 304), he struck a series of gold coins with obverse types directly copied from the gold staters of Alexander the Great (Fig. 8.29; Bérend 1998). Although Agathocles usually plays only a walk-on part (if that) in modern histories of the early Hellenistic period, he clearly saw himself – and was recognized by contemporaries – as the equal of Alexander's successors in the East (Plut. *Dem.* 25.7–8; Baron 2013: 93–105).

No less impressive is the coinage of Hieron II of Syracuse, who ruled over much of eastern Sicily from around 269 to 215 BC (Caltabiano, Carroccio and Oteri 1997; Arnold-Biucchi 2002). During Hieron's long reign, he consistently presented himself as a match for the Antigonid, Seleucid and Ptolemaic kings in the eastern Mediterranean. In 227 BC, when the city of Rhodes was levelled by an earthquake, Hieron was one of several Hellenistic kings (including Antigonus Doson, Seleucus II and Ptolemy III) to provide financial aid to the Rhodians (Polybius 5.88–90; Wilson 2013: 80–97). Hieron's bronze and silver coinage carried a portrait of the king in good Hellenistic royal style (Fig. 8.30); a substantial coinage in the name of

Figure 8.31. Silver tetradrachm in the name of Queen Philistis of Syracuse (c. 240–215 BC), with reverse legend BASILISSAS PHILISTIDOS, 'of Queen Philistis'. Note the royal diadem visible below the queen's veil. 13.55 g. ANS 1997.9.104.

Figure 8.32. Imitation of Ptolemaic bronze diobol, struck by Hieron of Syracuse (perhaps c. 264–260 BC). 18.27 g. ANS 1944.100.76065.

Hieron's wife, Queen Philistis, was also struck during this same period (Fig. 8.31). The coins of Philistis are strikingly similar to contemporary Ptolemaic coins bearing royal portraits of Arsinoe II and Berenice II (above, p. 152), and were surely based on Ptolemaic models. Remarkably, Hieron even seems to have struck outright copies of Ptolemaic bronzes early in his reign: a large issue of bronze coins with Ptolemaic types has recently been attributed to Hieron's Syracusan mint (Fig. 8.32; Wolf and Lorber 2011).

V   The return of the king

In the second and early first century BC, three minor kingdoms of central and northern Asia Minor (Cappadocia, Bithynia and Pontus) also produced extensive series of royal portrait coins, of a rather distinctive style (Figs. 8.33–8.37; Simonetta 2007; Callataÿ 2009b; Michels 2009: 151–251). The portraits show little sign of the idealization characteristic of other Hellenistic royal coin portraits. Several kings, notably Mithradates III of Pontus and Ariobarzanes I of Cappadocia (Figs. 8.35 and 8.37), are depicted as men in late middle age, with deeply furrowed brows and receding hair-lines. Nor do the portraits have any obvious divinizing attributes, aside from a small wing on the diadem of Prusias II (Fig. 8.34) – this may be an allusion to his marriage alliance with Philip V of Macedon, who claimed

Figure 8.33. Tetradrachm of Prusias I of Bithynia (*c.* 210–182). The king's underchin beard has no earlier parallels on Hellenistic royal coinage. 16.83 g. Oxford, SNG Ashmolean IX 434.

Figure 8.34. Tetradrachm of Prusias II of Bithynia (*c.* 177–149 BC). The king is depicted with two- or three-days' worth of stubble, perhaps a military 'campaign beard'. 16.72 g. ANS 1944.100.41891.

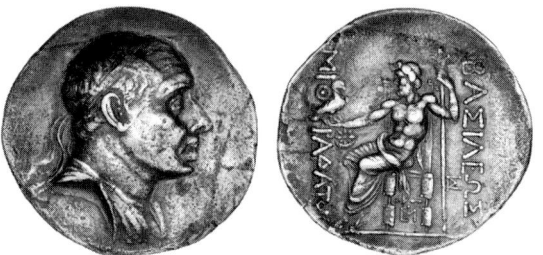

Figure 8.35. Tetradrachm of Mithradates III of Pontus (*c.* 220–200 BC). The reverse type is based on Alexander's tetradrachm coinage, but the individualized ruler portrait on the obverse is something entirely new. 16.10 g. ANS 1960.60.4.

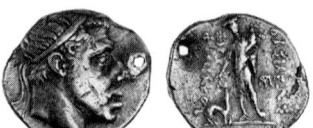

Figure 8.36. Drachm of Pharnaces I of Pontus (*c.* 200–169 BC). The identity of the deity on the reverse is uncertain. 4.12 g. ANS 1961.179.21.

Figure 8.37. Drachm of Ariobarzanes I of Cappadocia (*c.* 66 BC). On the reverse, Ariobarzanes carries the title Philorhōmaiou, 'friend of Rome', and his unusually 'veristic' portrait has sometimes been put down to Roman influence. 4.15 g. ANS 1944.100.62383.

descent from the hero Perseus (often depicted with a winged helmet) (Kaye 2013). These kings wished to be seen as real human beings, not as ideal royal archetypes.

Portrait coins, 'race' and morals

Modern discussions of Bithynian and Pontic coin portraits have a slightly curious tone to them. For Peter Green, 'Prusias I of Bithynia is porcine, crass and self-satisfied. The early kings of Pontus resemble nothing so much as a family of escaped convicts: Pharnaces I has the profile of a Neanderthaler, and Mithridates IV that of a skid-row alcoholic' (Green 1990: 350). Bert Smith thinks that Prusias I of Bithynia 'looks perhaps a little "foreign"', while the Pontic kings 'are clearly presented as un-Greek in race. . . One might guess that their un-Greek ethnic appearance reflects a need to conciliate a non-Greek power base, namely, an Iranian nobility' (Smith 1988: 113).

Otto Mørkholm agrees on the non-Greek physiognomy of the Pontic kings: the coinage of Mithradates I emphasizes 'his oriental features that are so different from Greek idealization or Macedonian heaviness' (Mørkholm 1991: 131). Norman Davis and Colin Kraay thought that the coin portrait of Pharnaces I of Pontus 'shows an ungracious and impatient face', and 'The portrait coins of Prusias II [of Bithynia] appear to confirm his reputation. . . as a poor creature' (Davis and Kraay 1973: 261, 266). Prusias II has had a particularly bad press. E. T. Newell found him to be 'a heavy, stupid looking person' (Newell 1937: 37), and Carl Schneider – a man with an interesting personal history (Murray 1969) – thought that he looked 'degenerate. . . rough and barbaric' (Schneider 1967: 788).

Racially un-Greek, degenerate, alcoholic, stupid – it is remarkable what one can tell about a man just by looking at his picture. (Callataÿ 2009b: 64; Michels 2009: 169)

Figure 8.38. Tetradrachm of Mithradates VI (*c.* 97 BC). This early undated issue carries a 'realistic' portrait of the king on the obverse. 16.33 g. ANS 1967.152.392.

Figure 8.39. Tetradrachm of Mithradates VI (July 74 BC). From 96/5 BC onwards, Mithradates' coins carry dates on the reverse, allowing us to chart the development of the king's coin portrait with unusual precision. 16.64 g. ANS 1944.100.41480.

The style of Pontic royal coinage changed with dramatic suddenness during the reign of Mithradates VI Eupator (119–63 BC) (Callataÿ 1997; Michels 2009: 202–15). Mithradates' earliest portrait coins (dating to the early 90s BC) fit into the broadly 'realistic' style of earlier Pontic royal coins, and depict a young man with unusually long hair and traces of side-whiskers (Fig. 8.38). But his coin portrait becomes increasingly idealized from the mid-80s BC onwards, and the later coins of Mithradates carry a startlingly fierce and dynamic image of the king (Fig. 8.39), with wild flying hair and a prominent Alexander-style *anastolē* or quiff (compare the portrait of Alexander on Fig. 8.17 above).

The reverse type of Mithradates' coins is also novel. The winged horse Pegasus is depicted bending down to drink, with a star and crescent moon to his left, accompanied by the legend Basileōs Mithradatou Eupatoros ('of King Mithradates Eupator'). The type is encircled by a wreath of ivy, perhaps recalling the ivy wreath on the cistophoric coinage of the Attalids (Chapter 5 above, pp. 77–82). John T. Ramsey has shown that this reverse type alludes to legends of Mithradates' birth and future greatness (Ramsey 1999). The Roman historian Justin tells us that the king's birth (135 BC) and accession to the throne (119 BC) were both marked by the appearance of blazing comets in the sky:

> The future greatness of Mithradates had been foretold even by heavenly portents. For both in the year in which he was born and in the year in which he first began to rule, a comet shone so brightly for 70 days that the entire sky seemed to be on fire. (Justin 37.2.1–2)

In a dazzling piece of historical detective work, Ramsey showed that the comet marking the king's birth (also attested in Chinese sources) must have appeared in the vicinity of the constellation Pegasus. The Pegasus-type on his coinage was therefore meant to evoke the celestial omens of Mithradates' birth – not to mention the widespread Near Eastern prophetic tradition that a bright light in the sky would foretell the birth of a saviour king (familiar to us from the Gospels).

In its first-century BC context, the idealized portrait of Mithradates is something of a throwback. It harks back to coin portraits of Alexander the Great, and presents the king as a charismatic warrior-king in the old Hellenistic style (McGing 1986: 89–108). Mithradates' coinage was part of a carefully constructed self-image as champion of the Greeks against Rome, most vividly expressed in the massacre in spring 88 BC of some 80,000 Italians in Asia Minor (App. *Mith.* 22–3; Kallet-Marx 1995: 153–8). The Mithradatic cause had a powerful appeal for many Greek city-states. As early as 97/6 BC, two partisans of Mithradates at Athens, Aristion and Philon, struck an issue of Athenian 'New Style' coinage with the Mithradatic Pegasus symbol on the reverse (Fig. 8.40), and the king himself was named on Athenian coins as a 'mint-magistrate' in 87/6 BC (Habicht 1997: 297–314; Mattingly 2004: 85–99).

Mithradates' revival of the old Alexandrine tradition of heroic royal iconography was short-lived. A small imitative coinage was struck by his son Ariarathes IX, who ruled sporadically over Cappadocia between 100 and 85 BC (Fig. 8.41; Callataÿ 1997: 200–9); the Mithradatic style of portraiture was also followed by the king's younger son, Pharnaces II, who ruled as Roman client-king of the Cimmerian Bosporus on the north shore of the Black Sea from 63 to 47 BC (Fig. 8.42; Golenko and Karyszowski 1972). Nonetheless, the coinage of Mithradates VI looks very much like the end of an era. Whatever attractions Mithradates' royal style

Figure 8.40. 'New Style' wreathed tetradrachm of Athens (97/6 BC), struck by the magistrates Aristiōn and Philōn. Aristion later led the unsuccessful Athenian resistance to Sulla in 87–86 BC, which ended in the sack of Athens in March 86 BC. 16.55 g. ANS 1944.100.24839.

Figure 8.41. Tetradrachm of Ariarathes IX of Cappadocia (c. 100–95 BC or c. 89–85 BC). Both the royal portrait and the reverse type of a grazing stag within a wreath (here, a vine wreath rather than an ivy wreath) are closely modelled on the coins of Mithradates VI. 16.47 g. ANS 1967.152.553.

Figure 8.42. Gold stater of Pharnaces II of the Cimmerian Bosporus (51/50 BC). The reverse legend reads Basileōs Basileōn Megalou Pharnakou, 'of Pharnaces, Great King of Kings'. 8.20 g. ANS 1967.152.383.

may have had for the Greek *poleis*, his coinage and its immediate imitations were the last of their kind. As we will see in Chapter 9, the coming of Roman rule to the eastern Mediterranean brought with it a whole new set of paradigms for the representation of power on late Hellenistic coins.

9

From Flamininus to Augustus

I   Ancient history from coins

Imagine for a moment that all written sources for Rome's conquest of the Hellenistic world had been lost. No Polybius, no Livy, no Cicero; no Illyrian Wars, no treaty of Apamea, no battle of Pydna. Imagine trying to reconstruct the political history of the eastern Mediterranean between, say, 229 and 30 BC from the coin evidence alone. What would Rome's arrival in the Greek East look like? Would we be able to spot the emergence of the earliest Roman provinces in the East, Macedonia from 146, Asia from 129, Syria, Cilicia and Bithynia-Pontus from 64? Whose impact would be most visible – Sulla, Pompey, Augustus?

There can be no doubt what the first coin to catch your eye would be. Around 196 BC, a very unusual issue of gold staters was struck somewhere in Greece, perhaps at Chalcis on Euboea. The ten known examples were struck from no fewer than five different obverse dies (and five reverse dies), suggesting that more than 100,000 coins may originally have been struck (Alföldi 1984; Callataÿ 2011a: 59–61). These coins carry on the obverse a portrait of a bearded male figure, without a diadem (Fig. 9.1). On the reverse, a Nike figure bearing a palm-frond (representing a military victory on land) is shown placing a wreath on the name T. Qvincti.

As the Latin legend on the reverse makes clear, these coins were struck by the great Roman general T. Quinctius Flamininus. Flamininus had defeated Philip V at the battle of Cynoscephalae in 197 BC – in effect marking the end of Antigonid Macedon as a major player in the Aegean world – and went on to proclaim the freedom of the mainland Greeks at the Isthmian games at Corinth the following year (Polybius 18.46.5). Flamininus' declaration of Greek freedom shows how well he had grasped the kind of Philhellenic rhetoric used by Hellenistic kings in their dealings with Greek cities (Walsh 1996); it is no surprise to find him equally able to speak the charismatic 'language' of Hellenistic royal coinage.

Aside from the use of Latin for the legend on the reverse, Flamininus' coinage is modelled on contemporary issues of Hellenistic kings in almost

Figure 9.1. Gold stater of T. Quinctius Flamininus (*c.* 196 BC). 8.44 g. *Numismatica Genevensis* 4 (2006), 130 (Callataÿ 2011a: 60, no. 5). Courtesy of Numismatica Genevensis SA.

every respect. Although attempts have been made to discern a distinctively 'Roman' style to his coin portrait (Kousser 2010: 527–8), this is little more than wishful thinking (Touchette 1992: 244). All of the elements of the portrait – the curly, ruffled hair, chiselled cheekbones, thin beard, beaky nose – find close parallels in Hellenistic royal coin portraits. Even the Latin legend on the reverse shows signs of having been cut by an engraver who did not know the Latin alphabet (on some examples, the Q of QVINCTI looks like a Greek letter *rho* lying on its side), and the use of the genitive (QVINCTI, rather than QVINCTIVS) is a Greek, not Roman phenomenon.

Wonderful object though it is, we ought not to linger too long over this famous coin. Its imitation of Hellenistic royal portraiture, explicit reference to Roman power and celebration of the personal charisma of a single Roman magistrate all turned out to be historical dead-ends. This was, if you like, the road *not* taken by Rome in the eastern Mediterranean during the last two centuries BC. The Latin alphabet seems not to be used again on Greek coins until the late 120s BC, and no other Roman magistrate would be depicted in Hellenistic style on a Greek coin for almost a century and a half (the next was Mark Antony: Fig. 9.17 below).

Flamininus aside, coins tell us remarkably little about the history of the early Roman provinces in the East – or, at least, so it appears at first sight. Silver and bronze coinage continued to be struck in large quantities in the Aegean and Asia Minor in the second and first centuries BC, but virtually none of it explicitly proclaims the change of regime. As this chapter will show, the basic pattern is continuity of earlier coin-types, many in 'fossilized' form. This continuity is a crucial and often neglected aspect of Rome's conquest of the Greek East. Whatever the real character of the political regimes in place in Macedonia and Greece after 146 BC, and in Asia Minor after 129 BC, the official story presented on coins was one of a restoration of Greek freedom, not of subjugation to Rome. We shall first look at the coinages of the two earliest eastern provinces in turn (Macedonia, then Asia), before turning to the evidence for the use of the Roman denarius in the East. The final part of this chapter will offer a brief glance forwards to the legacy of Hellenistic coinage in the Roman imperial period and beyond.

II Macedonia

In 167 BC, in the wake of King Perseus' defeat at Pydna the previous year, the Macedonian monarchy was dissolved. It was replaced by four nominally free Macedonian *merides*, literally 'Parts', usually translated as 'Republics' or 'Districts' (Livy 45.29). The First *meris* lay to the east of the Strymon river, with its capital at Amphipolis. The Second district was made up of the land between the Strymon and Axius rivers, including the Chalcidice peninsula and the city of Thessalonica. The Third *meris* covered the remainder of lower Macedonia, including Pella, and the Fourth *meris* consisted of the traditional cantons of Upper Macedonia.

Livy describes these four *merides* as Roman creations, but coin evidence suggests otherwise. In the early second century BC, probably in the last years of the reign of Philip V (*c.* 187–179 BC), several series of silver and bronze coins in the name of the 'Macedonians' began to be struck in various parts of Macedonia (Figs. 9.2–9.3; Kremydi-Sicilianou 2007). Among them were two splendid tetradrachm coinages. The first of these carried an image of Zeus wearing an oak wreath on the obverse, and Artemis riding a bull on the reverse, accompanied by the legend MAKEDONŌN PRŌTĒS, 'of the Macedonians, First (*meris*)' (Fig. 9.4; Kremydi-Sicilianou 2009). The other bore a Macedonian shield on the obverse and a club in an oak wreath on the reverse, with the legend MAKEDONŌN AMPHAXIŌN, 'of the Macedonians of Amphaxitis' (Fig. 9.5). The word 'Amphaxitis' literally means 'the land on

Figure 9.2. Silver tetrobol in the name of the Macedonians (*c.* 187–168 BC). The obverse carries the ethnic MA-KE and a club, placed on the boss of a Macedonian shield. 2.22 g. ANS 0000.999.7053.

Figure 9.3 Silver tetrobol in the name of the Macedonians (*c.* 187–168 BC). The reverse carries the ethnic MAKE-DONŌN flanking a ship's stern. The coin lacks any explicitly royal iconography. 2.19 g. ANS 1944.100.14155.

Figure 9.4. Tetradrachm of the First Macedonian *meris* (c. 187–168 BC), with Artemis Tauropolos on the reverse. The portrait of Zeus echoes the Poseidon of the royal coinage of Antigonus Gonatas (Figure 8.23 above). 16.62 g. ANS 1968.250.1.

Figure 9.5. Tetradrachm in the name of the Macedonians of Amphaxitis (c. 187–168 BC). 16.22 g. Oxford, SNG Ashmolean III 3288.

both sides of the Axius river', suggesting that this coinage was struck by either the Second or Third Macedonian *meris*.

These early second-century coinages in the name of the Macedonians clearly show that the four Macedonian 'Republics' were not a Roman invention, but already existed under the late Antigonid kings (Hatzopoulos 1996: I, 231–60; for a different view, see Juhel 2011). To all appearances, like their contemporary Eumenes II of Pergamum (Chapter 4 above, pp. 77–82), Philip V and Perseus tried to present their kingdom as a kind of quasi-voluntary league of Macedonian republics, no doubt influenced by the success and prestige of the mainland Greek *koina* of the period (Achaea and Aetolia in particular). This emphasis on the 'federal' nature of the Macedonian state fits nicely with the relatively uncharismatic style of these two kings' royal portrait coinages (Chapter 8 above, p. 160).

After the dissolution of the monarchy, an enormous new series of tetradrachms was struck in the name of the 'First' Macedonian district, with a much smaller issue in the name of the 'Second' (Prokopov 2012). The types

Figure 9.6. Tetradrachm of the First Macedonian *meris* (*c.* 167–158 BC). These coins were struck in very large quantities in the mid-second century BC, presumably by Roman authorities in Macedonia. 16.49 g. ANS 1957.172.715.

were adapted from the pre-167 Antigonid *meris* coinages, with a Macedonian shield and portrait of Artemis on the obverse, and club in oak wreath on the reverse (Fig. 9.6). This coinage gives the impression of seamless continuity in the governance of Macedonia. The official story, if you like, is one of national liberation: Rome has freed the Macedonian republics from their Antigonid overlords.

More striking still is the fact that this coinage continues seamlessly through the 140s BC and beyond. The establishment of the Roman province of Macedonia by Q. Metellus in *c.* 148 BC is, quite simply, invisible in the coin evidence. How surprising we find this depends on our conception of what a 'province' actually was in the mid-second century BC (Kallet-Marx 1995: 11–41). The Roman Republican provinces were not sharply legally defined entities, whose administration and governance were abruptly transformed by Roman 'annexation'. In the case of Macedonia, which had been paying annual tribute to Rome since 167, the only significant change after 148 was the arrival of a standing Roman legion and its proconsular commander. The invisibility of Rome on Macedon's post-167 coinage may in fact accurately reflect the absence of any meaningful Roman government in the region.

It is now clear that continuity also characterized the coinages of the rest of mainland Greece after 146 BC. In the past twenty years or so, the 'numismatic landscape' of the Greek mainland in the late Hellenistic period has been transformed beyond recognition (Warren 1999b). The traditional view was that the defeat of the Achaean League in 146 BC brought an abrupt end to most of the existing Greek federal and civic coinages of the Peloponnese and central Greece. As recently as the mid-1980s, the

Figure 9.7. Silver triobol of Messene (mid-second to mid-first century BC). The reverse bears the abbreviated civic ethnic ME-S with a tripod in a wreath. 2.39 g. ANS 1944.100.38830.

Figure 9.8. Silver triobol of the Achaean League, struck at Elis (mid-first century BC). On the reverse, the letters FA at left represent the ethnic of Elis, with magistrates' monograms above and to the right of the federal A-CH symbol (BCD Peloponnesos 682). 2.33 g. ANS 1944.100.38721.

Roman historian Michael Crawford could still claim (in his superb *Coinage and Money under the Roman Republic*) that 'as far as silver is concerned, after 146, Athens was the only mint active south of Thessaly, apart from a tiny issue of Chalcis' (Crawford 1985: 127). It is now clear that this is quite wrong. Several Peloponnesian cities (Messene, Argos, Sicyon, Patrae, Sparta, Megalopolis, Corone) continued minting civic silver triobols – in some cases in substantial quantities – right down through the late second and into the early first century BC (Fig. 9.7; Grandjean 2003: 130–52; Boehringer 2008). The main large-denomination coinage of the region, the 'New Style' tetradrachms of Athens (Chapter 3 above, p. 57), continued in an unbroken sequence from the 160s down to the 40s BC. Even the Achaean League, Rome's one-time staunchest enemy in mainland Greece, revived its federal silver coinage around 100 BC with the same basic types as its early second-century triobols (Fig. 9.8; Warren 1999a). Once again, 'subjugation' to Rome seems to have had little immediate effect on the minting activity of the cities of the Greek mainland.

This picture begins to change around the turn of the century. In the years around 100 BC, the first explicitly 'Roman' issue of Macedonian tetradrachms was struck. The basic types are familiar from the earlier *meris* coinages (bust of Artemis on shield boss and a club within an oak wreath), and the reverse still bears the Greek legend MAKEDONŌN ('of the Macedonians'), but now it also carries the additional three letters LEG in Latin script (Fig. 9.9; A. Burnett, *CH* VII 54–67; Psoma and Touratsoglou 2005: nos. 978–9). The significance of this legend is not clear. It could be an abbreviation of LEG(ATI), 'of the legate', indicating that the coin was struck

Figure 9.9. Tetradrachm of the Macedonians, with Latin legend Leg (*c.* 100 BC). The reverse type also carries a hand bearing an olive branch, the significance of which is uncertain. 16.84 g. ANS 1944.100.14272.

Figure 9.10. Tetradrachm of the Macedonians, in the name of Aesillas Q(uaestor) (*c.* 90–70 BC). The portrait of Alexander is very unlike earlier coin portraits, and may be based on a lost statue of the king. The *quaestor* Aesillas, the first Roman provincial official to put his name on a Greek coin-type, is not known from any other source. 16.60 g. ANS 1944.100.14282.

by a legate of the provincial governor; alternatively, it could represent Leg(io), referring to the Roman army in Macedonia. At any rate, this coinage marks an important turning point: these are the first coins struck on the Greek mainland to carry a Latin inscription since Flamininus' gold staters almost a century earlier.

This small issue was followed in around 90 BC by a wholly new Macedonian silver coin series, this time making no bones about its Roman origin (Bauslaugh 2000). These coins carry on the obverse a portrait of Alexander the Great, accompanied by the legend Makedonōn ('of the Macedonians') in Greek (Fig. 9.10). The reverse retains the wreath and club of the earlier Macedonian *meris* coinages, but now carries the name Aesillas Q(uaestor) in Latin. The *quaestor* was the chief financial officer

Figure 9.11. Tetradrachm of the Macedonians, in the name of Svvra Leg(atus) pro Q(uaestore) (*c.* 88–87 BC). The magistrate seems to be Q. Braetius Sura, legate to the Macedonian governor C. Sentius Saturninus (93–87 BC). 16.22 g. ANS 1964.156.1.

of the province, and the coins also bear two symbols of Aesillas' office, a chair (*sella*) and money chest (*cista*). These coins are a truly remarkable mix of Greek and Roman elements. The obverse type depicts the great Macedonian 'national' hero, Alexander, and declares (in Greek) that this is a coinage 'of the Macedonians'. The reverse type, by contrast, bears the name of a Roman financial magistrate in Latin, along with his official paraphernalia.

A year or two after the beginning of the 'Aesillas' series, the name Aesillas Q(uaestor) on the reverse was briefly replaced by Svvra Leg(atus) pro Q(uastore) (Fig. 9.11). To all appearances, this coin series was originally meant to bear a changing series of Roman magistrates' names on the reverse, reflecting the rotation of the province's financial officers. For whatever reason, this did not transpire. After the single Svvra issue, the legend Aesillas Q(uaestor) reappears on the coinage and remains unchanged for twenty years or so (*c.* 90–70 BC). No quaestor could have stayed in office for more than a couple of years at most, and so we must be dealing with a 'fossilization' of the first issue of the series. Hoard evidence suggests that much of the Aesillas coinage travelled northwards into inland Thrace (modern Bulgaria). Like the abundant Thasian-type tetradrachms minted in the same period (Chapter 2, p. 29; Callataÿ 2009a: 59–70), the Aesillas issues were probably struck to pay Thracian auxiliaries in the Roman army stationed in Macedonia. Once they had got used to receiving their pay in the form of Aesillas tetradrachms, the coins' chief users did not want any changes to the 'look' of their pay-packet.

Figure 9.12. Cistophoric tetradrachm, struck at Ephesus (129/8 BC). The coin is dated to Year 6 (the large C-shaped symbol on the reverse) of a civic era of Ephesus. 12.10 g. ANS 1951.5.33.

Figure 9.13. Cistophoric tetradrachm, struck at Ephesus (122/1 BC). The legend below the snakes and bow-case on the reverse reads C. Ati-n. C.f. 12.55 g. RBW collection (ex *CNG* 69, 396).

III Asia

Continuity is also evident in the coinages struck during the first hundred years or so of the Roman province of Asia. As we have seen (Chapter 4, pp. 77–82), the chief silver coinage of the second-century Attalid kingdom was the so-called cistophoric coinage, based on a very light drachm of *c.* 3.05 g. Cistophoric tetradrachms continued to be struck in large numbers after the Roman annexation of the Attalid realm (*c.* 129 BC), both by the old Attalid minting authorities (Ephesus, Pergamum, Tralles, Apamea and others) and by new cistophoric mints such as Synnada and Nysa (Kleiner 1978; 1979; Metcalf, forthcoming). The abundant post-Attalid cistophori of Ephesus are dated by a new civic era starting in 134/3 BC (Fig. 9.12; Rigsby 1979). Thanks to this, we can precisely date the first appearance of a Roman official on coins of the new Roman province of Asia. In 122/1 BC, the Ephesian mint struck a series of cistophori and gold staters bearing on the reverse (in Latin) the name C. At-in(ius) C.f. (Fig. 9.13; Callataÿ 2011a: 61). This man is presumably C. Atinius Labeo, praetor in Asia in either 122 or 121 BC; why his name should appear on this single issue of Ephesian coinage is impossible to say.

The post-Attalid cistophori were clearly in some sense the 'official' coinage of the Roman province. The dated cistophori of Ephesus show sharp peaks of production during or just after the First and Third Mithradatic Wars (83–79 BC and 70–67 BC), when Roman expenditure in Asia must have been particularly intense (Callataÿ 2011a: 71–3). As in Macedonia, Roman involvement in the minting of cistophori becomes increasingly evident in the course of the first century BC. The 'civic' cistophori of Ephesus, Tralles and Pergamum (and presumably other cities too) came to an abrupt end in 67/6 BC. From 58 to 49 BC, a new series of cistophori was struck at various mints, now bearing the names of Roman proconsuls of Asia and Cilicia (Fig. 9.14; Stumpf 1991: 17–55). The governor's name soon came to occupy the most prominent place on the reverse type: by the time of the Pergamene issues in the name of the general Metellus Pius in 49/8 BC (Fig. 9.15) there could no

Figure 9.14. Cistophoric tetradrachm, struck at Laodicea (51/50 BC). The reverse carries a familiar name: Tulliu(s) Imp(erator), none other than M. Tullius Cicero, governor of the Roman province of Cilicia in 51–50 BC. 11.38 g. ANS 1967.144.1.

Figure 9.15. Cistophoric tetradrachm, struck at Pergamum (49/8 BC). The reverse legend reads Q. Metellus Pius Scipio Imper(ator), and in place of the traditional bow-case, the snakes now curl around a legionary eagle. Metellus was governor of the new Roman province of Syria in 49 BC; these coins were struck while he wintered with his army in Asia at the end of that year. 11.98 g. ANS 1944.100.37493.

Figure 9.16. Cistophoric tetradrachm, perhaps struck at Pergamum (*c.* 48–39 BC). The reverse carries a large Q for Q(UAESTOR) and a Greek monogram, perhaps representing the Roman name ATRA(TINUS). 11.39 g. ANS 1951.5.101.

Figure 9.17. Cistophoric tetradrachm of Antony, struck at Ephesus (39 BC). The obverse bears the legend M. ANTONIUS IMP. COS. DESIG. ITER. ET TERT., 'M. Antonius, Imperator and Consul designate for the second and third time', while the reverse legend reads III. VIR. R(EI) P(UBLICAE) C(ONSTITUENDAE), '*triumvir* for reconstituting the Republic'. 11.89 g. ANS 1935.117.40.

longer be any doubt who was calling the shots. At an uncertain date between 48 and 39 BC, a further large issue of cistophori was struck in Asia, with no indication of mint at all, but simply a large Latin Q for QUAESTOR (Fig. 9.16; Metcalf 2009).

In the triumviral period and the reign of Augustus, the cistophorus was gradually transformed into a very different kind of coinage altogether. The last coins with recognizable cistophoric types are the cistophori struck by Mark Antony in 39 BC, bearing his own portrait and that of his wife Octavia, probably on the model of Hellenistic royal portrait coins (Figs. 9.17–9.18; *RPC I*, 2201–2). Coins of cistophoric weight continued to be struck in Asia right down to the Severan period (Fig. 9.19), albeit with iconography that owed nothing at all to their Attalid predecessors (Sutherland 1970; Metcalf 1980).

As in mainland Greece, several civic silver coinages also continued to be struck in western Asia Minor during the late second and early first century

Figure 9.18. Cistophoric tetradrachm of Antony, struck at Ephesus (39 BC). The legends are the same as on Figure 9.17. The jugate portrait of Antony and Octavia on the obverse echoes Hellenistic royal coin portraits in the same format (above, Figures 8.9–8.10, 8.15). 11.70 g. ANS 1944.100.7032.

Figure 9.19. 'Cistophoric' tetradrachm of Augustus, struck at Pergamum (18 BC). The reverse depicts the Pergamene temple of Roma and Augustus, with the inscription ROM. ET AVGVST. on the architrave, and the legend COM(MUNE) ASIAE, 'League of Asia' to left and right. The Roman province of Asia was still officially designated as a *koinon* or 'League' of Greek cities. 12.02 g. ANS 1944.100.39187.

BC. One of the few civic coinages which can be closely dated is the silver coinage of Alexandria Troas (Bellinger 1961: 93–104). Between 165/4 and 136/5 BC, Alexandria minted a small series of Attic-weight tetradrachms in the name of the chief civic deity, Apollo Smintheus, dated by years of a local civic era (Chapter 3 above, p. 62, Fig. 3.23). After a sixteen-year pause, the series recommenced in 119/18 BC, and continued down to 66/5 BC. (It is striking that this coinage stops at exactly the same time as the 'civic' cistophoric coinages of Asia: above, p. 178.) As Fig. 9.20 vividly illustrates, the quality of die-engraving at Alexandria went sharply downhill in the first century – but otherwise this long-lived civic coinage carries no trace of the momentous political changes that the Alexandrians experienced between the 160s and the 60s BC. Indeed, a few cities, like Antioch on the Maeander, may not even have started striking silver coins until after the creation of the Roman province (Fig. 9.21). Very little work has been done on the bronze

Figure 9.20. Civic tetradrachm of Alexandria Troas (69/8 BC). The reverse carries the name of a civic deity (APOLLŌNOS ZMITHEŌS) to left and right, with an era date (Year 233) just to the right of the standing figure of Apollo. 15.97 g. ANS 1944.100.43677.

Figure 9.21. Civic tetradrachm of Antioch on the Maeander (early first century BC). Antioch seems not to have struck any coinage in the second century; the dating of these Attic-weight issues to the first century BC is based on their reduced weight-standard (see above, Chapter 6, pp. 124–7). 14.91 g. ANS 1992.139.1.

coins of Asia Minor in the early years of Roman rule, but the general impression is of a new abundance of civic bronzes, like the large four-denomination bronze coinage of Apamea in Phrygia (Chapter 7 above, p. 133).

The overall picture of coin production in the early Roman province of Asia is very similar to what we have already seen in Macedonia and mainland Greece. For a generation or two after the end of the Antigonid and Attalid monarchies, the coinages of Macedonia and Asia show effectively no sign of the Roman presence at all. In practice, a large proportion of the Republican *meris* coinages and the post-Attalid cistophori must no doubt have ended up in the hands of Roman legionaries and auxiliaries, but the story told by the coins themselves is one of continuity rather than change.

In Macedonia, the shift to more explicitly 'Roman' coinages comes around the turn of the century, with the LEG tetradrachms and the large issues of Aesillas the *quaestor*. In Asia, the turning point was a few decades later: civic silver coinages largely disappeared in the mid-60s BC, and the

Figure 9.22. Tetradrachm imitating the types of Philip I, struck at Antioch (54/3 BC). The main reverse legend reads 'of King Philip Epiphanes Philadelphus'. The monogram KRA below Zeus' knee represents M. Licinius Crassus, proconsul of Syria in 54/3 BC. 15.59 g. ANS 1944.100.65449.

cistophori took on a much more explicitly Roman character from the early 50s. Between 66 and 62 BC, Pompey had massively expanded Rome's commitments in the East, creating new provinces in Syria, Pontus-Bithynia and Cilicia (Sherwin-White 1984: 186–234). The 'Romanization' of Asiatic coinage in the 60s and early 50s BC fits neatly into this sudden hardening of Roman power in the eastern Mediterranean.

In parts of the Roman East, coins lacking explicit Roman iconography continued to be struck right down to the principate of Augustus. The coinage of the early Roman province of Syria (from 64 BC) is arguably the most startling example of all. Here, Roman officials simply copied the silver coins of the last Seleucid king but two, Philip I Philadelphus (reigned *c.* 87–75 BC). Between 57 BC and 14/13 BC, the main tetradrachm coinages of the province of Syria carried the 'fossilized' types of Philip I, with only unobtrusive monograms on the reverse to indicate their Roman origin (Fig. 9.22; McAlee 2007: nos. 1–28; Houghton, Lorber and Hoover 2008: I, 2489–91). It is hard to think that the Roman governors of Syria positively wished to proclaim continuity with the hapless late Seleucid monarchs. Rather, as everywhere in the East, Roman coin policy seems to have been driven by purely practical considerations. If Philip's tetradrachms were the most widely accepted coins circulating in mid-first-century Syria, then Rome would cheerfully strike such tetradrachms too. The apparent 'meaning' of the types was simply not all that important.

IV The coming of the denarius – or not

Another way of approaching the transition to Roman rule in the eastern Mediterranean is to focus on changes in coin circulation, and in particular the movement of Roman coins into the Greek world. The Late Republican denarius was a silver coin weighing around 3.86 g, originally equivalent to ten bronze asses (the word *denarius* means 'tenner'), re-tariffed in *c.* 141 BC at sixteen asses (Woytek 2012). From the mid-second century BC onwards, denarii were struck in spectacular numbers at Rome, occasionally accompanied by smaller silver denominations such as the quinarius, a half-denarius piece (King 2007: 1–56).

In the second century BC, very few denarii travelled east of the Adriatic. The best-known body of evidence is a very large hoard of silver coins from Agrinion, in the far west of ancient Aetolia (*IGCH* 271; Thompson 1968a). This hoard – now partially held by the American Numismatic Society in New York – consists of some 1,348 silver coins, and seems to have been buried shortly after 129 BC (Warren 1999b: 376). The main bulk of the hoard is made up of Greek silver triobols on the 'symmachic' weight-standard (see above, Chapter 4, p. 69; Chapter 7, p. 140). More than half of the hoard consists of coins struck by cities of the Achaean League (838 triobols), with smaller numbers of civic triobols of Megalopolis in Arcadia (151), the Aetolian League (97), Sicyon (50) and others (Fig. 9.23–9.25). Crucially for its dating, the hoard also included 39 Athenian 'New Style' tetradrachms and, remarkably, 39 Roman Republican denarii (Figs. 9.26–9.28).

Figure 9.23. Silver triobol of the Achaean League, struck at Megalopolis (*c.* 192–188 BC), from the Agrinion hoard. 2.43 g. ANS 1963.31.1101.

Figure 9.24. Silver civic triobol of Megalopolis (*c.* 182–168 BC), from the Agrinion hoard. The reverse does not carry the ethnic of Megalopolis; the monogram AR at bottom left reflects Megalopolis' status as the chief city of Arcadia. 2.20 g. ANS 1963.31.1026.

Figure 9.25. Silver triobol of the Aetolian League (*c.* 205–150 BC), from the Agrinion hoard. 2.49 g. ANS 1963.31.115.

Figure 9.26. 'New Style' wreathed tetradrachm of Athens (130/29 BC), from the Agrinion hoard. This and the denarius of Q. Pilipus (Figure 9.28) are the latest datable coins in the hoard. 16.79 g. ANS 1963.31.270.

Figure 9.27. Roman denarius in the name of M. OPEIMI(US) (*c.* 131 BC), from the Agrinion hoard (*RRC* 254/1). 3.91 g. ANS 1963.31.38.

Figure 9.28. Roman denarius in the name of Q. PILIPUS (129 BC), from the Agrinion hoard (*RRC* 259/1). This coin is in near-mint condition, suggesting that the hoard was buried not long after 129 BC. 3.80 g. ANS 1963.31.39.

The Agrinion hoard has played an important role in fixing the chronology of several Greek issues, notably the early Achaean League coinage. But what is most striking about the hoard is its complete isolation in the second-century numismatic landscape (Callataÿ 2011a: 56–8). No other mainland Greek hoard before the Sullan period contains more than one or two stray denarii. It is best to see the Agrinion hoard – perhaps the accumulated pay and booty of a Roman soldier? – as the exception that proves the rule: in the late second century BC, Greece was still essentially a denarius-free zone.

Things gradually started to change in the last years of the Roman Republic. Greek civic silver issues were still being struck in abundant quantities during the Sullan period, but the large Peloponnesian silver triobol issues seem all to have come to an end by the 30s BC (Warren

1999b; Grandjean 1999). Denarii become increasingly abundant in Greek hoards of the mid-first century BC (Crawford 1985: 197), and the triumviral and Augustan periods may even have seen a few denarii being struck on the Greek mainland (*RPC I*, p. 245). The denarius makes its first appearances in Greek inscriptions around the middle of the century. An inscription from Messene concerning a new tax imposed by Rome (*c.* 70–30 BC) uses Greek monetary terminology in assessing the property of the tax-payers (staters, drachms, obols), but the total sum payable is given in denarii (Migeotte 1997). In Thessaly, the denarius did not replace the local Thessalian League staters (Chapter 4, p. 71) until well into the Augustan period: we have an edict of Augustus from the city of Pherae imposing a fixed conversion rate between Thessalian staters and denarii (Helly 1997).

All the evidence suggests that the movement of 'Roman' coinage into mainland Greece before the age of Augustus was slow and patchy at best. The same was true of the movement of currency in the other direction: there is no sign that Hellenistic Greek coins ever circulated in Italy to any great extent. A large hoard from Poggio Picenze in the central Appennines (*IGCH* 2056), buried in around 80 BC, contained what seems at first sight to be a quite extraordinary mix of Greek and Roman coins: around 200 Roman denarii, some 250 Achaean League triobols, 93 Athenian New Style tetradrachms (including 13 New Style imitations struck by Sulla in 86/5 BC), and 12 royal tetradrachms of Mithradates VI of Pontus, Ariarathes IV of Cappadocia and Nicomedes III of Bithynia. In fact, this hoard is very likely to be the pay and booty accumulated by a single Sullan legionary during service in the East in the mid-80s, and hence tells us very little about coin circulation in Italy.

In Asia Minor, hoard evidence (or rather its absence) suggests that the denarius was an even rarer sight than in mainland Greece. However, there is one suggestive pattern of evidence implying that the denarius was not completely unknown. The 40s and 30s BC saw a widespread (and unexpected) revival of Attic-weight tetradrachms in inland and southern Asia Minor. The Roman client-king Amyntas of Galatia (reigned 37/6–25 BC) struck a large issue of tetradrachms with types modelled on the abundant second-century coinage of Side in Pamphylia (Figs. 9.29–9.30). Anonymous imitations of Sidetan and other second-century Pamphylian tetradrachms were also struck in large quantities somewhere in southern Asia Minor, perhaps by Roman authorities in the region (Fig. 9.31; Meadows 2006; Meadows, 2014). These coins were all struck on a very light variant of the Attic weight-standard (*c.* 16.00 g), and may well have been intended to

Figure 9.29. Tetradrachm of Amyntas of Galatia (*c.* 37/6–25 BC). The reverse legend reads Basileōs Amyntou, 'of King Amyntas'. 15.96 g. ANS 1944.100.62286.

Figure 9.30. Tetradrachm of Side (*c.* 185–170 BC), with magistrate's name Kleu (charēs). The obverse bears a Seleucid anchor countermark on Athena's helmet. 16.43 g. ANS 1944.100.50927.

Figure 9.31. Late Republican imitation tetradrachm of Side (*c.* 40–20 BC). The magistrate's name, Kleuch(arēs), is copied from the genuine second-century tetradrachms of Side. 15.85 g. ANS 1944.100.50929.

circulate at par with four denarii. Similarly, several other late first-century coinages of southern Asia Minor seem to imitate the weight-standard of the Roman quinarius (the late drachms of the Lycian League, and silver coins of Stratonicea and Tabae in Caria). But the lack of hard evidence for the circulation of Roman denarii and quinarii in Asia makes this difficult to prove.

V   Survival and transformation

The Greek-speaking world of the eastern Mediterranean and western Asia underwent two great political transformations in the second half of the first millennium BC: the Macedonian conquest of the late fourth century, and the 'long' Roman conquest of the second and first centuries BC. Seen through the lens of coinage, as this chapter has tried to show, the two conquests look very different indeed. The conquest of the Persian empire by Alexander the Great led to a massive unification of the currency systems of Greece and the Near East. By the end of the fourth century BC, the Attic weight-standard held sway from the Balkans to the Hindu Kush; a homogeneous international style, based on the Alexander tetradrachm, was adopted by kings from Sicily to Arabia. By contrast, the Roman conquest of the Greek East is all but invisible in the sphere of coinage. Despite the political unification that came with Roman rule, Greek coinages of the second and first centuries BC saw no return to Alexander-style homogeneity. Instead, the early Roman governors of the eastern provinces faithfully preserved the local weight-standards and civic and royal types of the Greek East (Achaean League triobols, light-weight Asian cistophori, Seleucid royal tetradrachms...).

Eventually, of course, the eastern Roman coinages did settle into a distinctive new 'Graeco-Roman' style. From the reign of Augustus onwards, the bronze coinages of the Greek East usually carried a portrait of the reigning emperor on the obverse, with a local civic type on the reverse. Like the *polis* coinages of the Hellenistic period, these coins served as a means of expressing local identity and civic pride in a changed world (Howgego 2005). The example illustrated here (Fig. 9.32), from Apamea in Phrygia, depicts a local myth on the reverse, the landing of Noah's Ark on the hills around Apamea (Thonemann 2011: 88–98). Roman imperial coin portraits, too, owed a great deal to the traditions of Hellenistic royal portraiture. On the Apamean coin, the young emperor Severus Alexander is depicted in idealized right-facing profile, with a radiate crown on his head. The style and divinizing iconography would have been instantly familiar to any Hellenistic Greek viewer.

On the outer eastern fringes of the Roman empire, Hellenistic styles of coinage continued unbroken throughout the Roman imperial period. The Bosporan kingdom of the northern Black Sea – a small rump state carved out of the vast Pontic realm of Mithradates VI – survived as a Roman client-kingdom as late as the fourth century AD. The coins of the later Bosporan

Figure 9.32. Bronze coin of Apamea in Phrygia, struck under Severus Alexander (AD 222–35). Like many Hellenistic civic coin issues, the reverse bears the name of the magistrate who paid for the coinage, a certain P. Aelius Tryphon. 20.22 g. SNG Von Aulock 3506.

Figure 9.33. Gold stater of Sauromates I of the Cimmerian Bosporus (AD 120). The obverse carries a splendid Hellenistic-style royal portrait with the legend Βασιλεῶς Σαυρωματου, 'of King Sauromates'; the reverse depicts the Roman emperor Hadrian. 7.80 g. ANS 1944.100.41026.

Figure 9.34. Drachm of Artabanus IV of Parthia, struck at Ecbatana (AD 216–24). Although rendered in increasingly abstract fashion, the obverse and reverse types have hardly changed since the first century BC (Figures 5.9–5.10 above). 3.12 g. ANS 1944.100.83566.

kings stand in a direct line of descent from the late Hellenistic royal coinages of Mithradates VI and Pharnaces II (Chapter 8, Figs. 8.39 and 8.42): their splendid royal portraits show kings with Hellenistic diadems, shoulder-length 'Mithradatic' hair, and lush moustaches and beards (Fig. 9.33; Frolova and Ireland 2002; MacDonald 2005). In Mesopotamia and Iran, Parthian royal coinage remained faithful to its Hellenistic roots right down to the end of the dynasty in the third century AD (Fig. 9.34; Sinisi 2012: 288–9). The Sasanian Persian kings who succeeded the Parthians in the Near East carried on this particular strand of the

Figure 9.35. Sasanian gold dinar of Narseh (AD 293–303). The legend on the obverse reads 'The Mazda-worshipper, the divine Narseh, King of Kings of Iran, who is descended from the Gods'. The fire altar on the reverse also appears on the coins of the Hellenistic *fratarakā* in western Iran (Figures 5.1 and 5.3). 7.41 g. ANS 1967.154.7.

Figure 9.36. Arab-Sasanian silver drachm in the name of Ziyād bin Abī Sufyān, struck at Dārābgerd (AD 675). The obverse type is closely modelled on Sasanian coinage, but bears the Islamic legend 'in the name of Allah' on the lower right-hand rim. 3.78 g. ANS 1971.316.1391.

Figure 9.37. British 50 pence piece. The obverse legend reads Elizabeth II D(ei) G(ratia) Reg(ina) F(idei) D(efensor) 1997, 'Elizabeth II, Queen by the grace of God, Defender of the Faith'. The reverse type, designed by Christopher Ironside, depicts Britannia in good Hellenistic style.

Hellenistic coinage tradition deep into late antiquity, whence it would eventually be passed on to the early Islamic world (Figs. 9.35–9.36).

And the numismatic legacy of Alexander is still with us today. As I write this paragraph, I have in my pocket a slightly worn British 50 pence piece, dated 1997. On the obverse, it carries an idealized youthful portrait, in right-facing profile, of the reigning monarch; the reverse bears a seated

Figure 9.38. Tetradrachm of Lysimachus, struck at Pergamum (*c.* 287–282 BC). 16.96 g. ANS 1966.75.102.

deity with shield and trident, wearing a Corinthian helmet (Fig. 9.37; Eustace 2007). The monarch is Elizabeth II, and the seated figure is a personification of Britannia. But I imagine that the young Macedonian conqueror would have had little trouble in recognizing his distant descendant.

Guide to further reading

The best short introduction to Hellenistic history and culture is Frank Walbank's *The Hellenistic World* (London, 1981; revised edition, Cambridge, MA, 1993). For recent developments in the field, the collection of essays edited by Andrew Erskine, *A Companion to the Hellenistic World* (Malden, MA, 2003), is highly recommended. Graham Shipley's *The Greek World after Alexander, 323–30 BC* (London and New York, 2000) is particularly valuable for its close reading of documentary and literary sources. Michel Austin's *The Hellenistic World from Alexander to the Roman Conquest* (second edition, Cambridge, 2006) offers a wide selection of ancient sources in translation.

Specialized monographs on the various Hellenistic kingdoms abound. Among the countless biographies of Alexander the Great, Pierre Briant's *Alexander the Great and his Empire: a Short Introduction* (Princeton, 2010) stands out for its clarity and intelligence. There is no wholly satisfactory book on the 'successor' period (323–281 BC). For the Seleucid kingdom, the best starting point is the ground-breaking monograph by Susan Sherwin-White and Amélie Kuhrt, *From Samarkhand to Sardis: a New Approach to the Seleucid Empire* (London, 1993). Günther Hölbl's *A History of the Ptolemaic Empire* (London and New York, 2001) provides a lucid narrative of Ptolemaic history. My own *Attalid Asia Minor: Money, International Relations, and the State* (Oxford, 2013) is a recent collection of essays on the Attalids of Pergamum, with a particular focus on coinage.

The economic history of the Hellenistic world has flourished in recent years. A sense of the vitality of the field can be gained from three recent collections of essays edited by Zofia Archibald and others, *Hellenistic Economies* (London, 2001), *Making, Moving and Managing: the New World of Ancient Economies, 323–31 BC* (Oxford, 2005) and *The Economies of Hellenistic Societies, Third to First Centuries BC* (Oxford, 2011). A good overview of Hellenistic art can be found in J. J. Pollitt, *Art in the Hellenistic Age* (Cambridge, 1986), and royal coin portraiture is extensively treated in R. R. R. Smith, *Hellenistic Royal Portraits* (Oxford, 1988).

Incomparably the best introduction to ancient Greek and Roman coinage is Christopher Howgego's *Ancient History from Coins* (London and New York, 1995). There are several excellent papers in the volume edited by Andrew Meadows and Kirsty Shipton, *Money and its Uses in the Ancient Greek World* (Oxford, 2001); *The Oxford Handbook of Greek and Roman Coinage*, edited by W. E. Metcalf (Oxford, 2012), has a wide selection of good introductory essays. On Hellenistic coinage, Otto Mørkholm's *Early Hellenistic Coinage from the Accession of Alexander to the Peace of Apamea (336–188 BC)* (Cambridge, 1991) is detailed and authoritative. Much of the best specialized recent work on Hellenistic coinage can be found in the Bibliography under the names of François de Callatäy, Georges Le Rider and Andrew Meadows.

APPENDICES (by Andrew Meadows)

1 Glossary of numismatic terms

Authority The formal guarantor of the value of a coin. For civic coinages, the authority is generally presumed to be the government of the city itself. Within kingdoms and empires, the authority may be the supreme ruler (e.g. king or emperor), or an appointee (e.g. satrap or provincial governor).

Axis See **Die-axis**

Circulation The movement of coinage once it has been issued. The circulation of ancient coinage can be studied through the evidence of **hoards** and **single finds**, as well as from documentary sources.

Circulation wear The wear (or deterioration in condition) visible on a coin due to the time it has spent in **circulation**.

Control-mark A mark or symbol of some kind, generally on the **reverse** of a coin, apparently indicating some aspect of the administration of coin production.

Countermark A mark in the form of letter(s), a symbol, a **monogram** or a combination of these punched into a coin after its minting. The reason for the application of such marks is not always certain, and probably varied from case to case. Some served to reauthorize a coin for **circulation** in new areas. Others perhaps assigned new **denominations** to old coins.

Denomination The value of an ancient coin. These values are generally expressed in a standard set of units, subdivisions and multiples. See futher below: Denominational systems, pp. 197–8.

Die A piece of metal engraved with a design and then used to **strike** coins. Two dies were required to strike the two faces of a coin: the **obverse die** and the **reverse die**.

Die-axis The relative orientation of **obverse** and **reverse** images on a coin.

Die-engraver The artist responsible for the engraving of the design on to **dies**. They are generally anonymous on ancient coinage, although a few signatures are recorded, particularly in late fifth-century Sicily.

Die study A technical numismatic study of a coinage that involves the identification of the **dies** used to **strike** a coinage. Such studies allow for the establishment of the relative chronology of a coinage. They also permit quantification of a coinage by identifying the number of dies used to produce a given coinage.

Die-wear The wear, or damage, experienced by a **die** in the course of its use to **strike** coins. This may take the form of gradual deterioration or sudden breaks. It can be used by numismatists as part of a **die study** to determine the relative chronology of production.

Emergency hoard A hoard of coins, and perhaps other precious objects, secreted together in antiquity at a time of emergency. Such deposits tend to consist of a cross-section of coins in **circulation** at the time of deposit. They may thus serve as evidence for the nature of the coin supply at a given time.

Ethnic A **legend** indicating the collective group of people (usually the citizens of a city, but sometimes the members of a wider federal association) acting as the **authority** behind a coinage.

Exergue The area on a coin below the ground-line of a design.

Fiduciary Coinage that takes its value not from the character and quantity of the metal that it contains, but from the *fiat* of the **authority** behind it.

Field An empty area of a coin design where subsidiary symbols such as **mint-marks, control-marks** or **legends** may be placed.

Flan The metal blank from which a coin is struck.

Hoard A group of coins deposited together in antiquity, and thus forming a single archaeological context for multiple objects. The reasons for deposit are likely to have been varied, and are rarely recoverable with certainty from the archaeological deposits. Categories of hoard include (but are perhaps not limited to) **savings hoards, emergency hoards** and **ritual deposits**.

Imitation A coin that, more or less slavishly, copies the **types** of a model coinage, but is not a product of the same **authority** as its model.

Intrinsic Coinage that takes its value from the character and quantity (weight) of metal that it contains.

Issue Either the process of offcially placing a coin into circulation; or a specific subsection of a period of coin production, identifiable by specific **control-marks** or **mint-magistrates'** signatures.

Issuer The person administratively responsible for the production of a coin. The identity and indeed status of the issuer of an ancient coin is often unclear. The terms **moneyer** and **mint-magistrate** are often used to refer to officials known or assumed to have been responsible for the production of coin within a state.

Legend The inscription(s) that appear on a coin. These most often occur on the **reverse** on Archaic, Classical and Hellenistic Greek coins, but appear on Roman coins on the **obverse** too, whence the habit passed to the Eastern Roman provinces and, ultimately, to the modern world.

Mint A place where coins are produced. In the vast majority of ancient cases, no evidence exists for the nature or physical locations of mints, and many may not have consisted of permanent facilities. The term is therefore rather loosely used (at least for the ancient world) to indicate place and facility of production.

Mint-magistrate The official, whether elected or appointed, responsible for oversight of the production of coins within the **mint**. The names of many private individuals that appear on ancient coins are assumed to be those of mint-magistrates. See also **moneyer**.

Mint-mark A mark engraved, generally into the **reverse die**, to indicate the mint in which a coin was produced. Such marks may consist of letters, symbols or **monograms**. They may appear in association with **control-marks**.

Moneyer The official, whether elected or appointed, responsible for oversight of the production of coins within the **mint**. The term is most commonly used in ancient numismatics to refer to the **mint-magistrates** of the Roman Republican mint.

Monogram An identifying mark made up of a number of letters overlaid and/or ligatured. These are often found on coins as **mint-marks** or **control-marks**, or in **countermarks**.

Obverse The 'heads' side of a coin, produced by the **obverse die**. It is most often the side of the coin on which a portrait or other form of head is depicted, and sometimes thereby provides an indication of the **authority** behind the coin. See also **Reverse**.

Obverse die The die used to **strike** the **obverse** side of a coin.

Overstrike A coin produced by **striking** an existing coin with a new pair of **dies**. Overstrikes tend to be imperfect, and thus allow identification both of the designs of the original coin and of those struck over it.

Posthumous coinage A coinage produced in the name of a ruler, after his or her death.

Reverse The 'tails' side of the coin, produced by the **reverse die**. It is often the side of the coin bearing the **legend**, and thus provides a clear indication of where the coin was produced. See also **obverse**.

Reverse die   The die used to **strike** the **reverse** side of a coin.

Ritual deposit   A group of coins deposited together, not for the purpose of saving, but for religious purposes such as offerings to gods. Unlike many **hoards**, such deposits were arguably not intended to be recovered.

Savings hoard   A group of coins gathered together in a single deposit over a period of time, for the purpose of saving.

Single find   A coin found in isolation, either by accident, or by deliberate means such as metal-detecting. This may or may not occur within a controlled archaeological survey or excavation environment.

Strike   The process by which the majority of ancient coins were produced. This consisted of placing a blank of metal (**flan**) on the **obverse die**, positioning the **reverse die** on top of the blank, and then applying force in the form of hammer blows (striking) to imprint the designs of the two dies on to the piece of metal.

Test-cut   A cut made into an **intrinsic** value coin to ensure that it is made of solid metal, and not plated.

Type   The numismatic term for the design that appears on a coin; this may thus be subdivided into **obverse** and **reverse** types.

Weight-standard   The official system of weights in use in an ancient state. In an **intrinsic value** coinage, value depended on weight. Weight-standards thus become a means of unifying or dividing **circulation** of coinage, depending on decisions taken about adoption or rejection of specific weight-standards.

2 Denominational systems

(a) Greece

The Greek world was not, at any period, unified by a single monetary system. In the Archaic and Classical periods, different city-states adopted different weight-standards for their silver coinages. Moreover, different denominational structures were also used in different places. We are best informed about the denominations in use at the city of Athens, thanks to the spread of Athenian influence in the fifth century BC, and the fact that the Athenian (Attic) system was later adopted and spread by Alexander the Great.

The basic unit was the drachm ('handful'), which was sub-divided into six obols ('spits'). All other silver denominations were named by reference to these two basic units of account. The drachm and obol were not the most common denominations, however. In many states, Athens included, the main denomination was the tetradrachm (four drachms). Decadrachms (ten drachms), didrachms (two drachms), drachms (one drachm) and hemidrachms (half-drachms) were also produced. In addition to the obol, diobols (two obols), hemiobols (half-obols), tetartemoria (quarter-obols) and hemitetartemoria (eighth-obols) were also produced. Such small denominations, less than a drachm in value, are often described today as 'fractions'. In this extensive array of denominations, Athens was exceptional. Most states confined themselves to one or two denominations. The principal denomination in use in a state could also be referred to as a 'stater' or 'standard coin'.

For accounting purposes, units larger than the drachm were available. A 'mna' or 'mnaieion' consisted of 100 drachms, and a 'talent' was made up of 60 mnas or 6,000 drachms. The equivalences in grams of silver of the basic Athenian units of account were:

1 obol = 0.72 g
1 drachm = 6 obols = 4.30 g
1 mna = 100 drachms = 430 g
1 talent = 60 mnas = 600 drachms = 25.80 kg.

During the Hellenistic period bronze coinage became common in many states. At Athens the obol was divided into 8 bronze *chalkoi*. Half, one, two and four chalkous coins are known.

(b) Rome

The Roman monetary system before the Second Punic War (218–201 BC) was complex and unstable. The earliest silver coinage of the late fourth/early third century was essentially based on the Greek drachm system, on a variety of different standards. From the start this coinage was accompanied by bronze money in various forms. The basic Roman bronze unit was the 'as', originally weighing one Roman pound, or approximately 324 g (12 ounces). By the end of the third century the weight of the as had dropped to around 35 g. Around 212 BC the Roman state introduced a new silver denomination known as the denarius (ten as piece). This would remain the basic Roman silver coin until the third century AD. In 141 BC the denarius was re-tariffed at 16 asses. The full range of denominations issued in silver and bronze under the Republic can be set out as follows:

Silver
1 denarius = 10 or 16 asses
1 quinarius = half denarius = 5 or 8 asses
1 sestertius = quarter denarius = 2 1/2 or 4 asses

Bronze
1 as (= 1/10 or 1/16 denarius)
1 semis = half as
1 triens = quarter as
1 quadrans = third as
sextans = sixth as
uncia = twelfth as

Under Augustus the bronze coinage was reformed to produce the following denominations:

Sestertius (4 asses or 1/4 denarius)
Dupondius (2 asses or half sestertius)
As (quarter sestertius)
Semis (half as)
Quadrans (quarter as)

In addition the gold aureus, which had started to be produced in serious quantities by Julius Caesar, was standardized at a value of 25 denarii.

3 The manufacture and material of ancient coinage

Ancient coinage was hand made, in two senses. First, the actual process of striking the coins was carried out by hand. A coin was produced by placing a blank piece of metal on a die set within an anvil, or similar anchoring device. This is known to numismatists as the 'obverse die', or sometimes the 'anvil die'. A second die on the end of a punch (the 'reverse die') was then placed on top of the blank and hit forcefully with a hammer, probably several times. The result was a flat, roundish piece of metal with, usually, designs or 'types' on both sides (Fig. 10.1).

The second hand-crafted element of coin production was the engraving of the designs that appeared on ancient coins. Unlike modern coin dies, which are all mechanically copied from a single master engraving, each ancient die was individually engraved and thus different from every other. These two elements of hand production create an interesting mixture of results. On the one hand, there is an individuality of design of dies, which allows us to trace the products of an ancient mint in a way that is impossible for modern coins. It also allows us to count the number of dies used to produce a particualr coinage, and thus to quantify it. On the other hand, manual striking, although not nearly so fast as modern machine production, allows for the production of thousands of identical or closely similar objects within a very short space of time. Coins, in this sense, are one of the very rare examples from the pre-modern world of mass production.

The substance of ancient coinage was also profoundly different from that of today's coins. In origin, coinage was a monetary instrument of intrinsic value. The earliest coins, produced in Asia Minor from the mid-seventh to mid-sixth century BC were made of carefully controlled amounts of electrum, the alloy of gold and silver. Subsequently, most probably under the influence of the prevailing monetary tradition of the Near East, coinage came largely to be produced in high-quality silver (from the latter part of the sixth century BC through to the first century AD), with gold being produced when circumstances of supply or demand particularly prompted it.

The fact that these precious metal coins took their value from their weight often made it possible for them to circulate over wide areas, and beyond the borders of the political authorities that had produced them. Nevertheless, there were constraining factors. The novelty of coinage, in

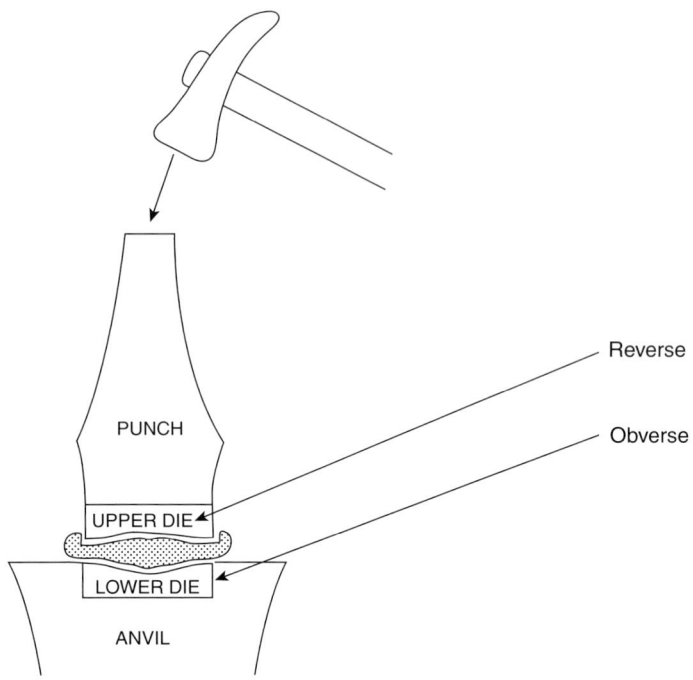

Figure 10.1. The minting of ancient coins.

contrast to the earlier Near Eastern practice of making payments with weighed amounts of silver bullion, lay both in the carefully regulated weights (denominations) at which coins were produced, which added facility of use, and in the designs that were struck on them, which provided clear statement of origin, and thus guaranteed their metal quality (value). While both developments added convenience and functionality, they also served potentially to constrain monetary behaviour. The localized system of weight-standards of the ancient world, according to which ancient coins were denominated, could serve to fragment as well as to unify monetary behaviour. Similarly a mark of guarantee could only function where it was recognized. This became particularly important after the phenomenon of bronze coinage arose in the latter part of the fifth century BC. Such coinages were, on the whole, produced as fiduciary instruments, whose value lay not so much in their metal content, which was far less tightly controlled than in precious metal coinage, but in the guaranteed system in which they circulated. Such fiduciary coinages depended for their value essentially on the confidence of the recipients of the coin in their ability to re-use it later.

Bibliography

Adams, J. P. (1980) 'Aristonikos and the cistophori', *Historia* 29: 302–14.

Ager, S. L. (2005) 'Familiarity breeds: incest and the Ptolemaic dynasty', *JHS* 125: 1–34.

Alföldi, M. R.- (1984) 'Der Stater des T. Quinctius Flamininus', *Numismatische Zeitschrift* 98: 19–26.

Allen, D. F. and Nash, D. (1980) *The Coins of the Ancient Celts.* Edinburgh.

Amedick, R. (2005) 'Iesus Nazarenus Rex Iudaiorum: Hellenistische Königsikonographie und das Neue Testament', in *Picturing the New Testament*, ed. A. Weissenrieder, F. Wendt and P. von Gemünden. Tübingen: 53–66.

Aperghis, G. G. (2001) 'Population – production – taxation – coinage: a model for the Seleukid economy', in *Hellenistic Economies*, ed. Z. H. Archibald, J. Davies, V. Gabrielsen and G. J. Oliver. London and New York: 69–102.

(2004) *The Seleukid Royal Economy: the Finances and Financial Administration of the Seleukid Empire.* Cambridge.

Archibald, Z. H. (2011) 'Mobility and innovation in Hellenistic economies', in *The Economies of Hellenistic Societies, Third to First Centuries BC*, ed. Z. H. Archibald, J. K. Davies and V. Gabrielsen. Oxford: 42–65.

Arnold-Biucchi, C. (2002) Review of Caltabiano, Carroccio and Oteri 1997, *BMCR* 05.08.2002.

Arslan, M. and Devecioğlu, Ü. (2011) 'Der hellenistische Münzschatz von Apameia: ein Vorbericht', in *Kelainai-Apameia Kibotos: Développement urbain dans le contexte anatolien*, ed. L. Summerer, A. Ivantchik and A. von Kienlin. Bordeaux: 309–15.

Ashton, R. H. J. (2001) 'The coinage of Rhodes 408–*c*. 190', in *Money and its Uses in the Ancient Greek World*, ed. A. Meadows and K. Shipton. Oxford: 79–115.

(2006) 'The beginning of bronze coinage in Karia and Lykia', *NC* 166: 1–14.

(2007) 'The pre-imperial coinage of Iasos', *NC* 167: 47–78.

(2012a) 'Cyme in Aeolis: Persic-weight didrachms, Seleucid Attic-weight coinage, and contemporary autonomous bronzes', *NC* 172: 27–34.

(2012b) 'The Hellenistic world: the cities of mainland Greece and Asia Minor', in *The Oxford Handbook of Greek and Roman Coinage*, ed. W. E. Metcalf. Oxford: 191–210.

(2013) 'The use of the cistophoric weight-standard outside the Pergamene kingdom', in *Attalid Asia Minor: Money, International Relations, and the State*, ed. P. Thonemann. Oxford: 245–64.

(forthcoming) 'The late Hellenistic brass and bronze coinage of Phrygian Apameia', in *Kelainai-Apameia Kibotos*, vol. II, ed. A. Ivantchik, A. von Kienlin and L. Summerer. Bordeaux.

Ashton, R. H. J. and Kinns, P. (2003) 'Opuscula Anatolica II', *NC* 163: 1–47.

(2004) 'Opuscula Anatolica III', *NC* 164: 71–83.

Ashton, R. H. J. and Meadows, A. (2008) 'The Letoon deposit', *NC* 168: 111–34.

Assar, G. F. (2006) 'A revised Parthian chronology of the period 91–55 BC', *Parthica* 8: 55–104.

Audouin, R. and Bernard, P. (1974) 'Trésor de monnaies indiennes et indo-grecques d'Aï Khanoum (Afghanistan)', *RN* 16 (6th series): 6–41.

Austin, M. (1986) 'Hellenistic kings, war, and the economy', *CQ* 36: 450–66.

(2006) *The Hellenistic World from Alexander to the Roman Conquest: a Selection of Ancient Sources in Translation*, second edition. Cambridge.

Badian, E. (1981) 'The deification of Alexander the Great', in *Ancient Macedonian Studies in Honor of C. F. Edson*, ed. H. J. Dell. Thessaloniki: 27–71.

Baldus, H. R. (1996) 'Die Münzfunde', in *Didyma III.1: Ein Kultbezirk an der Heiligen Strasse von Milet nach Didyma*, ed. K. Tuchelt. Mainz am Rhein: 217–23.

Bardill, J. (2012) *Constantine: Divine Emperor of the Christian Golden Age*. Cambridge.

Baron, C. A. (2013) *Timaeus of Tauromenium and Hellenistic Historiography*. Cambridge.

Bauslaugh, R. A. (2000) *Silver Coinage with the Types of Aesillas the Quaestor*. New York.

Bellinger, A. R. (1961) *Troy, Supplementary Monograph 2: the Coins*. Princeton.

Bérend, D. (1998) 'De l'or d'Agathocle', in *Studies in Greek Numismatics in Memory of Martin Jessop Price*, ed. R. Ashton and S. Hurter. London: 37–41.

Bergmann, M. (1998) *Die Strahlen der Herrscher. Theomorphes Herrscherbild und politische Symbolik im Hellenismus und in der römischen Kaiserzeit*. Mainz.

Bhandare, S. (2007) 'Not just a pretty face: interpretations of Alexander's numismatic imagery in the Hellenic East', in *Memory as History: the Legacy of Alexander in Asia*, ed. H. P. Ray and D. T. Potts. New Delhi: 208–56.

Billows, R. (2003) 'Cities', in *A Companion to the Hellenistic World*, ed. A. Erskine. Malden, MA: 196–215.

Bingen, J. (2007) *Hellenistic Egypt: Monarchy, Society, Economy, Culture*. Edinburgh.

Bloch, M. and Parry, J. (1989) 'Introduction', in *Money and the Morality of Exchange*, ed. J. Parry and M. Bloch. Cambridge: 1–32.

Boehringer, C. (2008) 'Quelques remarques sur la circulation monétaire dans le Péloponnèse au IIe et au Ier siècle a.C.', in *Le Péloponnèse d'Épaminondas à Hadrien*, ed. C. Grandjean. Bordeaux: 83–9.

Boiy, T. (2004) *Late Achaemenid and Hellenistic Babylon*. Leuven.

Bopearachchi, O. (1991) *Monnaies gréco-bactriennes et indo-grecques: catalogue raisonné.* Paris.

(1998) *Sylloge Nummorum Graecorum. The Collection of the American Numismatic Society, Part 9: Graeco-Bactrian and Indo-Greek Coins.* New York.

Bosworth, A. B. (2002) *The Legacy of Alexander: Politics, Warfare, and Propaganda under the Successors.* Oxford.

Boudet, R. and Depeyrot, G. (1997) *Monnaies gauloises à la croix.* Wetteren.

Bracey, R. (2011) 'New histories of central and south Asia', in *The British Museum and the Future of UK Numismatics*, ed. B. Cook. London: 44–52.

Bresson, A. (1999) 'Rhodes and Lycia in Hellenistic times', in *Hellenistic Rhodes: Politics, Culture, and Society*, ed. V. Gabrielsen, P. Bilde, T. Engberg-Pedersen, L. Hannestad and J. Zahle. Aarhus: 98–131.

(2005) 'Coinage and money in the Hellenistic age', in *Making, Moving and Managing: the New World of Ancient Economies, 323–31 BC*, eds. Z. H. Archibald, J. K. Davies and V. Gabrielsen. Oxford: 44–72.

(2006) 'The Athenian mint in the second century BC and the Amphictionic decree', *Annali* 52: 45–85.

Briant, P. (1982) *Etat et pasteurs au Moyen-Orient ancien.* Cambridge and Paris.

(2002) *From Cyrus to Alexander: a History of the Persian Empire.* Winona Lake, IN.

(2006) 'L'Asie Mineure en transition', in *La transition entre l'empire achéménide et les royaumes hellénistiques*, ed. P. Briant and F. Joannès. Paris: 309–51.

(2010) *Alexander the Great and his Empire: a Short Introduction.* Princeton.

Bryce, T. R. (1986) *The Lycians: a Study of Lycian History and Civilisation to the Conquest of Alexander the Great, I: the Lycians in Literary and Epigraphic Sources.* Copenhagen.

Burnett, A. M. (1986) 'The iconography of Roman coin types in the third century BC', *NC* 146: 67–75.

Cabanes, P. (1976) *L'Épire de la mort de Pyrrhos à la conquête romaine (272–167 av. J.C.).* Paris.

Callataÿ, F. de (1994a) 'Réflexions sur les ateliers d'Asie Mineure d'Alexandre le Grand', in *Trésors et circulation monétaire en Anatolie antique*, ed. M. Amandry and G. Le Rider. Paris: 19–35.

(1994b) *Les tétradrachmes d'Orodès II et de Phraate IV.* Paris.

(1997) *L'histoire des guerres mithridatiques vue par les monnaies.* Louvain-la-Neuve.

(1998) 'Les monnaies hellénistiques en argent de Ténédos', in *Studies in Greek Numismatics in Memory of Martin Jessop Price*, ed. R. Ashton and S. Hurter. London: 99–114.

(2000) 'Guerres et monnayages à l'époque hellénistique', in *Économie antique. La guerre dans les économies antiques*, ed. J. Andreau, P. Briant and R. Descat. Saint-Bertrand de-Comminges: 337–64.

(2004) 'Le premier monnayage de la cité d'Amastris (Paphlagonie)', *SNR* 83: 57–86.

(2005) 'A quantitative survey of Hellenistic coinages: recent achievements', in *Making, Moving and Managing: the New World of Ancient Economies, 323–31 BC*, ed. Z. H. Archibald, J. K. Davies and V. Gabrielsen. Oxford: 73–91.

(2008) 'Les tétradrachmes hellénistiques au nom des Thasiens et la circulation monétaire en Thrace aux IIe et Ier s. av. J.-C.', *RBN* 154: 31–54.

(2009a) 'Armies poorly paid in coins (the Anabasis of the Ten-Thousands) and coins for soldiers poorly transformed by the markets (the Hellenistic Thasian-type tetradrachms) in ancient Greece', *RBN* 155: 51–70.

(2009b) 'The first royal coinages of Pontos (from Mithridates III to Mithridates V)', in *Mithridates VI and the Pontic Kingdom*, ed. J. M. Høtje. Aarhus: 63–94.

(2011a) 'More than it may seem: the use of coinage by the Romans in late Hellenistic Asia Minor (133–63 BC)', *AJN* 23: 55–86.

(2011b) 'Quantifying monetary production in Greco-Roman times: a general frame', in *Quantifying Monetary Production in Greco-Roman Times*, ed. F. de Callataÿ. Bari: 7–29.

Callieri, P. (2007) *L'archéologie du Fārs à l'époque hellénistique*. Paris.

Callot, O. (2010) 'A new chronology for the Arabian Alexanders', in Huth and van Alfen 2010: 383–402.

Caltabiano, M. C., Carroccio, B. and Oteri, E. (1997) *Siracusa Ellenistica. Le monete 'regali' di Ierone II, della sua famiglia e dei Siracusani*. Messina.

Cannadine, D. (1983) 'The context, performance and meaning of ritual: the British monarchy and the "invention of tradition", *c.* 1820–1977', in *The Invention of Tradition*, ed. E. Hobsbawm and T. Ranger. Cambridge: 101–64.

Carlsson, S. (2010) *Hellenistic Democracies: Freedom, Independence and Political Procedure in Some East Greek City-States*. Stuttgart.

Carney, E. D. (2013) *Arsinoë of Egypt and Macedon: a Royal Life*. Oxford.

Carradice, I. A. and La Niece, S. (1988) 'The Libyan War and coinage: a new hoard and the evidence of metal analysis', *NC* 148: 33–52.

Cartledge, P. and Spawforth, A. (2002) *Hellenistic and Roman Sparta: a Tale of Two Cities*, second edition. London and New York.

Casabonne, O. (2004) *La Cilicie à l'époque achéménide*. Paris.

Casevitz, M. and Frontisi-Ducroux, F. (1989) 'Le masque du "Phallen": Sur une épiclèse de Dionysos à Méthymna', *Revue de l'histoire des religions* 206/2: 115–27.

Ceccarelli, P. (2013) *Ancient Greek Letter Writing: a Cultural History (600–150 BC)*. Oxford.

Chandezon, C. (2000) 'Foires et panégyries dans le monde grec classique et hellénistique', *REG* 113: 70–100.

Chaniotis, A. (1995) 'Sich selbst feiern?' Die städtischen Feste des Hellenismus im Spannungsfeld zwischen Religion und Politik', in *Stadtbild und Bürgerbild im Hellenismus*, ed. P. Zanker and M. Wörrle. Munich: 147–72.

(2003) 'The divinity of Hellenistic rulers', in *A Companion to the Hellenistic World*, ed. A. Erskine. Malden, MA: 431–45.

(2005) *War in the Hellenistic World*. Malden, MA.

Chrubasik, B. (2013) 'The Attalids and the Seleukid kings, 281–175 BC', in *Attalid Asia Minor: Money, International Relations, and the State*, ed. P. Thonemann. Oxford: 83–119.

Çizmeli-Öğün, Z. and Marcellesi, M.-C. (2011) 'Résaux d'échanges réginaux en Asie Mineure occidentale: l'apport des monnaies de fouilles', in *Nomisma. La circulation monétaire dans le monde grec antique*, ed. T. Faucher, M.-Chr. Marcellesi and O. Picard. Athens: 297–342.

Clark, A. J. (2007) *Divine Qualities: Cult and Community in Republican Rome*. Oxford.

Cohen, G. M. (2013) *The Hellenistic Settlements in the East from Armenia and Mesopotamia to Bactria and India*. Berkeley, Los Angeles and London.

Coleman, K. M. (1990) 'Fatal charades: Roman executions staged as mythological enactments', *JRS* 80: 44–73.

Collis, J. (2003) *The Celts: Origins, Myths and Inventions*. Stroud.

Colvin, S. (2011) 'The koine: a new language for a new world', in *Creating a Hellenistic World*, ed. A. Erskine and L. Llewellyn-Jones. Swansea: 31–45.

Crawford, M. H. (1985) *Coinage and Money under the Roman Republic*. London.

Cribb, J. (2007) 'Money as a marker of cultural continuity and change in central Asia', in *After Alexander: Central Asia before Islam*, ed. J. Cribb and G. Herrmann. Oxford: 333–75.

Cunliffe, B. (2001) *The Extraordinary Journey of Pytheas the Greek*. London.

Curti, E., Dench, E. and Patterson, J. R. (1996) 'The archaeology of central and southern Roman Italy: recent trends and approaches', *JRS* 86: 170–89.

Curtis, V. S. (1998) 'The Parthian costume and headdress', in *Das Partherreich und seine Zeugnisse*, ed. J. Wiesehöfer. Stuttgart: 61–73.

(2007) 'Religious iconography on ancient Iranian coins', in *After Alexander: Central Asia before Islam*, ed. J. Cribb and G. Herrmann. Oxford: 413–34.

Cutroni Tusa, A. (1990) 'Monete macedoni ed ellenistische nei ripostigli siciliani', *Annali: Istituto Italiano di Numismatica* 37: 49–80.

Dąbrowa, E. (2008) 'The political propaganda of the first Arsacids and its targets', *Parthica* 10: 25–31; reprinted in Dąbrowa 2011: 89–97.

(2010) 'The Parthian kingship', in *Concepts of Kingship in Antiquity*, ed. G. B. Lanfranchi and R. Rollinger. Padua: 123–34; reprinted in Dąbrowa 2011: 111–21.

(2011) *Studia Graeco-Parthica*. Wiesbaden.

Dahmen, K. (2010) 'The numismatic evidence', in *A Companion to Ancient Macedonia*, ed. J. Roisman and I. Worthington. Malden, MA: 41–62.

Dany, O. (1999) *Akarnanien in Hellenismus: Geschichte und Völkerrecht in Nordwestgriechenland*. Munich.

Davesne, A. and Le Rider, G. (1989) *Gülnar II: Le trésor de Meydancıkkale (Cilicie Trachée, 1980)*. Paris.

Davis, N. and Kraay, C. M. (1973) *The Hellenistic Kingdoms: Portrait Coins and History*. London.

Delrieux, F. (2007) 'Frappes monétaires et cités grecques d'Asie Mineure occidentale de la mort d'Alexandre le Grand à la paix d'Apamée', *Pallas* 74: 129–59.

Depeyrot, G. (1999) *Les monnaies hellénistiques de Marseille*. Wetteren.

Derow, P. (2003) 'The arrival of Rome: from the Illyrian wars to the fall of Macedon', in *A Companion to the Hellenistic World*, ed. A. Erskine. Malden, MA: 51–70.

Doyen, C. (2012) *Étalons de l'argent et du bronze en Grèce hellénistique*. Louvain-la-Neuve.

Dubois, L. (1996) *Inscriptions grecques dialectales d'Olbia du Pont*. Geneva.

Ebert, J. (1972) *Griechische Epigramme auf Sieger an gymnischen und hippischen Agonen*. Berlin.

Engels, D. (2013) 'A new Frataraka chronology', *Latomus* 72/1: 28–80.

Engels, J. (2010) 'Macedonians and Greeks', in *A Companion to Ancient Macedonia*, ed. J. Roisman and I. Worthington. Malden, MA: 81–98.

Erickson, K. (2013) 'Seleucus I, Zeus and Alexander', in *Every Inch a King: Comparative Studies on Kings and Kingship in the Ancient and Medieval Worlds*, ed. L. Mitchell and C. Melville. Leiden and Boston: 109–27.

Erickson, K. and Wright, N. L. (2011) 'The "royal archer" and Apollo in the East: Greco-Persian iconography in the Seleukid empire', in *Proceedings of the XIV International Numismatic Congress*, ed. N. Holmes. Glasgow: 163–8.

Erim, K. T. (1989) 'The mint of Morgantina', in *Morgantina Studies II: the Coins*, by T. V. Buttrey, K. T. Erim, T. D. Groves and R. Ross Holloway. Princeton: 1–67.

Errington, M. A. (2008) *A History of the Hellenistic World: 323 – 30 BC*. Oxford and Malden, MA.

Erskine, A. (2002) 'O brother where art thou? Tales of kinship and diplomacy', in *The Hellenistic World: New Perspectives*, ed. D. Ogden. Swansea: 97–117.

(ed.) (2003) *A Companion to the Hellenistic World*. Malden, MA.

Eustace, K. (2007) 'Britannia: some high points in the history of the iconography on British coinage', *BNJ* 76: 323–36.

Ferrary, J.-L. (1988) *Philhellénisme et impérialisme. Aspects idéologiques de la conquête romaine du monde hellénistique*. Rome.

Feugère, M. and Py, M. (2011) *Dictionnaire des monnaies découvertes en Gaule méditerranéene*. Montagnac and Paris.

Finley, M. I. (1970) 'Aristotle and economic analysis', *Past and Present* 47: 3–25.

Fischer-Bossert, W. (2005) 'Die Lysimacheier des Skostokos', *RBN* 151: 49–74.

Fowler, R. (2005) '"Most fortunate roots": tradition and legitimacy in Parthian royal ideology', in *Imaginary Kings: Royal Images in the Ancient Near East, Greece and Rome*, ed. O. Hekster and R. Fowler. Stuttgart: 125–55.

Franke, P. R. (1961) *Die antike Münzen von Epirus*. Wiesbaden.

Frazer, E. J. and van der Touw, J. (2010) '"The Random Walk": a study of coins lost and found in an urban environment', *NC* 170: 375–405.

Fröhlich, P. (2004) *Les cités grecques et le contrôle des magistrats (IVe–Ier siècle avant J.-C.)*. Geneva and Paris.

Frolova, N. A. and Ireland, S. (2002) *The Coinage of the Bosporan Kingdom: From the First Century BC to the Middle of the First Century AD*. Oxford.

Fronda, M. P. (2010) *Between Rome and Carthage: Southern Italy during the Second Punic War*. Cambridge.

Gabrielsen, V. (2007) 'Trade and tribute: Byzantium and the Black Sea straits', in *The Black Sea in Antiquity: Regional and Interregional Economic Exchanges*, ed. V. Gabrielsen and J. Lund. Aarhus: 287–324.

Gaslain, J. (2010) 'Éléments de réflexion sur la conquête et l'occupation arsacides de la Mésopotamie (IIe siècle av. N.È.)', *Parthica* 12: 9–16.

Geus, K. (2003) 'Space and geography', in *A Companion to the Hellenistic World*, ed. A. Erskine. Malden, MA: 232–45.

Gitler, H. and Kahanov, Y. (2002) 'The Ascalon 1988 hoard (*CH* 9.548): a periplus to Ascalon in the late Hellenistic period', *CH* 9: 259–68.

Golenko, K. V. and Karyszowski, P. J. (1972) 'The gold coinage of King Pharnaces of the Bosporus', *NC* 12: 25–38.

Grandjean, C. (1995) 'Les comptes de Pompidas (*IG* VII 2426). Drachmes d'argent symmachique et drachmes de bronze', *BCH* 119/1: 1–26.

(1999) 'Les dernières monnaies d'argent du Péloponnèse', in *Travaux de numismatique grecque offerts à Georges Le Rider*, ed. M. Amandry and S. Hurter. London: 139–46.

(2003) *Les Messéniens de 370/369 au 1er siècle de notre ère: monnayages et histoire*. Athens and Paris.

Grandjean, C. and Moustaka, A. (eds.) (2013) *Aux origines de la monnaie fiduciaire. Traditions métallurgiques et innovations numismatiques*. Bordeaux.

Graninger, D. (2011) *Cult and Koinon in Hellenistic Thessaly*. Leiden.

Green, P. (1990) *Alexander to Actium: the Hellenistic Age*. London.

Gruen, E. (1984) *The Hellenistic World and the Coming of Rome* (2 vols.). Berkeley and London.

(1985) 'The coronation of the Diadochoi', in *The Craft of the Ancient Historian*, ed. J. W. Eadie and J. Ober. Lanham, MD: 253–71.

(1993) 'Hellenism and persecution: Antiochus IV and the Jews', in *Hellenistic History and Culture*, ed. P. Green. Berkeley: 238–64.

(2000) 'Culture as policy: the Attalids of Pergamon', in *From Pergamon to Sperlonga: Sculpture and Context*, ed. N. T. de Grummond and B. S. Ridgway. Berkeley, Los Angeles and London: 17–31.

Guillaume, O. (1990) *Analysis of Reasonings in Archaeology.* Oxford.

Gupta, P. L. and Hardaker, T. R. (1985) *Indian Silver Punchmarked Coins: Magadha-Maurya Karshapana Series.* Nashik.

Haaff, P. A. van't (2007) *Catalogue of Elymaean Coinage ca. 147 BC–AD 228.* Lancaster, PA and London.

Habicht, C. (1997) *Athens from Alexander to Antony.* Cambridge, MA.

Hall, J. M. (2002) *Hellenicity: Between Ethnicity and Culture.* Chicago.

Hansen, M. H. and Nielsen, T. H. (2004) *An Inventory of Archaic and Classical Poleis.* Oxford.

Harding, D. W. (2007) *The Archaeology of Celtic Art.* London and New York.

Hatzopoulos, M. B. (1996) *Macedonian Institutions under the Kings* (2 vols). Athens.

(2011) 'Macedonians and other Greeks', in *Brill's Companion to Ancient Macedon: Studies in the Archaeology and History of Macedon, 650 BC–300 AD*, ed. R. J. Lane Fox. Leiden: 43–78.

Hauser, S. R. (2012) 'The Arsacid (Parthian) empire', in *A Companion to the Archaeology of the Ancient Near East*, vol. II, ed. D. T. Potts. Oxford: 1001–20.

Heipp-Tamer, C. (1993) *Die Münzprägung der lykischen Stadt Phaselis in griechischer Zeit.* Saarbrücken.

Helly, B. (1997) 'Le *diorthôma* d'Auguste fixant le conversion des statères thessaliens en deniers', *TOPOI* 7/1: 63–91.

Hiebert, F. T. and Cambon, P. (2008) *Afghanistan: Hidden Treasures from the National Museum, Kabul.* Washington, DC.

Höghammar, K. (2007) 'A group of Koan issues from c. 200 BC', *NC* 167: 79–92.

Hölbl, G. (2001) *A History of the Ptolemaic Empire.* London.

Hollander, D. B. (2007) *Money in the Late Roman Republic.* Leiden and Boston.

Holt, F. L. (1984) 'The so-called "pedigree coins" of the Bactrian Greeks', in *Ancient Coins of the Graeco-Roman World: the Nickle Numismatic Papers*, ed. W. Heckel and R. Sullivan. Waterloo, Ont.: 69–91.

(1999) *Thundering Zeus: the Making of Hellenistic Bactria.* Berkeley, Los Angeles and London.

(2003) *Alexander the Great and the Mystery of the Elephant Medallions.* Berkeley, Los Angeles and London.

(2012) *Lost World of the Golden King: In Search of Ancient Afghanistan.* Berkeley, Los Angeles and London.

Hoover, O. D. (2002) 'The identity of the helmeted head on the "victory" coinage of Susa', *SNR* 81: 51–60.

(2007) 'A revised chronology for the late Seleucids at Antioch (121/0–64 BC)', *Historia* 56: 280–301.

(2008a) 'Countermarks on Seleucid and foreign silver coins', in Houghton, Lorber and Hoover 2008: II, 157–93.

(2008b) 'Overstruck Seleucid coins', in Houghton, Lorber and Hoover 2008: II, 209–30.

(2011) 'Never mind the bullocks: taurine imagery as a multicultural expression of royal and divine power under Seleukos I Nikator', in *More than Men, Less than Gods: Studies on Royal Cult and Imperial Worship*, ed. P. P. Iossif, A. S. Chankowski and C. C. Lorber. Leuven, Paris, and Walpole, MA: 197–228.

Hoover, O. D. and Iossif, P. P. (2008) 'Metrological study of Seleucid tetradrachms of Antioch and Phoenicia', in Houghton, Lorber and Hoover 2008: II, 1–8.

Hoover, O. D. and MacDonald, D. (1999–2000) 'Syrian imitations of New Style Athenian tetradrachms struck over Myrina', *Berytus* 44: 109–17.

Hornblower, S. (1996 [2003]) 'Hellenism, Hellenization', in *The Oxford Classical Dictionary, Third Edition Revised*, ed. S. Hornblower and A. Spawforth. Oxford: 677–9.

Houghton, A. (2004) 'Seleucid coinage and monetary policy of the second century BC', in *Le roi et l'économie: autonomies locales et structures royales dans l'économie de l'empire séleucide* (Topoi: Orient-Occident, Suppl. 6), ed. V. Chankowski and F. Duyrat. Lyons: 49–79.

Houghton, A. and Lorber, C. C. (2002) *Seleucid Coins: a Comprehensive Catalogue, Part I: Seleucus I through Antiochus III*. New York.

Houghton, A., Lorber, C. and Hoover, O. D. (2008) *Seleucid Coins: a Comprehensive Catalogue, Part II: Seleucus IV through Antiochos XIII* (2 vols). New York.

Howgego, C. (1990) 'Why did ancient states strike coins?', *NC* 150: 1–25.

(1995) *Ancient History from Coins*. London and New York.

(2005) 'Coinage and identity in the Roman provinces', in *Coinage and Identity in the Roman Provinces*, ed. C. Howgego, V. Heuchert and A. Burnett. Oxford: 1–17.

(2013) 'The monetization of temperate Europe', *JRS* 103: 16–45.

Hoyos, D. (2007) *Truceless War: Carthage's Fight for Survival, 241 to 237 BC*. Leiden.

Huth, M. (2010) 'Athenian imitations from Arabia', in Huth and van Alfen 2010: 227–56.

Huth, M. and van Alfen, P. G. (eds.) (2010) *Coinage of the Caravan Kingdoms: Studies in the Monetization of Ancient Arabia*. New York.

Invernizzi, A. (2007) 'The culture of Parthian Nisa between steppe and empire', in *After Alexander: Central Asia before Islam*, ed. J. Cribb and G. Herrmann. Oxford: 163–77.

Iossif, P. P. and Lorber, C. C. (2012) 'The rays of the Ptolemies', *Revue numismatique* 169: 197–224.

Isayev, E. (2007) *Inside Ancient Lucania: Dialogues in History and Archaeology*. London.

Jackson, A. E. (1971) 'The bronze coinage of Gortyn', *NC* 11: 37–51.

Jakobsson, J. (2010) 'Antiochus Nicator, the third king of Bactria?', *NC* 170: 17–33.

James, S. (1999) *The Atlantic Celts: Ancient People or Modern Invention?* London.

Jenkins, G. K. (1974) 'Coins of Punic Sicily, Part 2', *SNR* 53: 23–41

(1977) 'Coins of Punic Sicily, Part 3', *SNR* 56: 5–65

(1978) 'Coins of Punic Sicily, Part 4', *SNR* 57: 5–68

(1980) 'Hellenistic gold coins of Ephesos', *Anadolu* 21: 183–8.

(1989) 'Rhodian plinthophoroi: a sketch', in *Kraay-Mørkholm Essays: Numismatic Studies in Memory of C. M. Kraay and O. Mørkholm*, ed. G. Le Rider, G. K. Jenkins, N. Waggoner and U. Westermark. Louvain-la-Neuve: 101–19.

Johnson, C. G. (1999) 'The divinization of the Ptolemies and the gold octadrachms honoring Ptolemy III', *Phoenix* 53: 50–6.

Jones, C. P. (2000) 'Diodoros Pasparos revisited', *Chiron* 30: 1–14.

(2004) 'Events surrounding the bequest of Pergamon to Rome and the revolt of Aristonicos', *JRA* 17: 469–85.

Jones, N. F. (1979) 'The autonomous wreathed tetradrachms of Magnesia on Maeander', *ANSMN* 24: 63–109.

Juhel, P. O. (2011) 'Un fantôme de l'histoire hellénistique: le "district" macédonien', *GRBS* 51: 579–612.

Kallet-Marx, R. (1995) *Hegemony to Empire: the Development of the Roman Imperium in the East from 148 to 62 BC*. Berkeley, Los Angeles and Oxford.

Kay, P. (2013) 'What did the Attalids ever do for us? The view from the *aerarium*', in *Attalid Asia Minor: Money, International Relations, and the State*, ed. P. Thonemann. Oxford: 123–48.

(2014) *Rome's Economic Revolution*. Oxford.

Kaye, N. (2013) 'The silver tetradrachms of Prousias II of Bithynia', *AJN* 25: 21–48.

Keay, S. and Terrenato, N. (2001) *Italy and the West: Comparative Issues in Romanization*. Oxford.

Keegan, J. (1987) *The Mask of Command: a Study of Generalship*. London.

Keen, A. (1998) *Dynastic Lycia: a Political History of the Lycians and their Relations with Foreign Powers c. 545–362 BC*. Leiden.

Keller, D. (1996) 'Gedanken zur Datierung und Verwendung der Statere Philipps II. und ihrer keltischen Imitationen', *RSN* 75: 101–17.

Kim, H. S. (2002) 'Small change and the moneyed economy', in *Money, Labor and Land: Approaches to the Economies of Ancient Greece*, ed. P. Cartledge, E. E. Cohen and L. Foxhall. London and New York: 44–51.

Kim, H. S. and Kroll, J. H. (2008) 'A hoard of archaic coins of Colophon and unminted silver (CH I.3)', *AJN* 20: 53–103.

King, C. E. (2007) *Roman Quinarii from the Republic to Diocletian and the Tetrarchy*. Oxford.

Kinns, P. (1980) 'Studies in the coinage of Ionia: Erythrae, Teos, Lebedus, Colophon, c. 400–30 BC', Ph.D. thesis, Cambridge University

(1983) 'The Amphictionic coinage reconsidered', *NC* 143: 1–22.

(1989a) 'Ionia: the pattern of coinage during the last century of the Persian empire', *REA* 91/1–2:183–93.

(1989b) 'Two studies in the silver coinage of Magnesia on the Maeander', in *Kraay-Mørkholm Essays: Numismatic Studies in Memory of C. M. Kraay and O. Mørkholm*, ed. G. Le Rider, G. K. Jenkins, N. Waggoner and U. Westermark. Louvain-la-Neuve: 137–48.

(2006) 'A new third century BC didrachm of Chios in Ionia', *NC* 166: 31–9.

Kitchen, K. (2001) 'Economics in ancient Arabia, from Alexander to the Augustans', in *Hellenistic Economies*, ed. Z. H. Archibald, J. Davies, V. Gabrielsen and G. J. Oliver. London and New York: 157–73.

Kleiner, F. S. (1978) 'Hoard evidence and the late cistophori of Pergamum', *ANSMN* 23: 77–106.

(1979) 'The late cistophori of Apamea', in *Greek Numismatics and Archaeology: Essays in Honor of M. Thompson*, ed. O. Mørkholm and N. Waggoner. Wetteren: 119–30.

Kleiner, F. S. and Noe, S. P. (1977) *The Early Cistophoric Coinage*. New York.

Klose, D. O. A. (1998) 'Zur Chronologie der thessalischen Koinonprägungen im 2. und 1. Jh. v. Chr.', in *Stephanos Nomismatikos: Edith Schönert-Geiss zum 65. Geburtstag*, ed. U. Peter. Berlin: 333–50.

Klose, D. O. A. and Müseler, W. (2008) *Statthalter, Rebellen, Könige: Die Münzen aus Persepolis von Alexander dem Grossen zu den Sasaniden*. Munich.

Knapp, R. C. (2005) 'Introduction: archaeonumismatics and Nemea', in R. C. Knapp and J. D. Mac Isaac, *Excavations at Nemea III: the Coins*. Berkeley, Los Angeles and London: 11–61.

Knoepfler, D. (1979) 'Contributions à l'épigraphie de Chalcis', *BCH* 103: 165–88.

(2010) 'Les agonothètes de la Confédération d'Athéna Ilias', *Studi Ellenistici* 24: 33–62.

Konuk, K. (2011) 'War tokens for silver? Quantifying the early bronze issues of Ionia', in *Quantifying Monetary Supplies in Greco-Roman Times*, ed. F. de Callataÿ. Bari: 151–61.

(2013) 'Coinage and identities under the Hekatomnids', in *4th Century Karia: Defining a Karian Identity under the Hekatomnids*, ed. O. Henry. Paris: 101–21.

Kosmetatou, E. (2003) 'The Attalids of Pergamon', in *A Companion to the Hellenistic World*, ed. A. Erskine. Malden, MA: 159–74.

Kosmin, P. (2013) 'Rethinking the Hellenistic gulf: the new Greek inscription from Bahrain', *JHS* 133: 61–79.

Kousser, R. (2010) 'Hellenistic and Roman art, 221 BC–AD 337', in *A Companion to Ancient Macedonia*, ed. J. Roisman and I. Worthington. Malden, MA: 522–42.

Kremydi, S. (2011) 'Coinage and finance', in *Brill's Companion to Ancient Macedon: Studies in the Archaeology and History of Macedon, 650 BC–300 AD*, ed. R. J. Lane Fox. Leiden: 159–78.

Kremydi-Sicilianou, S. (2007) 'ΜΑΚΕΔΟΝΩΝ ΠΡΩΤΗΣ ΜΕΡΙΔΟΣ: evidence for a coinage under the Antigonids', *RN* 163: 91–100.

(2009) 'The Tauropolos tetradrachms of the first Macedonian *meris*: provenance, iconography and dating', in *ΚΕΡΜΑΤΙΑ ΦΙΛΙΑΣ. Τιμητικός Τόμος για τον Ιωάννη Τουράτσογλου.* Athens: I, 191–201.

Kroll, J. H. (1976) 'Aristophanes' πονηρὰ χαλκία: a reply', *GRBS* 17: 329–41.

(1993) *The Athenian Agora Volume XXVI: The Greek Coins.* Princeton.

(2007) 'The Emergence of Ruler Portraiture on Early Hellenistic Coins', in *Early Hellenistic Portraiture: Image, Style, Context*, ed. P. Schultz and R. von den Hoff. Cambridge: 113–22.

(2009) Review of Warren 2007, *JHS* 129: 192–3.

(2011) 'The reminting of Athenian silver coinage, 353 BC', *Hesperia* 80: 229–59.

(2013) 'On the chronology of third-century BC Athenian silver coinage', *RBN* 159: 33–44.

Kropp, A. J. M. (2013) *Images and Monuments of Near Eastern Dynasts, 100 BC–AD 100.* Oxford.

Lane Fox, R. (1996) 'Text and image: Alexander the Great, coins, and elephants', *BICS* 41/1: 87–108.

(2007) 'Alexander the Great, last of the Achaemenids?', in *Persian Responses: Political and Cultural Interaction With(in) the Achaemenid Empire*, ed. C. Tuplin. Swansea: 267–311.

Larsen, J. A. O. (1968) *Greek Federal States: Their Institutions and History.* Oxford.

Le Rider, G. (1965) *Suse sous les Séleucides et les Parthes. Les trouvailles monétaires et l'histoire de la ville.* Paris.

(1966) *Monnaies crétoises du Ve au Ier siècle av. J.-C.* Paris.

(1977) *Le monnayage d'argent et d'or de Philipp II frappé en Macédoine de 359 à 294.* Paris.

(1993) 'Les deux monnaies macédoniennes des années 323–294/290', *BCH* 117: 491–500.

(1996) *Monnayage et finances de Philippe II: un état de la question.* Athens and Paris.

(1999) *Antioche de Syrie sous les Séleucides: corpus des monnaies d'or et d'argent. I: De Séleucos I à Antiochos V, c. 300–161.* Paris.

(2001a) *La naissance de la monnaie: pratiques monétaires de l'Orient ancien.* Paris.

(2001b) 'Sur un aspect du comportement monétaire des villes libres d'Asie Mineure occidentale au IIe siècle', in *Les cités d'Asie Mineure occidentale au IIe siècle a.C.*, ed. A. Bresson and R. Descat. Paris and Bordeaux: 37–63.

(2007) *Alexander the Great: Coinage, Finances, and Policy* (translated by W. E. Higgins). Philadelphia.

Le Rider, G. and Callataÿ, F. de (2006) *Les Séleucides et les Ptolémées: l'héritage monétaire et financier d'Alexandre le Grand.* Monaco.

Lee, I. (2000) 'Entella: the silver coinage of the Campanian mercenaries and the site of the first Carthaginian mint 410–409 BC', *NC* 160: 1–66.

Lerner, J. D. (1999) *The Impact of Seleucid Decline on the Eastern Iranian Plateau.* Stuttgart.

Lewis D. M. (1962) 'The chronology of the Athenian New Style coinage', *NC* 2: 275–300.

Lorber, C. C. (2005) 'A revised chronology for the coinage of Ptolemy I', *NC* 165: 45–64.

(2011) 'Theos *Aigiochos*: the aegis in Ptolemaic portraits of divine rulers', in *More than Men, Less than Gods: Studies on Royal Cult and Imperial Worship*, ed. P. P. Iossif, A. S. Chankowski and C. C. Lorber. Leuven, Paris, and Walpole, MA: 293–356.

(2012a) 'The coinage of the Ptolemies', in *The Oxford Handbook of Greek and Roman Coinage*, ed. W. E. Metcalf. Oxford: 211–34.

(2012b) 'Dating the portrait coinage of Ptolemy I', *AJN* 24: 33–44.

Lorber, C. C. and Hoover, O. D. (2003) 'An unpublished tetradrachm issued by the Artists of Dionysos', *NC* 163: 59–68.

Lund, H. S. (1992) *Lysimachus: a Study in Early Hellenistic Kingship.* London.

Ma, J. (2000) 'Fighting *poleis* of the Hellenistic world', in *War and Violence in Ancient Greece*, ed. H. van Wees. London: 337–76.

(2002) *Antiochos III and the Cities of Western Asia Minor*, revised edition. Oxford.

(2003a) 'Kings', in *A Companion to the Hellenistic World*, ed. A. Erskine. Malden, MA: 177–95.

(2003b) 'Peer polity interaction in the Hellenistic age', *Past and Present* 180: 9–39.

McAlee, R. (2007) *The Coins of Roman Antioch.* Lancaster, PA and London.

MacDonald, D. (2005) *An Introduction to the History and Coinage of the Kingdom of the Bosporus.* Lancaster, PA and London.

MacDowall, D. W. (2007) 'Coinage from Iran to Gandhāra', in *On the Cusp of an Era: Art in the Pre-Kusāna World*, ed. D. M. Srinivasan. Leiden: 234–65.

Mackil, E. (2013) *Creating a Common Polity: Religion, Economy, and Politics in the Making of the Greek Koinon.* Berkeley, Los Angeles and London.

Mackil, E. and van Alfen, P. (2006) 'Cooperative coinage', in *Agoranomia: Studies in Money and Exchange Presented to John H. Kroll*, ed. P. van Alfen. New York: 201–46.

McNicoll, A. W. (1997) *Hellenistic Fortifications from the Aegean to the Euphrates.* Oxford.

Mairs, R. (2011) *The Archaeology of the Hellenistic Far East: a Survey.* Oxford.

Manning, J. G. (2010) *The Last Pharaohs: Egypt under the Ptolemies, 305–30 BC.* Princeton.

Manov, M. and Damyanov, V. (2013) 'The first mint of Cavarus, the last king of the Celtic kingdom in Thrace', *AJN* 25: 11–19.

Marcellesi, M.-C. (2004) *Milet des Hécatomnides à la domination romaine. Pratiques monétaires et histoire de la cité du IVe au IIe siècle av. J.-C.* Mainz am Rhein.

(2012) *Pergame de la fin du Ve au début du Ier siècle avant J.-C.* Studi Ellenistici 26. Pisa and Rome.

Mari, M. (2008) 'The ruler cult in Macedonia', in *Studi Ellenistici XX*, ed. B. Virgilio. Pisa and Rome: 219–68.

Marinescu, C. A. (1996) 'Making and spending money along the Bosporus: the Lysimachi coinages minted by Byzantium and Chalcedon', Ph.D. thesis, Columbia University.

(2000) 'The posthumous Lysimachi coinage and the dual monetary system at Byzantium and Chalcedon in the third century BC', in *XII. Internationaler Numismatischer Kongress, Berlin 1997: Akten*, ed. B. Kluge and B. Wiesser. Berlin: I, 333–7.

Martin, T. R. (1985) *Sovereignty and Coinage in Classical Greece*. Princeton.

Masson, O. (1986) 'Quelques noms des magistrats monétaires grecs. V. Les monétaires de Kymé d'Éolide', *RN* 28: 51–64.

Mattingly, D. J. (2011) *Imperialism, Power, and Identity: Experiencing the Roman Empire*. Princeton.

Mattingly, H. B. (1993) 'The Ma'Aret En-Nu'man hoard, 1980', in *Essays in Honour of Robert Carson and Kenneth Jenkins*, ed. M. J. Price, A. Burnett and R. Bland. London: 69–86.

(2004) *From Coins to History: Selected Numismatic Studies*. Ann Arbor.

(2011) Review of Warren 2007, *NC* 171: 494–7.

Mauss, M. (1990 [1925]) *The Gift*, translated by W. D. Halls, with a foreword by Mary Douglas. London and New York.

Meadows, A. (1998) 'Parion', in R. Ashton, A. Meadows, K. Sheedy and U. Wartenberg, 'Some Greek coins in the British Museum', *NC* 158: 37–51, at 41–6.

(2001) 'Money, freedom, and empire in the Hellenistic world', in *Money and its Uses in the Ancient Greek World*, ed. A. Meadows and K. Shipton. Oxford: 53–63.

(2002) 'Stratonikeia in Caria: the Hellenistic city and its coinage', *NC* 162: 79–134.

(2004) 'The earliest coinage of Alexandria Troas', *NC* 164: 47–70.

(2006) 'Amyntas, Side, and the Pamphylian Plain', in *Agoranomia: Studies in Money and Exchange Presented to John H. Kroll*, ed. P. van Alfen. New York: 151–75.

(2009a) 'The Hellenistic silver coinage of Clazomenae', in *Ancient History, Numismatics and Epigraphy in the Mediterranean World: Studies in Memory of Clemens E. Bosch and Sabahat Atlan and in Honour of Nezahat Baydur*. Istanbul: 247–62.

(2009b) 'Money in an ideal world: Plato's *Laws* and the dual nature of coinage', in *ΚΕΡΜΑΤΙΑ ΦΙΛΙΑΣ. Τιμητικός τόμος για τον Ιωάννη Τουράτσογλου*. Athens: 25–31.

(2011) 'The Chian revolution: changing patterns of hoarding in 4th-century BC western Asia Minor', in *Nomisma. La circulation monétaire dans le monde grec antique*, ed. T. Faucher, M.-C. Marcellesi and O. Picard. Athens: 273–95.

(2013) 'The closed-currency system of the Attalid kingdom', in *Attalid Asia Minor: Money, International Relations, and the State*, ed. P. Thonemann. Oxford: 149–205.

(2014) 'Imitative coinage in first-century Pamphylia', in *First International Congress of the Anatolian Monetary History and Numismatics, 25–28 February 2013, Antalya: Proceedings*, ed. K. Dörtlük, O. Tekin and R. Boyraz Seyhan. Istanbul: 409–22.

Meadows, A. and Houghton, A. (2010) 'The Gaziantep hoard, 1994 (*CH* 9.527; 10.308)', *CH* 10: 173–223.

Metcalf, W. E. (1980) *The Cistophori of Hadrian*. New York.

(2009) 'A note on the later Republican cistophori', *SNR* 88: 205–10.

(forthcoming) 'The cistophori of Nysa', in *Essays in Honor of R. Witschonke*.

Michels, C. (2009) *Kulturtransfer und monarchischer 'Philhellenismus'. Bithynien, Pontos und Kappadokien in hellenistischer Zeit*. Göttingen.

Migeotte, L. (1992) *Les souscriptions publiques dans les cités grecques*. Geneva.

(1997) 'La date de l'*oktôbolos eisphora* de Messène', *TOPOI* 7/1: 51–61.

Millar, F. (1978) 'The Background to the Maccabean Revolution', *Journal of Jewish Studies* 29: 1–21; reprinted in *Rome, the Greek World and the East, Volume III: The Greek World, the Jews, and the East*. Chapel Hill, 2006: 67–90.

(1983) 'The Phoenician cities: a case-study of Hellenisation', *PCPS* 29: 55–71.

(1993) *The Roman Near East 31 BC–AD 337*. Cambridge, MA and London.

Miller, R. P. (2010) 'East Arachosia (Quetta) hoard, 2002 (*CH* 10.275)', *CH* X: 105–7.

Minns, E. H. (1913) *Scythians and Greeks*. Cambridge.

Mitchell, S. (2003) 'The Galatians: representation and reality', in *A Companion to the Hellenistic World*, ed. A. Erskine. Malden, MA: 280–93.

Morel, J.-P. (1989) 'The transformation of Italy, 300–133 BC: the evidence of archaeology', in *The Cambridge Ancient History, Second Edition, Vol. VIII: Rome and the Mediterranean to 133 BC*, ed. A. E. Astin, F. W. Walbank, M. W. Frederiksen and R. M. Ogilvie. Cambridge: 477–516.

Morgan, C. (2003) *Early Greek States beyond the Polis*. London and New York.

Mørkholm, O. (1984a) 'The chronology of the New Style coinage of Athens', *ANSMN* 29: 29–42.

(1984b) 'Some Pergamene coins in Copenhagen', in *Festschrift für Leo Mildenberg: Numismatik, Kunstgeschichte, Archäologie*, ed. A. Houghton, S. Hurter, P. E. Mottahedeh and J. A. Scott. Wetteren: 181–92.

(1991) *Early Hellenistic Coinage from the Accession of Alexander to the Peace of Apamea (336–188 BC)*. Cambridge.

Mørkholm, O. and Zahle, J. (1972) 'The coinage of Kuprlli: a numismatic and archaeological study', *ActaArch* 43: 57–113.

(1976) 'The coinages of the Lycian dynasts Kheriga, Kherei and Erbbina: a numismatic and archaeological study', *ActaArch* 47: 47–90.

Morris, S. P. (2001) 'The prehistoric background of Artemis Ephesia: a solution to the enigma of her "breasts"?', in *Der Kosmos der Artemis von Ephesos*, ed. U. Muss. Vienna: 135–51.

Mullen, A. (2013) *Southern Gaul and the Mediterranean: Multilingualism and Multiple Identities in the Iron Age and Roman Periods*. Cambridge.

Müller, C. (2011) 'Autopsy of a crisis: wealth, Protogenes, and the city of Olbia in *c.* 200 BC', in *The Economies of Hellenistic Societies, Third to First Centuries BC*, ed. Z. H. Archibald, J. K. Davies and V. Gabrielsen. Oxford: 324–44.

Murray, O. (1969) Review of Schneider 1967, *CR* 19: 69–72.

Nash, D. (1987) *Coinage in the Celtic World*. London.

Nercessian, Y. T. (2006) *Silver Coinage of the Artaxiad Dynasty of Armenia*. New York.

Newell, E. T. (1927) *The Coinages of Demetrius Poliorcetes*. London.
    (1937) *Royal Greek Portrait Coins*. New York.

Noreña, C. F. (2011) 'Coins and communication', in *The Oxford Handbook of Social Relations in the Roman World*, ed. M. Peachin. Oxford: 248–68.

Ober, J. (2008) *Democracy and Knowledge: Innovation and Learning in Classical Athens*. Princeton.

Olivier, J. and Lorber, C. (2013) 'Three gold coinages of third-century Ptolemaic Egypt', *RBN* 159: 49–150.

Osborne, R. (2008) 'Reciprocal strategies: imperialism, barbarism and trade in Archaic and Classical Olbia', in *Meetings of Cultures – Between Conflicts and Coexistence*, ed. P. G. Bilde and J. H. Petersen. Aarhus: 333–46.

Palagia, O. (2006) 'Art and royalty in Sparta of the 3rd century BC', *Hesperia* 75: 205–17.

Panagopoulou, K. (2001) 'The Antigonids: patterns of a royal economy', in *Hellenistic Economies*, ed. Z. H. Archibald, J. Davies, V. Gabrielsen and G. J. Oliver. London and New York: 313–64.

Parker, R. (2004) 'New "Panhellenic" festivals in Hellenistic Greece', in *Mobility and Travel in the Mediterranean from Antiquity to the Middle Ages*, ed. R. Schlesier and U. Zellmann. Münster: 9–22.

Petac, E. and Vîlcu, A. (2012) 'Syrian wars and the beginning of Lysimachus-type staters at Tomis', *Istros* 18: 51–63.

Peter, U. (1997) *Die Münzen der thrakischen Dynasten (5.-3. Jahrhundert v. Chr.)*. Berlin.

Picard, O. (1979) *Chalcis et la Confédération eubéenne*. Athens and Paris.

Pirngruber, R. (forthcoming) *The Babylonian Economy in the Late Achaemenid and Seleucid Periods, ca. 400-140 BC*. Cambridge.

Poddighe, E. (2009) 'Alexander and the Greeks: the Corinthian League', in *Alexander the Great: a New History*, ed. W. Heckel and L. A. Tritle. Chichester and Malden, MA: 99–120.

Potts, D. T. (1999) *The Archaeology of Elam*. Cambridge.

(2007) 'Foundation houses, fire altars and the *frataraka*: interpreting the iconography of some post-Achaemenid Persian coins', *Iranica Antiqua* 42: 271–300

(2010) 'The circulation of foreign coins within Arabia and of Arabian coins outside the peninsula in the pre-Islamic era', in Huth and van Alfen 2010: 65–82.

Prag, J. R. W. (2006) 'Poenus plane est – but who were the "Punickes"?', *PBSR* 74: 1–37.

(2010) 'Siculo-Punic coinage and Siculo-Punic interactions', in *Meetings between Cultures in the Ancient Mediterranean*, ed. M. Dalla Riva. *Bollettino di Archeologia on line*, Volume speciale: http://151.12.58.75/archeologia/bao_document/articoli/2_PRAG.pdf

(2012) 'Sicilian identity in the Classical and Hellenistic periods: epigraphic considerations', in *Epigraphical Approaches to the Post-Classical Polis*, ed. P. Martzavou and N. Papazarkadas. Oxford: 37–53.

Prag, J. R. W. and Quinn, J. C. (eds.) (2013) *The Hellenistic West: Rethinking the Ancient Mediterranean*. Cambridge.

Price, M. J. (1991) *The Coinage in the Name of Alexander the Great and Philip Arrhidaeus* (2 vols). Zurich and London.

Price, S. R. F. (1984) *Rituals and Power: the Roman Imperial Cult in Asia Minor*. Cambridge.

Prokopov, I. (2006) *Die Silberprägung der Insel Thasos und die Tetradrachmen des 'thasischen Typs' vom 2.–1. Jahrhundert v.Chr.* Berlin.

(2011) 'The imitations of late Thasian tetradrachms: chronology, classification and dating', in *Proceedings of the XIV International Numismatic Congress*, ed. N. Holmes. Glasgow: 337–44.

(2012) *The Silver Coinage of the Macedonian Regions, 2nd–1st Century BC*. Wetteren.

Psoma, S. (2007a) 'À propos de drachmes d'argent du décret amphictyonique *CID* IV 127', *ZPE* 160: 79–88.

(2007b) 'Profitable networks: coinages, *panegyris* and Dionysiac artists', *MHR* 22/2: 237–55.

(2008) '*Panegyris* coinages', *AJN* 20: 227–55.

(2012) 'Greece and the Balkans to 360 BC', in *The Oxford Handbook of Greek and Roman Coinage*, ed. W. E. Metcalf. Oxford: 157–72.

(2013) 'War or trade? Attic-weight tetradrachms from second-century BC Attalid Asia Minor in Seleukid Syria', in *Attalid Asia Minor: Money, International Relations, and the State*, ed. P. Thonemann. Oxford: 265–300.

Psoma, S. and Touratsoglou, I. (2005) *Sylloge Nummorum Graecorum, Greece 4. Numismatic Museum, Athens: The Petros Z. Saroglos Collection, Volume I: Macedonia*. Athens.

Psoma, S. and Tsangari, D. (2003) 'Monnaie commune et états fédéraux: la circulation des monnayages frappés par les états fédéraux du monde grec', in *The Idea of European Community in History, Vol. II: Aspects of Connecting Poleis and Ethnē in Ancient Greece*, ed. K. Buraselis and K. Zoumboulakis. Athens: 111–42.

Purcell, N. (2013) 'On the significance of East and West in today's "Hellenistic" history', in Prag and Quinn 2013: 367–90.

Rajak, T. (1990) 'The Hasmoneans and the uses of Hellenism', in *A Tribute to Geza Vermes: Essays on Jewish and Christian Literature*, ed. P. R. Davies and R. T. White. Sheffield: 261–80; reprinted in T. Rajak, *The Jewish Dialogue with Greece and Rome*. Leiden, 2001: 61–80.

Ramsey, J. T. (1999) 'Mithridates, the banner of Ch'ih-yu, and the comet coin', *HSCP* 99: 197–253.

Rapin, C. (2007) 'Nomads and the shaping of central Asia: from the early Iron Age to the Kushan period', in *After Alexander: Central Asia before Islam*, ed. J. Cribb and G. Herrmann. Oxford: 29–72.

Reger, G. (2011) 'Inter-regional economies in the Aegean basin', in *The Economies of Hellenistic Societies, Third to First Centuries BC*, ed. Z. H. Archibald, J. K. Davies and V. Gabrielsen. Oxford: 368–89.

Regling, K. (1927) *Die Münzen von Priene*. Berlin.

Rhodes, P. J. and Osborne, R. (2003) *Greek Historical Inscriptions 404–323 BC*. Oxford.

Rigsby, K. J. (1979) 'The era of the province of Asia', *Phoenix* 33: 39–47.

(1996) *Asylia: Territorial Inviolability in the Hellenistic World*. Berkeley, Los Angeles and London.

Ripollès, P. P. (2008) 'The X4 hoard (Spain)', *Israel Numismatic Research* 3: 51–64.

(2012) 'The ancient coinages of the Iberian peninsula', in *The Oxford Handbook of Greek and Roman Coinage*, ed. W. E. Metcalf. Oxford: 356–74.

Rizakis, A. D. (2008) *Achaïe III, les cités achéennes: épigraphie et histoire*. Athens.

Robert, L. (1951) *Études de numismatique grecque*. Paris.

(1966) *Monnaies antiques en Troade*. Geneva and Paris.

(1973) 'Les monétaires et un décret hellénistique de Sestos', *RN* 15: 43–53.

Robinson, E. S. G. (1954) 'Cistophori in the name of King Eumenes', *NC* 6/14: 1–8.

Root, M. C. (1979) *The King and Kingship in Achaemenid Art*. Leiden.

Rousset, D. (2010) *Fouilles de Xanthos X: De Lycie en Cabalide*. Geneva.

Rumscheid, F. and Koenigs, W. (1998) *Priene: a Guide to the 'Pompeii of Asia Minor'*. Istanbul.

Runciman, W. G. (1990) 'Doomed to extinction: the *polis* as an evolutionary dead-end', in *The Greek City from Homer to Alexander*, ed. O. Murray and S. Price. Oxford: 347–67.

Rutter, N. K. (ed.) (2001) *Historia Numorum: Italy*. London.

Sacks, K. S. (1985) 'The wreathed coins of Aeolian Myrina', *ANSMN* 30: 1–43.

Schneider, C. (1967) *Kulturgeschichte des Hellenismus, Erster Band*. Munich.

Scholten, J. B. (2000) *The Politics of Plunder: Aitolians and their Koinon in the Early Hellenistic Era, 279–217 BC*. Berkeley, Los Angeles and London.

Schuol, M. (2000) *Die Charakene: Ein mesopotamisches Königreich in hellenistisch-parthischer Zeit*. Stuttgart.

Seldeslachts, E. (2004) 'The end of the road for the Indo-Greeks?', *Iranica Antiqua* 39: 249–96.

Sellwood, D. G. (1980) *An Introduction to the Coinage of Parthia*. London

Sellwood, D. G. and Simonetta, A. M. (2006) 'Notes on the coinage and history of the Arsacids from the advent of Orodes II to the end of the reign of Phraates IV', *NAC* 35: 283–315.

Sergueenkova, V. (2006) 'The stylis on the gold of Alexander the Great', *NAC* 35: 165–78.

Shayegan, M. Rahim (2011) *Arsacids and Sasanians: Political Ideology in Post-Hellenistic and Late Antique Persia*. Cambridge.

Sherwin-White, A. N. (1984) *Roman Foreign Policy in the East, 168 BC to AD 1*. London.

Sherwin-White, S. (1985) 'Ancient archives: the edict of Alexander to Priene, a re-appraisal,' *JHS* 105: 69–89.

Sherwin-White, S. and Kuhrt, A. (1993) *From Samarkhand to Sardis: a New Approach to the Seleukid Empire*. London.

Shipley, G. (2000) *The Greek World after Alexander: 323–30 BC*. London and New York.

Simonetta, A. M. (2007) 'The coinage of the Cappadocian kings: a revision and a catalogue of the Simonetta collection', *Parthica* 9: 9–152.

Sinisi, F. (2012) 'The coinage of the Parthians', in *The Oxford Handbook of Greek and Roman Coinage*, ed. W. E. Metcalf. Oxford: 275–94.

Slater, W. (2010) 'Paying the pipers', in *L'argent dans les concours du monde grec*, ed. B. Le Guen. Paris: 249–81.

Smith, R. R. R. (1988) *Hellenistic Royal Portraits*. Oxford.

Sosin, J. D. (2004) 'Alexanders and *stephanephoroi* at Delphi', *Classical Philology* 99: 191–208.

Stewart, A. F. (1993) *Faces of Power: Alexander's Image and Hellenistic Politics*. Berkeley and Los Angeles.

Stolyarik, E. (2000) 'The gold coinage of the Bosporan kingdom under the late Spartocids', in *XII. Internationaler Numismatischer Kongress, Berlin 1997: Akten*, ed. B. Kluge and B. Wiesser. Berlin: I, 378–83.

(2004/5) 'Silver coinage of the Bosporan king Spartocus', *AJN* 16–17:75–85.

Stumpf, G. R. (1991) *Numismatische Studien zur Chronologie der römischen Statthalter in Kleinasien (122 v.Chr.–163 n.Chr.)*. Saarbrücken.

Sutherland, C. H. V. (1970) *The Cistophori of Augustus*. London.

Tarn, W. W. (1913) *Antigonos Gonatas*. Oxford.

Temin, P. (2013) *The Roman Market Economy*. Princeton.

Thompson, D. J. and Buraselis, K. (2013) 'Introduction', in *The Ptolemies, the Sea and the Nile: Studies in Waterborne Power*, ed. K. Buraselis, M. Stefanou and D. J. Thompson. Cambridge: 1–18.

Thompson, M. (1954) 'A countermarked hoard from Büyükçekmece', *ANSMN* 6: 11–34.

(1961) *The Athenian New Style Coinage* (2 vols.) New York.

(1968a) *The Agrinion Hoard*. Numismatic Notes and Monographs 159. New York.

(1968b) 'The mints of Lysimachus', in *Essays on Greek Coinage Presented to Stanley Robinson*, ed. C. M. Kraay and G. K. Jenkins. Oxford: 163–82.

(1983) *Alexander's Drachm Mints I: Sardes and Miletus*. New York.

(1984) 'Paying the mercenaries', in *Festschrift für Leo Mildenberg: Numismatik, Kunstgeschichte, Archäologie*, ed. A. Houghton, S. Hurter, P. E. Mottahedeh and J. A. Scott. Wetteren: 241–7.

Thonemann, P. (2005) 'The tragic king: Demetrios Poliorketes and the city of Athens', in *Imaginary Kings: Royal Images in the Near East, Greece and Rome*, ed. O. Hekster and R. Fowler. Stuttgart: 63–86.

(2008) 'Cistophoric geography: Toriaion and Kormasa', *NC* 168: 43–60.

(2011) *The Maeander Valley: a Historical Geography from Antiquity to Byzantium*. Cambridge.

(2013a) 'The Attalid state, 188–133 BC', in *Attalid Asia Minor: Money, International Relations, and the State*, ed. P. Thonemann. Oxford: 1–49.

(2013b) 'Phrygia: an anarchist history, 950 BC–AD 100', in *Roman Phrygia: Culture and Society*, ed. P. Thonemann. Cambridge: 1–40.

Touchette, L.-A. (1992) Review of Smith 1988, *JRS* 82: 243–5.

Touratsoglou, I. P. (2004) Review of Le Rider 2007 (original French edition, 2003) *SNR* 83: 180–92.

Troxell, H. A. (1982) *The Coinage of the Lycian League*. New York.

(1997) *Studies in the Macedonian Coinage of Alexander the Great*. New York.

Tsangari, D. I. (2007) *Corpus des monnaies d'or, d'argent et de bronze de la Confédération étolienne*. Athens.

van Alfen, P. G. (2005) 'Problems in ancient imitative and counterfeit coinage', in *Making, Moving and Managing: the New World of Ancient Economies, 323–31 BC*, ed. Z. H. Archibald, J. K. Davies and V. Gabrielsen. Oxford: 322–54.

(2010) 'A die study of the "Abiel" coinage of eastern Arabia', in Huth and van Alfen 2010: 549–94.

van Bremen, R. (2007) 'The entire house is full of crowns: Hellenistic *agōnes* and the commemoration of victory', in *Pindar's Poetry, Patrons and Festivals*, ed. S. Hornblower and C. Morgan. Oxford: 345–75.

(2008) 'The date and context of the Kymaian decrees for Archippe', *REA* 110: 357–82.

Vismara, N. (1989–96) *Monetazione arcaica della Lycia I–III*. Milan.

Visona, P. (1998) 'Carthaginian coinage in perspective', *AJN* 10: 1–27.

Vlassopoulos, K. (2013) *Greeks and Barbarians*. Cambridge.

Voegtli, H. (1990) 'Zwei Münzfunde aus Pergamon', *SNR* 69: 41–50.

von Reden, S. (2007) *Money in Ptolemaic Egypt, from the Macedonian Conquest to the End of the Third Century BC*. Cambridge.

(2010) *Money in Classical Antiquity*. Cambridge.

Waggoner, N. M. (1983) 'Further reflections on Audoleon and his Alexander mint', *RBN* 129: 5–21.

Walbank, F. W. (1976/7) 'Were there Greek federal states?', *SCI* 3: 27–51; reprinted in F. W. Walbank, *Selected Papers: Studies in Greek and Roman History and Historiography*. Cambridge, 1985: 20–37.

(1981) *The Hellenistic World*. Fontana.

(2000) 'Hellenes and Achaeans: "Greek nationality" revisited', in *Further Studies in the Ancient Greek Polis*, ed. P. Flensted-Jensen. Stuttgart: 19–33.

Wallace-Hadrill, A. (2008) *Rome's Cultural Revolution*. Cambridge.

Walsh, J. J. (1996) 'Flamininus and the propaganda of liberation', *Historia* 45: 344–63.

Warren, J. A. W. (1999a) 'The Achaean league silver coinage controversy resolved: a summary', *NC* 159: 99–109.

(1999b) 'More on the "new landscape" in the late Hellenistic coinage of the Peloponnese', in *Travaux de numismatique grecque offerts à Georges Le Rider*, ed. M. Amandry and S. Hurter. London: 375–93.

(2007) *The Bronze Coinage of the Achaian Koinon: the Currency of a Federal Ideal*. London.

(2008) 'The framework of the Achaian koinon', in *Le Péloponnèse d'Épaminondas à Hadrien*, ed. C. Grandjean. Bordeaux: 91–9.

Weinstock, S. (1971) *Divus Julius*. Oxford.

Welles, C. B. (1934) *Royal Correspondence in the Hellenistic Period*. New Haven.

Westermark, U. (1961) *Das Bildnis des Philetairos von Pergamon. Corpus der Münzprägung*. Stockholm.

(1989) 'Remarks on the regal Macedonian coinage ca. 413–359 BC', in *Kraay-Mørkholm Essays: Numismatic Studies in Memory of C. M. Kraay and O. Mørkholm*, ed. G. Le Rider, G. K. Jenkins, N. Waggoner and U. Westermark. Louvain-la-Neuve: 301–15.

(1995) 'On the Pergamene bronze coins in the name of Athena Nikephoros', *StCercNum* 11: 29–35.

Wheatley, P. V. (2003) 'The Year 22 tetradrachms of Sidon and the date of the battle of Gaza', *ZPE* 144: 268–76.

Widemann, F. (2009) *Les successeurs d'Alexandre en Asie centrale et leur héritage culturel*. Paris.

Wiesehöfer, J. (1996) '"King of kings" and "Philhellên": kingship in Arsacid Iran', in *Aspects of Hellenistic Kingship*, ed. P. Bilde, T. Engberg-Pedersen, L. Hannestad and J. Zahle. Aarhus: 55–66.

(2009) 'The Achaemenid Empire', in *The Dynamics of Ancient Empires: State Power from Assyria to Byzantium*, ed. I. Morris and W. Scheidel. Oxford: 66–98.

(2011) 'Frataraka rule in early Seleucid Persis: a new appraisal', in *Creating a Hellenistic World*, ed. A. Erskine and L. Llewellyn-Jones. Swansea: 107–21.

Wigg-Wolf, D. (2008) 'Coinage on the periphery', in *Roman Coins outside the Empire: Ways and Phases, Contexts and Functions*, ed. A. Bursche, R. Ciolek and R. Wolters. Wetteren: 35–47.

Williams, J. H. C. and Burnett, A. M. (1998) 'Alexander the Great and the coinages of western Greece', in *Studies in Greek Numismatics in Memory of Martin Jessop Price*, ed. R. Ashton and S. Hurter. London: 379–93.

Wilson, R. J. A. (2013) 'Hellenistic Sicily, c. 270–100 BC', in Prag and Quinn 2013: 79–119.

Wolf, D. and Lorber, C. (2011) 'The "Galatian Shield without Σ" series of Ptolemaic bronze coins', *NC* 171: 7–53.

Woolf, G. (1998) *Becoming Roman: the Origins of Provincial Civilization in Gaul*. Cambridge.

Wörrle, M. (2000) 'Pergamon um 133 v. Chr.', *Chiron* 30: 543–76.

Worthington, I. (2008) *Philip II of Macedonia*. New Haven and London.

Woytek, B. E. (2012) 'The denarius coinage of the Roman Republic', in *The Oxford Handbook of Greek and Roman Coinage*, ed. W. E. Metcalf. Oxford: 315–34.

Yarrow, L. M. (2013) 'Heracles, coinage and the West: three Hellenistic case studies', in Prag and Quinn 2013: 348–66.

Zimmermann, K. (2001) 'Zur Münzprägung "der Libyer" während der Söldnerkrieges', in *Punica – Libyca – Ptolemaica: Festschrift für Werner Huss*, ed. K. Geus and K. Zimmermann. Leuven: 235–52.

Index